TWAYNE'S WORLD AUTHORS SERIES

A Survey of the World's Literature

Sylvia E. Bowman, Indiana University

GENERAL EDITOR

DENMARK

Leif Sjöberg
State University of New York at Stonybrook

EDITOR

Søren Kierkegaard

TWAS 392

Søren Kierkegaard
(Drawing by Chr. Kierkegaard)

SØREN KIERKEGAARD

By BRITA K. STENDAHL

Radcliffe Institute

TWAYNE PUBLISHERS

A DIVISION OF G. K. HALL & CO., BOSTON

Library of Congress Cataloging in Publication Data

Stendahl, Brita K
    Søren Kierkegaard.

    (Twayne's world authors series ; TWAS 392 : Denmark)
    Bibliography: pp. 225–29.
    Includes index.
    1. Kierkegaard, Søren Aabye, 1813–1855.
B4377.S73   1976   198'.9   76–6860
ISBN 0–8057–6234–5

Contents

About the Author

Brita K. Stendahl was born in Stockholm, Sweden, in 1925. She attended Uppsala University where she received a teol. fil. ex. (1945); a teol. kand. degree (1949); a fil. kand. degree (1954). In 1954 the family moved to the United States where her husband, now the dean of the Divinity School, became a professor at Harvard. In 1956 Mrs. Stendahl taught a course in Swedish Language and Literature at Harvard. This experience sparked her interest in the study of comparative literature. In 1959–60 she formalized this study at Uppsala, Sweden, and from 1961–63 she was a Radcliffe Scholar at the Institute for Independent Study. She then taught in the Freshman Seminar Program at Harvard and presently teaches in the Radcliffe Seminar Program where she introduced a course in the literature of Søren Kierkegaard that became the basis for this book.

Preface

Kierkegaard is not easy to read. His complicated personality, reflected in the wide variety of styles he used and in the great number of *personae* he invented, constantly mystifies the reader and erects barriers for him. Once familiar with Kierkegaard's indirect method of presentation, however, readers often find his works both exhilarating and rewarding. The intention of this book is to provide an introduction to his changing moods and to the various modes of his thought and writing. Since he is anything but aphoristic, I have tried to make a virtue of the necessity of quoting him *in extenso* by selecting characteristic passages that will also help the reader build up a "Kierkegaard memory," that is, a vocabulary of Kierkegaardian terms and ideas that will facilitate further study of his works. Moreover, I have tried in every case to quote from the most readily available American paperback editions of his works so that one can easily consult these passages in their larger context.

We are accustomed to look to thinkers for answers to the large general questions that form the basis of Western philosophy. Because Kierkegaard ignored most traditional questions— or rather approached them from an unconventional angle—we must learn to read him not for direct answers, but for the many questions he poses and for the shape in which he wraps them. Therefore it is perhaps best to view him first as a literary figure and to make an unhurried appraisal of his various styles, giving ample time to his questions and counterquestions; for Kierkegaard was, above all, a poet who used his imagination for the high purpose of the spiritual enlightenment of the individual. He became convinced that the most important things in life, those pertaining to ethics and religion, could not be argued. But they could be brought into view. One could point out a way, indicate a model. He used his literary talents and his brilliant intellect to project situations and to create possibilities that the reader can recognize and explore. He invented characters whose dilemmas we share. While he may seem to repeat himself, greater familiarity with his work shows that by constantly changing and rearranging the same material he was really attempting to clarify the issues; thereby he hoped to deepen our understanding of important concepts, such as fear and pity, sin and despair, love and faith. Indeed, Kierkegaard is a supreme poet-dialectician when it comes to illustrating the tension between such pairs. He makes us both see and feel how they are connected. My material for this study is organized around the so-called aesthetic works, but in the interest of wholeness I have also included crucial data from his life, as well as key terms from his other works.

Chapter 1 analyzes Kierkegaard's particular and personal choice, selecting the term "witness to the truth" as a vital expression for what he wanted to become for his age. If this concept of his mission has made him a source of inspiration to countless individuals, it has also made him a source of embarrassment to the academic disciplines, since it led him into the shadowy no-man's-land somewhere between the boundaries of literature, philosophy, and theology.

Chapter 2 surveys Kierkegaard's apprenticeship. He has been called an "author's author," a title he earned, not because of any esoteric strain in his voluminous output, but because of his meticulous and self-conscious approach to "authorship." Before he ventured into writing, he was fully aware of the enormous difficulties involved in achieving the stylistic mastery and the philosophical maturity of a genuine author whose work would be not merely interesting and amusing but truly great and immortal. Since he was quite aware that his moment for becoming such a genuine author had not yet arrived, he considered his earliest writings only a preparation for his later literary mission. These early works contain a preview of what was to come.

Chapter 3 deals with the four crises in Kierkegaard's life that not only assured him of his identity, but also precipitated his feverish literary activity. These events yielded the experience he needed before undertaking genuine "authorship." Like many other great authors, Kierkegaard wrote, not fiction, but transcendent autobiography, that is, he consciously wrote about himself—not as a personality, but as a typical human case. After much recollection and reflection upon what he had experienced, he translated, rearranged, and experimented with his material from various points of view. He undertook this task in solitude and with the utmost seriousness—before God.

These first three chapters form a unit, which contains the necessary background material for an intelligent reading of any Kierkegaardian text. Chapters 4, 5, and 6 examine in some detail the texts of *Either/Or, Fear and Trembling,* and *Stages on Life's Way,* dealing primarily with the questions that might arise during a first reading. Thus I do not attempt to offer definitive solutions to the riddles posed by the *personae* and the pseudonymous editors or authors of these works. Rather, I try to present the riddles in a way congenial to Kierkegaard's own method, letting the categories of his thought emerge from the text so that by the end of the second unit of the book the reader should be reasonably familiar with his philosophical framework.

Chapter 7 links the two units of the book by examining the relations among three of Kierkegaard's *personae.* While he was publishing his aesthetic works under various pseudonyms, he simultaneously wrote a series of essays that he called "edifying discourses." These he published under the name of S. Kierkegaard. The puzzle of the pseudonyms only becomes complicated when we approach Climacus (the author of *Concluding Unscientific Postscript*) and Anti-Climacus (author of the psychological treatise *Sickness unto Death* and of the edifying work entitled *Training in Christianity*). Unlike other *personae,* these two represent a point of view strikingly similar to what we normally conceive of as Kierkegaard's own position. In this chapter, I attempt to disentangle Kierkegaard from these two pseudonyms and thus to reveal the actual nature of his intellectual and spiritual quest.

Chapter 8, finally, is both a review and a practical application of the approach to Kierkegaard that I recommend. It is an exercise, if you will, in the "Kierkegaard memory." For that purpose I have chosen one of his early aesthetic works, *Repetition,* which has always been considered a difficult text. This chapter functions both as a recapitulation of Kierkegaard's themes and as a confirmation of his aims.

For all his modernity, Kierkegaard was still very much the product of his own time. There is little to suggest, for example, that when he established the category of "the individual" he ever supposed that this role could be filled by a woman or that women could be considered the intellectual equals of men. Nothing is to be gained by trying to synchronize such aspects of his thought with the contemporary world. Also, though I refer from time to time to Kierkegaard's relation to romantic philosophy, any attempt to make a detailed assessment of the connections between his thought and that of his predecessors— Lessing, Hamann, Fichte, and Hegel, to name a few of the most important—is beyond the scope of this book. Moreover, in an effort to give a presentation of Kierkegaard's thought, I have purposely avoided involving the reader in scholarly debates about his merits as a philosopher. The question I ask in this book is "Why did Kierkegaard adopt this peculiar mode of writing?" I feel that the best way to seek an answer to such a question is simply to ascend the spiral staircase of his dialectics, taking due note of the principles that underlie its construction. Because this is a guided tour, I have consistently used the pronoun "we" to emphasize my feeling that at the top of the stairs the reader and I both enter a world of unanswered questions.

At Harvard I had the privilege of listening to two excellent teachers in Scandinavian studies: Barry Jacobs and Göran Printz-Påhlson. Many aspects of my interpretation of Kierkegaard are owing to their clear grasp of his works. I am also truly grateful to Professor Jacobs and to Professor Paul L. Holmer, whose helpful criticisms of the manuscript have been incorporated into the final form of the book. I also wish to thank Joyce Townsend and Ole Lokensgard for their painstaking scrutiny of my text and Louise Pfeiffer for executing the final typing of the book. Finally, I must express my abiding gratitude to the Radcliffe Institute, which gave me not only the opportunity to teach, but also the encouragement to write.

Cambridge, Massachusetts   BRITA K. STENDAHL

Acknowledgments

I am grateful to the following publishers for permission to make quotations from works to which they hold the copyright:

Princeton University Press for the following works by Søren Kierkegaard: *Either/Or*, Volume I translated by David F. Swenson and Lillian Marvin Swenson, Volume II translated by Walter Lowrie, translations revised by Howard A. Johnson (copyright © 1959); *Fear and Trembling* and *The Sickness Unto Death*, translated by Walter Lowrie (copyright © 1954); *Training in Christianity*, translated by Walter Lowrie (copyright © 1967); *Philosophical Fragments or A Fragment of Philosophy*, 2nd. ed., translated by David F. Swenson, revised by Howard V. Hong (copyright © 1962); *Stages on Life's Way*, translated by Walter Lowrie (copyright © 1969); *On Authority and Revelation: The Book on Adler, or a Cycle of Ethico-Religious Essays*, translated by Walter Lowrie (copyright © 1955); *Repetition: An Essay in Experimental Psychology*, translated by Walter Lowrie (copyright © 1969); *Concluding Unscientific Postscript*, translated by David F. Swenson and Walter Lowrie (copyright © 1969), reprinted by permission of Princeton University Press and the American Scandinavian Foundation; *Mimesis: The Representation of Reality in Western Literature* by Erich Auerbach, translated by Willard Trask (copyright © 1953), and *Kierkegaard's Thought* by Gregor Malantschuk, translated by Howard V. Hong and Edna H. Hong (copyright © 1971).

Harper & Row for quotations from the following by Søren Kierkegaard: *The Point of View For My Work As An Author*, translated by Walter Lowrie; *Works of Love*, translated by Howard V. Hong and Edna H. Hong; *The Journals of Kierkegaard*, translated by Alexander Dru; *The Concept of Irony*, translated by Lee M. Capel; and *Kierkegaard* by Walter Lowrie. Indiana University Press for quotations from *Armed Neutrality and An Open Letter*, translated by Howard V. Hong and Edna

Chronology

1813   May 5. S.K. born in Copenhagen.

1830   October 30. Matriculated in the university.

1833   April. Takes his examinations.

1837   May. Sees Regine for the first time.

1838   August 9. His father dies.

        September 7. Publication of *From the Papers of One Still Living*.

1840   July 3. Takes his examination.

        July 19–August 6. Tour in Jutland.

        September 8–10. Woos Regine and becomes engaged.

1841   August 11 (*circa*). Sends back the ring to Regine.

        September 29. Defense of his thesis, *The Concept of Irony*.

        October 11. Final breach with Regine.

        October 25–March 6. Visit to Berlin.

1843   February 20. Publication of *Either/Or*.

        April 16. At evensong at Easter Regine nods.

        May 16. Publication of *Two Edifying Discourses*.

        May?–June? Short visit to Berlin.

        October 16. Publication of *Repetition, Fear and Trembling*, and *Three Edifying Discourses*.

        December 6. Publication of *Four Edifying Discourses*.

1844   March 5. Publication of *Two Edifying Discourses*.

        June 8. Publication of *Three Edifying Discourses*.

        June 13. Publication of *Fragments*.

        June 17. Publication of *The Concept of Dread, Prefaces*.

        August 31. Publication of *Four Edifying Discourses*.

1845   April 29. Publication of *Three Discourses on Imagined Occasions*.

        April 30. Publication of *Stages on Life's Way*.

        May 13–24. Visit to Berlin.

        December 20. Criticism in *Gæa* of "Guilty?/Not Guilty?"

        December 27. S.K.'s reply in *Fædrelandet*.

December 29. P. L. Møller's reply in *Fædrelandet*.

1846 January 2. First article against S.K. in *The Corsair*.

January 10. S.K.'s reply in *Fædrelandet*.

February 27. Publication of *Concluding Unscientific Post-script*.

March 30. Publication of *A Literary Review*.

May 2–16. Visit to Berlin.

July 12. Buys Magister Adler's books.

October 2. Goldschmidt retires from *The Corsair*.

1846– *The Book on Adler* written.
1847

1847 March 18. Publication of *Edifying Discourses in Various Spirits*.

September 29. Publication of *The Works of Love*.

November 3. Regine married to Schlegel.

December 23. Goldschmidt begins publication of *North and South*.

December 24. S.K. sells home on Nytorv.

1848 April 26. Publication of *Christian Discourses*.

July 24–27. Publication of *The Crisis and A Crisis in the Life of an Actress*.

1848– *The Point of View for My Work as an Author* written.
1849

1849 May 14. Publication of second edition of *Either/Or, The Lilies of the Field*.

May 19. Publication of *Two Minor Ethico-Religious Treatises*.

July 30. Publication of *The Sickness unto Death*.

1850 April 30. Moves to new home at Nørregade.

September 27. Publication of *Training in Christianity*.

December 20. Publication of *An Edifying Discourse*.

1851 August 7. Publication of *About My Work as an Author* and *Two Discourses at the Communion*.

September 10. Publication of *For Self-Examination*.

1851– *Judge for Yourself* written.
1852

1854 January 30. Bishop Mynster dies.

December 18. Article against Martensen published in *Fædrelandet*.

Chronology

1855 January–May. Polemic in *Fædrelandet*.
May–September. The nine numbers of *The Instant* issued.
November 4. His death.

CHAPTER 1

The Vital Expression

I *Witness to the Truth*

IN the last years of his short life, Søren Kierkegaard came upon an expression that stopped him short: he meditated on it, and in the end it took possession of him. This expression was "witness to the truth" (*Sandhedsvidne*).[1] Kierkegaard had a passion for the truth, and that it be rightly expressed was of vital importance to him, a matter of life and death. His two teachers, Socrates and Christ, were both put to death for witnessing.

To be a witness, then, is dangerous business. It offends the established order. Kierkegaard knew and understood that the Greek word for "witness" translated also as "martyr." When meditating upon this relationship, he also came to understand that the method that he had used all along in his writing was incapable of fulfilling his responsibility as a Christian—which was of paramount importance to him. He had learned his method of questioning from Socrates' maieutic method (maieutic = related to midwifery), and he had perfected it into a style. This style of hide and seek came to dominate both the structure of his writing and the way in which he organized his life. We may wonder whether anyone in the nineteenth century was more explicitly concerned about "life style" than Kierkegaard.

But he became increasingly aware that he would have to come out into the open sooner or later; that he would have to become a witness to the truth in a direct, unambiguous manner. In 1848—seven years before his death—he had already written in his notebook, and the broken syntax reveals his agony over the question:

Ultimately the user of the maieutic will be unable to bear the responsibility, for the maieutic approach still remains rooted in human

17

sagacity, however sanctified and dedicated in fear and trembling this may be. God becomes too powerful for the maieutic practitioner and then he is a witness, different from the direct witness only in what he has gone through to become a witness.[2]

When Kierkegaard finally comes to the point of speaking out openly against the established order, the object of his witness is not the state but the church: the Church of Denmark. He had begun his studies in theology; all the time he was writing his dissertation on irony and his novels and essays and discourses, he had been concerned with religious matters and observed the shortcomings of the church. However, he had not spoken out directly. But when he heard that powerful phrase, "witness to the truth," applied to a bishop in a Copenhagen funeral eulogy then the fuse burning in Kierkegaard reached its point of explosion. However educated the aristocratic old bishop might have been, he had not been a witness to the truth. That was a lie and a blasphemy. An expression like "witness to the truth" was too vital to be applied casually to an urbane pillar of the established ecclesiastical order. This funeral oration marked an end to Kierkegaard's "armed neutrality"; he was finally induced to drop his reserve.[3]

Why was his reaction so intense? We hope that this introduction to Kierkegaard will make it clear that his entire *oeuvre* was one intensive, extensive undertaking in the art of expressing truth. He knew how difficult it was. The glibness of ecclesiastical rhetoric struck him as cheap while the truth, he had learned, was dear.

We shall attempt to trace—in chronological order—the Kierkegaardian experiment. We shall try to analyze the charade that he felt obliged to act out in his life and his work in order to make us really understand exactly what he was aiming at— and what he was *not* aiming at. For him, it was a necessary performance inasmuch as we need distance and time in order to grasp the expression fully. He was not content merely to define a concept for his readers; he wished to make them know it, personally, inwardly, so that the word became flesh. It was a matter of overwhelming importance to Kierkegaard. Nothing, for him, was more serious than words.

II *The Stimulant*

A teacher of Scandinavian literature who writes an introduction to Kierkegaard must grapple with problems different from those that are usually encountered. Normally, one introduces a complete unknown and explains his or her position by analogy and in terms of "intellectual influences" and stimuli. In the case of Kierkegaard, one is dealing rather with a figure who influenced and stimulated others. And he is by no means unknown. This pertains not only to literature, but also to theology, philosophy, and psychology. There is hardly a respectable *From X to Y* survey that does not include Kierkegaard's name in the index, invoking some reverent words about him as an interesting corrective, as the originator of a fascinating concept, etc.[4] His name—with its standing epithets, "the melancholy Dane" and "the father of existentialism"—is often bandied about.

Articles about Kierkegaard have appeared in likely and unlikely journals, from the *Harvard Theological Review* to *The New Yorker*. Each year students write papers on "Kierkegaard and ——": Kierkegaard and Rilke, Kierkegaard and Dürrenmatt, Nabokov and Kierkegaard, and so forth. The ribs of his umbrella reach far.[5]

Kierkegaard, Kierkegaard—where does he belong? What is his primary discipline? Theology, philosophy, psychology, literature, or history of ideas? Who has adopted him? No one. No discipline has accepted his entire corpus, nor is he truly respectable in any though the number of books and dissertations relating to his works continues to mount. This creates an awkward situation, for Kierkegaard is arrogant enough to ask for either total acceptance or angry rejection; he saw his work as of whole cloth, and would stand for no cutting. In a sense he was right in this insistence, for, indeed, his work will not yield if the whole is not duly considered.

Theologians find him most suggestive, and he no doubt influenced such later Christian thinkers as Barth, Tillich, and Gogarten, as well as such Jewish thinkers as Buber and Heschel.[6] Yet, among theologians, Kierkegaard is often considered limited in that he is concerned almost exclusively with two doctrines: that of the Fall and that of Incarnation.

It is precisely his stress upon these two doctrines that makes Kierkegaard an aberration in other disciplines. For scholars in the history of ideas, Kierkegaard becomes an interesting corrective to Hegel, but he is regarded as too singular to represent more than a footnote in the development of great Western European thought.

Philosophers have had a problem because of the "father" image often attached to him. Kierkegaard is supposed to be the source of the existentialism of Heidegger, Jaspers, and Sartre, writers he influenced; but all of these philosophers have used his work piecemeal. Only recently have scholars begun to distinguish Kierkegaard from his alleged followers. We find in him a thinker who is passionately concerned with "the expression"—not merely with what is said, but *how* it is said and *when* it is said. He has no interest in the ominous, nor in the void, nor in the unutterable *per se*. The how and when of expression concern him, for he feels that they reveal authenticity. Thus, style, to him, is much more than stylistic rules.[7]

Kierkegaard is out to quash the superficial and the sentimental. He wants to clarify the two existential categories and expose the confusion of the ethical and the religious. He saw that confusion as a natural consequence of the Hegelian largesse that lumped them into the aesthetic category as readily accessible to cognition. Kierkegaard began his philosophical studies as a Hegelian, but his dissertation research and what happened to him personally at this time of his life led him to break with the Hegelian school and choose Socrates for his teacher. "Know thyself" became his first commandment. He took infinite care to see that his thesis, "truth is subjectivity," should be understood not "aesthetically," in which case it makes no sense, but, rather, existentially—that is, ethically and religiously. Thus, to speak of existentialism is a contradiction to the intention of his philosophical work. An existential "system" is a contradiction in terms.[8]

All of Kierkegaard's writing was based on intensive self-examination, and his never-slackening interest in human behavior makes him a gold mine for psychologists. *The Concept of Dread* and *The Sickness unto Death* were intended as textbooks in psychology: fifty years before Freud, Kierkegaard described in them the stirrings of the unconscious and the split of the self into ego and superego. He was acutely aware of the internalizing process; "inwardness" was the forming of the superego through models, heroes, and prototypes.[9] He understood the necessity of that process, for good or for evil. He used no fancy anthropological terminology but spoke of the age-old division of body, soul, and spirit—the body being the physical and the soul, the psychological. When this psychosomatic unity is moved by the spirit, the "self" acts. If a person is constantly directed from outside, then the spirit is not given a chance to act and react freely and decisively. Such a person is hardly a human being: not yet a "self." Only when persons listen inwardly and answer to their own spirit did Kierkegaard consider them to be individuals. Spirit, however, is not easy to have nor to handle. It lends its imagination to the body-soul combination, and the result is less often joyous than it is despairing and melancholy.[10]

Kierkegaard speaks much about melancholy: not in order to depress us, nor to make us feel sorry for him, but because this was a discovery he made which he did not think had been given proper attention. The "melancholy Dane" might be an adequate epithet for Hamlet, but it is a misnomer for Kierkegaard, who was clinical about melancholy. The response of his spirit to melancholy fascinated him. He observed the occasions on which melancholy was *not* the response but when instead the spirit was freed and moving and the self was becoming the image it longed to be. Such happy, full acceptance was possible.[11]

We might suppose that literary critics would claim Kierkegaard eagerly, counting him among the classics in literary criticism. Here we have a writer's writer who has not only composed highly original works, but who has also described what he was doing. A meta-novelist who carefully staked out the categories, assisting the floundering reader in every way. Knowledgeable in aesthetic theory, Kierkegaard gave due credit to Aristotle and to Hegel, whose *Aesthetik* he found superb. He greatly admired Lessing, and Hamann remained the ultimate humorist for him—humor being a category to which he attached special meaning. One might imagine that Kierkegaard would be the ideal subject for a literary critic: offering not only the story, but the entire critical apparatus in the bargain!

But no. We hear some appreciative words. But not many. Northrop Frye, for instance: we would presume that he might feel an affinity to Kierkegaard because of Kierkegaard's delineation of stages, his use of heroes, his careful analysis of irony as the instrument with which poets coordinate and master their work; because of his cyclical view of ages, and his treatment of myths. Yet Frye makes only fleeting reference to him in *The Anatomy of Criticism*.[12]

In any case, Kierkegaard has made his way into the minds of many people without the benefit of support from any one discipline. He has made an impact without becoming a staple in any curriculum. His fame is due to "discoveries." Any time there is crisis and uncertainty, people will discover Kierkegaard and find his insights overwhelmingly powerful. This was true in Germany at the turn of the century and in the Anglo-American world of the thirties.

But it is the Danes we must thank for the impressive scholarship on Kierkegaard. It is their imagination, their faithfulness to the cause, and their pride in a fellow citizen that stand as the cornerstone to this hall of fame. The critic Georg Brandes, who personally did not share Kierkegaard's Christianity, wrote a very incisive and imaginative book about Kierkegaard which was soon translated and which not only sparked the interest that arose in Germany but also gave him a second hearing in Scandinavia. Faithful but less flamboyant laborers—who have issued excellent editions and epoque-making monographs—are Himmelstrup, Thulstrup, and Malantschuk. Copenhagen is the Mecca of Kierkegaard scholarship.[13]

But the unsung heroes in the struggle to bring Kierkegaard to the bookshelves—not only in libraries but in homes all over the world—are the translators. Kierkegaard is very difficult to translate. The task demands sustained energy (for he can be tortuous and long-winded) and vision as well as knowledge. In English the work is almost completed, thanks to tireless efforts by Howard and Edna Hong. It began in the late thirties with Lowrie, Dru, and Swenson, and by now the bibliography is impressive.[14] Kierkegaard was Danish, to be sure, but English is becoming his second language. It is now possible to get an impression of his work without moving to Copenhagen and learning Danish.

III   *The Poet*

What then was Kierkegaard? He was a poet (*Digter*). He said so himself. By poet he does not mean a person who writes verse, of course. No, a poet is a person who grows up with an insatiable need to understand and to create out of understanding. Everybody and everything that comes into view is observed and reflected and set by the imagination into a scheme that is so fascinating that the poet moves from the immediate world into the imaginary (in transcribed Greek, "*poiein*," to make). The immediate can become a hindrance, interfering with the rapid movement of the spirit. Poets need to be free, to forget themselves during the moment of creation. Their one wish is to be so volatile that at any moment they can swing into the world of possibility. To be dragged down by actuality—the momentary milieu—is pain. To his own amazement, Kierkegaard discovered the high degree to which he was able to survive poised in this lofty position without being knocked down by actuality. But he also saw from the start that this could mean living in dream, a temptation that had to be checked by actuality. Hence, he conducted a gigantic experiment with his own life as the laboratory; it is this that makes him a "religious" poet. It is not, in the first instance, the fact that he wrote about religion, but his adherence to the poetic task that allows him to call himself a "religious poet." To put it another way: his faithfulness to his poet's calling made him worthy of the title.

There is an interesting contemporary trend away from fiction and toward biography. The underlying motive could very well be that people have tired of fiction because often it does not seem to be any more than just that; curiously enough, many people read in order to learn about real life and to gather insight and even guidance. With modern fiction, they are not sure about what they read. It could all be a fraud; therefore, a book that purports to portray real life gives more, as it calls for true empathy. In Kierkegaard's case this relation between imagination and actuality was conscious, and was dominated by his quest for truth. Kierkegaard fully understood the poet's responsibility to tell the truth. He carries on a dialogue with what he calls "his poet," splitting himself in two, checking himself by displaying the other side.

His greatness as a poet does not depend on his style: at times it can be marvelous, poetic, witty, revealing an uncanny gift for the perfect metaphor, but at other times (and in the same paragraph), it may be as heavy, labored, and tortuous as any German philosopher's discourse.[15] What is great is his choice of themes and of heroes. At this some will balk, saying: What is so great about that? It all seems very old and familiar: Socrates, Jesus, Abraham, Job, Don Juan, Faust, lilies in the field and birds in the air? But this is exactly the point.

This is at the heart of his greatness. He was angry with "modern" writers who craved the new, who scrutinized and pulverized their experience. Kierkegaard is not interested in anything new; he doubts whether true novelty is possible. For him, the miracle is that the old becomes new for each generation; that repetition is not dreary, but a marvelous thing. The fact that it is the same and yet not the same lends religious significance to repetition. And it is in this wonder that Kierkegaard wants his reader to participate. It is to this end that he applies all his cunning.

Kierkegaard came to distinguish between "genuine," essential, or authentic authors and "premise-authors." "Genuine" authors are those who can see things in their total connection, who have a point of view congruent with the way in which they live, and, thus, they can give to their age what it needs. "Premise-authors," on the other hand, merely take from the age the experience they need and give only a quick display of playing with matches.[16]

IV The Present Age

One way to begin reading Kierkegaard is to pick up a literary review he once wrote called *The Two Ages*. Part of the review is published in English under the title *The Present Age*.[17] It was written in 1846, i.e., two years before the revolutionary year 1848, during which so many of Europe's established institutions overturned. Anticipation and anguish filled the age. Some called it a revolutionary age. No, declared Kierkegaard; changes would occur, but not revolution, because revolution meant radical change. And Kierkegaard did not think his age capable of such change.

When Kierkegaard was growing up, Denmark comprised two "nations" in terms of education and belief. On the one hand, there were the well-to-do, the nobility and the professionals, the lawyers, doctors, and scientists, all of whom shared in an inherited and imported culture and in the Latin language that was its symbol. In the beginning of this review, *The Present Age*, Kierkegaard stated:

If we had statistical tables of the consumption of intelligence from generation to generation as we have for [alcoholic] spirits, we should be astounded at the enormous amount of scruple and deliberation consumed by small, well-to-do families living quietly, and at the amount which the young, and even children, use. For just as the children's crusade may be said to typify the Middle Ages, precocious children are typical of the present age.[18]

Kierkegaard knew what he was writing about; he grew up among such people.

On the other hand, he did not fail to notice that, alongside the educated, there were the servants, the farmers, the lower-middle class, and also the majority of the women. All these people had little or no education. Their world view was that of the Bible. Denmark was (and is) a Protestant country with a state Lutheran Church. It was in church that the two groups met, listening to sermons by the only people forced to straddle the chasm between the exciting world of ideas—of progress and development and rising expectations—and the cyclical world of the farmers, the poor and the lowly among whom expectation of rise and conquest meant little, but content and discontent were very real. The clergy, themselves educated, joined with the educated and spoke like them. It took Kierkegaard a long time to realize that the educated rich do not apprehend Biblical messages in the same manner as the common man. A Biblical message speaks immediately to the poor while, in their sophistication the educated "translate" it. When that eventually became clear to him, it became his own one-man revolution.

Kierkegaard addressed *The Present Age*, however, to his educated peers from whom he had heard much talk but little evidence of what alone in his estimation could bring about revolution—namely, passion. He observed that when the aim is single, not ambiguous, and when the vision is focused and bright, not double and blurred, revolution can come. Kierkegaard's purpose in writing *The Present Age* was not to advocate revolution, but to correct what he felt to be gross misuse of the term. It was in order to overcome the confusion that he contributed an analysis of "the present age."

In his review, Kierkegaard sees the age characterized not by revolutionary passion but by "leveling." By "leveling," he means the capacity always to see two sides to everything: a "both/and." Reflection enters in. But it is by no means automatically true that reflecting before a decision makes it come out right. On the contrary, we then see that both sides have merits and drawbacks, and the more we discuss the harder it is to decide. The case that at first seems to be so clear reduces itself to a mere "on the one hand/on the other hand," a "both/and." Therefore Kierkegaard feels that reflection often hinders action. Leveling is a silent, abstract process that chisels away at the human spirit. There might be sudden outbursts of enthusiasm, but these are instantly rebuffed and reflected upon, so that in the end the individual feels powerless, and things grind on. Leveling is a kind of entropy. Its abstract power cannot be halted.

In contrast to the Age of Enlightenment, when there was a genuine passion for learning, and to the Age of the French Revolution, when there was genuine enthusiasm for violent overthrow, Kierkegaard's age, he wrote, was pervaded by leveling: The age is not revolutionary, for it is too calculating. The age is not joyous, for it is too serious. The age is not heroic, for it is too intelligent. The age is not for learning; it is too busy for that. In other words, the age is ambiguous because although everybody is able to criticize everything, everything is still left standing and empty. A revolutionary age would "pull everything down."

In such an age as his, people search for values and morality. But, said Kierkegaard, we cannot look *about* for values; we must look *inward*:

Morality is character, character is that which is engraved (charásso); but the sand and the sea have no character and neither has abstract intelligence, for character is really inwardness. Immorality, as energy, is also character; but to be neither moral nor immoral is merely ambiguous, and ambiguity enters into life when the qualitative distinctions are weakened by a gnawing reflection. The revolt of the passions is elemental, the dissolution brought about by ambiguity is a silent sorites [a form of sophism leading by gradual steps from truth to absurdity] that goes on night and day. The distinction between good and evil is enervated by a superficial, superior and theoretical knowledge of evil, and by a supercilious cleverness which is aware that goodness is neither appreciated nor worth while in this world, that it is tantamount to stupidity. No one is any longer carried away by the desire for the good to perform great things, no one is precipitated by evil into atrocious sins, and so there is nothing for either the good or the bad to talk about, and yet for that very reason people gossip all the more, since ambiguity is tremendously stimulating and much more verbose than rejoicing over goodness or repentance over evil.

The springs of life, which are only what they are because of the qualitative differentiating power of passion, lose their elasticity. The distance separating a thing from its opposite in quality no longer regulates the inward relation of things. All inwardness is lost . . .[19]

In the present age, to be a subject has come to mean "to be a third party," an observer; it should mean participation, choosing sides, knowing one's role. Instead of going about their tasks with enthusiasm, Kierkegaard observed, people are torn apart by envious discontent. This envy, this resentment, results in leveling.

In a social context in which leveling has set in, hierarchies lose their meaning, and a bland playacting of roles takes place. When people no longer fill their roles but merely play them, exhaustion, boredom, and despair overcome those roles and result in unhealthy tensions among the people involved. Relationships cannot be happy. A father is embarrassed to command his children. Being obedient to their parents annoys children. To be a ruler is made to be sham, and to be a citizen is made to be a chore. Nobody dares admire wholeheartedly. Instead of enthusiasm in joint enterprise, resentment arises that poisons the will and hinders people from making decisions.

Twice in this review Kierkegaard says that reflection in itself is not evil, but that it can become so if it tries, by some half-digested doctrine, to abolish concrete observation and diminish

real contradictions that confront people everywhere in life. He
believes that, as there is a time for everything, there must first
be a time for silence, for private digestion—then comes the
time for speech. Leveling degrades that "vital" difference, the
time and the tension that should exist between the moment at
which some event is perceived by individuals and the moment
at which they respond to it in an innate manner, showing
character. Only in this way do we come to know in our "selves"
the vital difference between private and public, form and content, concealment and manifestation, love and debauchery. By
talking too soon and thus not letting the differences arise and
make themselves felt to us, all is reduced to trivia. Gossip,
formlessness, superficiality, flirtation, and mere "reasoning" result.
Rather than a revolutionary age, this is an age of advertisement,
writes Kierkegaard, of endless abstraction and concern for the
temporal. Money, in itself only representational, becomes the
single object of desire.[20]

What is the remedy? There is none, answers Kierkegaard.
When the leveling process has entrenched itself, it cannot be
stopped. Some might hope for a great hero to appear, a person
who could lead, but they are mistaken in their hope. A house
infected with termites will eventually fall when it is hollowed
out. The days of spectacular heroes such as Holger Danske or
Martin Luther are over. No association or party would agree on
their merits. Objective debate passes back and forth; the Press
informs the Public, and the majority agrees with the majority.
No "individual" can withstand such abstract power without
acknowledging the sham and evil. But those who become such
individuals "leap" from the temporal to the eternal, choosing
standards above the general din. The majority will not accept
such persons. Rather it is more probable that such individuals
will be put to death, as Socrates once was in a time equally
sophisticated and rich in culture, yet just as barren, as the
present age.

At the end of his analysis, Kierkegaard begins to speak of
one special individual called the "unrecognizable," the "secret
servant" or the "spy":

Only by suffering can the "unrecognizable" dare to help on the
levelling process and, by the same suffering action, judge the instru-

ments. He dare not overcome the levelling process directly, that would be his end, for it would be the same as acting with authority. But he will overcome it in suffering and in that way express once more the law of his existence, which is not to dominate, to guide, to lead, but to serve in suffering and help indirectly. Those who have not made the leap will look upon his unrecognizable action, his suffering, as failure; those who have made the leap will suspect that it was victory, but they can have no certainty, for they could only be made certain by him, and if he gave that certainty to a single person it would be the end of him, because he would have been unfaithful to the divinity in desiring to play at being authority: that would mean that he had failed; not only by being unfaithful to God in trying to use authority, but because he did not obey God and teach men to love one another by compelling himself, so that even though they begged him to do so he should not have deceived them by exerting authority.[21]

Such a passage is a good guide to Kierkegaard's life and work. Here we find all his favorite credentials: to speak "without authority," to "communicate indirectly," to serve "in suffering," and even to dare to "help on" the leveling process. To do this is faithful service to God. To overcome the leveling process directly, however, would bring death. That would mean becoming a martyr.

This position is not an easy one to adopt or explain. If he were so clever, why didn't he say so directly? Indirect communication had come to have enormous value and religious meaning for him. To be open to God was to be concealed to others. There was an inner journey, an inwardness, that had to be completed before there could be a time for speech, e.g., for witnessing. Kierkegaard came to use the word "suffering" more and more for this mode of being. In his lonely and painstaking search, he was actually pleading for time.

Kierkegaard went to great lengths to clarify that, when he wrote, he did so "without authority." He was not an apostle. He desired no disciples. He had no word from God. He was only a poet.[22] Moreover, he was "the unrecognizable." For years he played hide and seek with the people of Copenhagen. While he labored arduously with his books, he also managed to take time out to be seen, to appear as an idler and a dandy, fre-

quenting the theater or walking the streets as if he had nothing
in common with the inward process to which his books bore
witness. Furthermore, his major works were not published
under his own name, but were pseudonymous; so that even if
people knew he was the author, they remained uncertain about
his relationship to the various pseudonyms.

Shortly before the publication of the review *The Two Ages*,
Kierkegaard's public image had undergone a dramatic metamorphosis. He had become the fool ridiculed by a weekly
journal, and as a consequence people laughed at him and
pestered him in the street, picking up cues from the journal,
The Corsair.[23] Kierkegaard had provoked the attack himself;
he hints at this when he says that he has to "help on," e.g., to
speed up the leveling process. At home in his study, he worked
on his religious writing. Outside, he was laughed at as the fool.
He was, indeed, the unrecognizable.

This was all according to his scheme. His person, he felt,
should not intrude upon his works. He was a secret servant, a
spy—in disguise—for God.

Why all these theatrics? The answer to this question belongs
to "the poetry"—what he made of himself while faithfully waiting for God to let him speak directly "in character." The moment
finally came in the last year of his life when, in answer to the
"witness to the truth" challenge (of which we spoke earlier),
Kierkegaard issued a little journal called *The Moment*.[24]

Thoroughly polemical, *The Moment* was against the Church
and its handling of the sacraments, against the sophisticated
clergy and the clergy's entrenched mores and bourgeois habits
which he would have nothing to do with—considering them
even a betrayal of the Christianity of the New Testament.

We should not overlook the fact that when at last he spoke
directly, he addressed himself to the common people with whom
he could finally identify himself completely. Precisely because by
now he was poor and feeling old and tired, he could easily
transmit the message. The ecclesiastical establishment seemed
a hoax to him, a shameful disguise, a deception and a terrible
confusion. He wanted simple honesty.[25] He wanted the kind
of honesty he saw among the people, but not among the
educated who were the leveled and the levelers. At this point

Kierkegaard obviously was not looking back in memory and reflection but living only for the moment and the future.

Although the search he undertook was universal, it was also highly personal. It had to be experienced, and Kierkegaard was coy about what he was doing. But in the end there was not a shred of reluctance. There had been a long time for silence; he had simply had to be sure. Both as an author and as a person he had to go through a phenomenal balancing act before he could make the leap.

The chapters that follow primarily concern this balancing act, its beauty, its pain, and its rewards.

CHAPTER 2

The Preparation

WHAT are precocious children? We conjure up a picture of lonely children growing up with loving parents guiding and guarding their every step, admiring their progress. When we hear wise and knowledgeable remarks from such children, we smile, yet shake our heads, wondering what will become of these little grown-ups.

What happens to children who have it all in advance, those who learn by rote instead of by experience? This is the question. The ones who know more than their contemporaries—what do they do when they encounter these contemporaries? Luckily, some of them—perhaps the majority—stop themselves, adjust to the situation, relearn, and find their places in society as is. Making such an adjustment is necessarily a difficult and lonely process.

Some of these children enjoy the feeling of superiority and cleverness that comes from overwhelming others with a better argument, faster repartée, particularly when their only defense is a quick tongue; it becomes a great temptation for them to rely on this unique but deadly strength. "You might beat me up, but I'll annihilate you first with a single comment!" These children elicit fear and respect, but they seldom get what they so desperately need (although they may not know it): that is, friendship. Lonely children like this remain lonely children though they grow up admired, envied, and feared.

Such gifted children learn what they learn secretly because they can never let on to anyone that they are learning something they did not already know. The manner of testing new knowledge in itself becomes a whole production that must be staged and acted out, so carefully prepared that nothing goes awry, exposing ignorance. Such children learn by observing others and experimenting with them rather than by direct confrontation.

Kierkegaard belonged to this species of lonely children, and he knew it. He was master of the deadly repartée, the unmasking and exposing of others. As he grew into manhood, his quick, witty tongue made him a celebrity in the salons of Copenhagen. He had plenty of material to play with, and like the finest juggler, he could keep it all in the air, giving a breathtaking exhibition. When he returned home, alone, he would react to his own behavior, his all too perfect memory replaying every scene. He reflected on the manner in which he had dealt with things and recognized the danger of such a style, not only for the "victims" and for those he bedazzled, but also for himself. Perhaps he occasionally regarded such behavior as healthy. While alienating some persons—the dense and the slow-witted—he received telepathic messages of tacit agreement from intelligent and sensitive individuals in the form of smiles and sudden glances. Eyes met and spoke.

I Papers of One Still Living

One of the most venerated figures of Kierkegaard's time was Hans Christian Andersen, for whom doors opened wherever he went. Andersen, who was ten years older than Kierkegaard, would become the center of the family circle, telling his fairy tales to the children while keeping an eye on the adult listeners. He amused them and held them all spellbound.

Andersen did not want to be "merely" an author of children's books. He had enormous ambition; he wanted to conquer. He wanted to write the best novels and to dominate the stage. He yearned to befriend the "finest people": royalty, nobility, and artists. He wished to travel and to visit the greatest palaces and the quaintest towns. And everything he wanted, and everything he dreamed, came true. He did it all. And then there was the victorious return to his hometown, Odense, illuminated in his honor. Yet it often seemed to him as if none of it were true, as if he had to pinch himself and ask: Is this actually happening to me? (*Mit Livs Eventyr*).[1]

He tried five times to write his true story in novel form. But epic proved a genre he could not master. The ugly duckling that became a swan makes a wonderful fairy tale, but as a novel, peopled with ordinary characters, it becomes boring—no matter

how many grizzly adventures and sudden elevations take place.
When Kierkegaard ventured to try his pen for the first time, it
is typical that his chosen target was none other than the renowned H. C. Andersen, whose novel *Only A Fiddler* had recently been published.[2] Kierkegaard demolished in order to
produce a clean beginning. He did a thorough job—so thorough
that few have managed to finish reading his little book. For
this reason, the title is often misunderstood. *Papers of One Still
Living* does not in the least mean that Kierkegaard was concerned merely with his own life span. Not at all. The idea
behind this twisted title is very different.[3]

It lies at the very center of his criticism of Andersen's novel,
which is built around the belief that geniuses—well-met, nour-
ished, and helped along—will develop their talents and grow
miraculously before the very eyes of their benefactors. If, on
the other hand, genius is spurned and relegated to abject poverty
to freeze and starve, then the talent will wither and die, and
the world will be so much the poorer for it. The fiddler in the
novel is just such a poor, rejected genius whose miserable funeral
procession—bearing him, like Mozart, to a pauper's grave—mo-
mentarily halts the grand equipage of his former beloved, who
is now a successful, rich, and famous singer. She bows her head
for the deceased, believing he was *only a fiddler.*

The book portrays two gifted children of the same background
who are treated differently by life. The one who was pampered
and spoiled became successful. The other was deprived and
eventually succumbed. In his analysis, Kierkegaard states that
such ideas are clearly nonsense. As he saw it, Mr. Andersen had
not the foggiest notion of what constitutes a genius. For
Kierkegaard, adversity does not thwart a genius. Genius feeds on
adversity and overcomes it. Nothing can stop true genius; it
will have its own way.[4] Andersen had simply wrapped the story
too much around his own life without testing it for any universal
validity. Truly great epic artists, however, forget about their
personal life and live their story's point of view. Epic authors
should die from themselves in order to resurrect life in their
works that present a vision greater than the authors themselves.
They must die from the inessential and live transfigured in the
essential.[5]

Such authors have found a key to life's meaning. They have caught a second breath. Their work provides the center they have found, a center around which everything else takes form. They have died from the world only to be resurrected in their work.

In this light Kierkegaard diagnosed the three forms of story-telling: the lyric, the epic, and the drama. Of these, the lyric—the most immediate—speaks principally to feeling. The lyric poet sings for the moment and creates a mood. There is no need to express a coherent life view. The epic poet, however, aims at cognition, and here the author reveals his point of view, his philosophy of life (or his lack of one). Finally, the drama speaks of the conflict between points of view and the clashing of wills. Therefore, as the most complicated form of storytelling, drama demands the most; an ability to express point of view dialectically.

Kierkegaard was of the opinion that Andersen lacked a center of gravity, a life view which epic poets must have so that their work does not run out in sand and dust. He felt that Andersen—if he wanted to continue to write novels—must find a sustaining life view. Hence, Kierkegaard offered Andersen a choice between either a humanistic life view or a Christian conviction. No matter what he chose, he must face a moment when his life needed to be understood through an idea, and this idea would then be the key, the "Governance" that guided his works. He could not go on toying with both.

The title, *Papers of One Still Living*, then explains itself. Kierkegaard hints that he, Kierkegaard, has not yet died from himself. He himself cannot yet write as an epic poet. He designates his book as merely the papers of a still-living man.

This was Kierkegaard's first book. Although not a success, it attracted a good deal of attention. And it hurt the sensitive Andersen so much that four years later, when he staged a comedy, he had a character, a barber, read from Kierkegaard's book. In the audience at the time, Kierkegaard stood up to receive recognition. His biting wit made people aware of the sentimentality and the hunger for love that so often made Andersen awkward and cloying in society.

Andersen and Kierkegaard are Denmark's greatest and most

renowned authors. It is a strange coincidence that Kierkegaard's career should start with an attack on the only other writer who could challenge his reputation as their country's top genius. As writers, they certainly stood opposite each other. Andersen wrote by instinct, believing his heart and his ear, disregarding logic and dialectics. Andersen distrusted science and found the university world cold and inhospitable; he emphasized friendliness, goodness. He trusted in Providence and asserted that everything would work out in the end. He was for the underdog, the poor, the weak, and the humble. At times he rewarded them (provided they were honest and generous) with a happy landing among the rich. Consider the ugly duckling which became a swan and lived in the king's pond.[6]

In the light of this criticism, how curious it is to think of the reinforcing influence Andersen's stories have had upon millions of people who have read them and told them as bedtime stories to their children. In terms of philosophy, these tales are not much better than those of Horatio Alger; and yet because they are so much better written and are so much more imaginative, their message—that things will all work out in the end—has often crept in undetected and unchallenged.

Some will say that, so long as Andersen and other writers content themselves with tea parties and tin soldiers, their effect is inconsequential. Yet the moment they innocently, but consistently, begin to attach ethical and religious meaning to what they write, we had better wonder whether they mean what they say. In Andersen's case, we must side with Kierkegaard; there is not much evidence of the man's knowing much about what he professed: goodness, heaven, Providence.

II   The Concept of Irony

The world around us is diffuse, multifaceted, and infinitely complex. For survival, each one of us makes a mental picture of the world. We assemble bits of learning from experience, from books, from the media, and order them into a coherent picture to the best of our ability. New information and insights lead to reordering. We have a great desire to communicate where we are in the world, but making others aware poses problems. Our primary means of communication is verbal. The moment we begin to speak, we are already twice removed from what actually hits us. We find ourselves in the land of signs and symbols. The more complicated the experience we want to communicate, the more involved become our metaphors. The more involved our metaphors, the greater the risk of losing our listeners—those with whom we wish to communicate. Our most earnest efforts lead to boredom in our listeners. We stay with our discourse at our own peril.

And at our own peril, we begin to play tricks. We say what we don't mean and watch the startled reactions. We lose some who refuse to follow by taking us literally, but we gain immensely by the response of those who do follow. Our audience, our reader or listener, comes alive and seems to be getting the point. Through negative means, we have established a positive contact. Even though we haven't said anything, something stirs in the other person. This is indirect communication and the birthplace of irony.

Irony and satire—these ambiguous means of communication—helped Kierkegaard come out of himself and made him a success in society. They left him the master of many occasions. But were they good or evil? With that question he began an investigation that lasted for years, and as his work grew, he grew into it. His dissertation at the university is entitled *The Concept of Irony.*[7]

Kierkegaard did not find it difficult to discover indirect communication. He became more and more aware of his power in verbal communication and delighted in his increasing skills. But who were his "readers"? This worried him. Who got the point? Over the years, he found that those he had trusted and taken for granted as being enlightened and intelligent and fully capable of laughing with him, did not follow him, did not get the point. They laughed but were not roused. Many did not understand what he meant by what he wrote; for instance, many did not see that the book about Andersen was not just about Andersen or for him alone. The seriousness under the surface was often missed.

Nevertheless, indirect communication and irony merged into a point of view that Kierkegaard began to embrace to such a degree that it eventually became an organizing principle of

his life from which he could not tear himself loose even though
he prayed to be saved from it.

The Concept of Irony has the subtitle With Constant Reference to Socrates. According to Kierkegaard's thesis, the concept
of irony has its inception in the person Socrates. Socrates' special
value is his personality. Yet the irony lies in the fact that even
though this personality has had tremendous import, there is
virtually nothing left from which history can judge Socrates.
Only silence. He wrote nothing. Forming a conception of
Socrates is therefore different from forming a conception of
other individuals and philosophers who have left writings from
which we can deduce their points of view.

. . . as there are now thousands of years between him and us, and
since not even his contemporaries could grasp him in his immediacy,
so it is easy to see how doubly difficult it is for us to reconstruct
his existence, for we must endeavor to apprehend through a new
integral [calculus] this already complicated conception. If we next
say that the substantial aspect of Socrates' existence was irony, and
if we postulate further, that irony is a negative concept then one only
sees how difficult it becomes to secure an image of him.[8]

Kierkegaard said that it is a little like seeing "an elf wearing
a hat that makes him invisible." Yet this is the task that
Kierkegaard put before us. We must struggle to see the invisible
and to recognize the hat.

As a dissertation, The Concept of Irony adheres to the common
requirements of scholarship. It contains textual analysis and
debates with leading authorities, particularly Hegel and his
Danish adherents.[9] Kierkegaard wrote it in Danish as opposed
to Latin and, what is more remarkable, he defended this dissertation in Danish, a practice so unusual at the time that he had
to receive special permission.[10]

The book has two parts. The first centers on Socrates and ways
in which he can be understood in the light of what was written
about him around the time that he lived. The second part deals
with irony as seen and used by the Romantic movement.

Who was Socrates? And what was he about? Three outstanding
authors, contemporaries of Socrates, have given us their render-

ings: Plato, Xenophon, and Aristophanes. In his *Memorabilia*, Xenophon's purpose was to prove to the Athenians how wrong they had been in putting this good man to death. In defending Socrates, Xenophon makes him not only innocent but also harmless. Kierkegaard feels that Xenophon—by taking the danger away from Socrates—manages to make the whole drama trivial. A pragmatist, Xenophon's interest lay in stressing the useful in the words and deeds of Socrates.

Instead of the good we have the useful; for the beautiful, the serviceable; for the true, the established [*Bestaaende*]; for the sympathetic, the lucrative; and for the harmonious unity, sobriety.[11]

Xenophon takes the long road, parasang after parasang, in the horizontal forward march of empiricism. If we had no other account of Socrates than Xenophon's, our image of Socrates would have been that of an honorable and well-intentioned sophist, and we might feel that the reason the Athenians put him to death could very well have been, not that they feared him, but that he bored them. What clinches Kierkegaard's argument that Xenophon misunderstood Socrates is his observation that Xenophon's writing contains not a trace of irony.

Turning to Plato, Kierkegaard asks the familiar question of the possible relation between the actual Socrates and Plato's version of the man. Plato no doubt made an image of Socrates that he used to his own purpose. Was the dialogue form an invention of Plato? Kierkegaard got around this question by asking: What is the meaning of asking questions? Either one does it in order to get a reply, so that another question can be asked and then answered, and the dialogue arrives at last at something given (the Idea). Or one begins with questioning further and further, so that one finally arrives at emptiness (Irony). Kierkegaard saw Socrates practicing this latter method; Socrates always began by stating that he knew nothing, and after exhaustive questioning, he always returned to this point of knowing nothing, a point that the other participants had by then realized and come to share. There are "no results." Socrates conception is fully negative in all the early dialogues. Plato's understanding, however, differs. It implies that Socrates was given the Idea. "Where empiricism ends Socrates begins."[12] From the *Republic* and in all later dialogues, this image dominates. But Kierkegaard attributes this image to Plato rather than to the actual Socrates who might have been a man with no speculative needs. Socrates, he thinks, is to be found exactly in the middle, in irony, which oscillates between the ideal and the empirical.

In order to strengthen the ground for this impression, Kierkegaard turned to Aristophanes, who, in *Clouds*, has given us a comic picture of Socrates as the greatest of the sophists. It is told that during a performance of *Clouds*, Socrates stood up so people could find out for themselves what possible resemblance might exist between the man and the character of the play.[13] Kierkegaard is not one to make light of Aristophanes' satire. He gives a lengthy analysis of Aristophanes' ability to reach reality by the comic route. As an image, clouds are perfect symbols of directionless thought. They shape themselves this way and that, resembling everything, but being nothing in themselves. Aristophanes has intuitively understood Socrates as irony. Irony becomes comical the moment one tries to attach results to it, and Kierkegaard points out therefore that the sophists in the play seem comical indeed; however, Socrates remains separated, hovering between heaven and earth in his hammock, crying: Give me a place to stand.[14] The sophists are types, but Socrates has personality. He is comical, to be sure, but nevertheless he has a particular character. His teaching is nonsense, but his dialogue echoes actuality—as when he claims that instead of believing in the gods, one must believe in nothing; and when one speaks, one should speak about nothing.

What Aristophanes had caught instinctively in Socrates' personality was named by both Xenophon and Plato. They discussed Socrates' *daimon* to which he himself had constantly referred. According to Plato, Socrates' *daimon* warned him, restrained him, and urged him to abstain from doing things. According to Xenophon it compelled and urged him to do things. Actually, these are two sides of the same coin, but, according to Kierkegaard, we have here another example of Xenophon's limpness of thought when he opted for the positive while Plato understood the driving force behind the negative.

People in early Greece who were in trouble turned to the

oracle that then commanded them, telling them what to do. Instead, Socrates had his *daimon* within him restraining him. In his inwardness grew a consciousness of self. Socrates' "place to stand" was his subjectivity; he was fully subjective, maintaining a negative relation to everything established: to religion, to the state, to the family, etc. Everything was drawn into question, not because Socrates had a better solution, but because he himself did not know and wanted to know.

Thus Kierkegaard found the Socrates of the *Apology* the most convincing and closest to the actual Socrates. Hegel had argued that Socrates was guilty of the crimes of which he stood accused. Hegel meant that Socrates understood his guilt and accepted the death penalty, thus becoming a tragic hero. Kierkegaard did not agree. According to him, Socrates was incompatible with the state, indifferent to power. Merely because he could convince others that they knew nothing did not mean that he knew anything himself. His task was to free the individual from every commitment. He erased the blackboard with all its signs and equations. But he did not fill it up again. It was not a scholarly life he pursued when he acted out his maieutic role by questioning everything. He pulled people out of the established world. But he did not build or promise a better world. He stood aside and watched them. The expression "know thyself" should be interpreted "separate thyself."[15] This is what Socrates did. He was wholly himself. Not even life and death had a hold on him. Socrates always behaved in the same manner. He questioned beliefs, and during the questioning process he proved that others did not believe either. When he stood trial, he used the same tactic, and the whole enterprise was somehow outside of him—without reality.

Kierkegaard wanted to prove over against Hegel that Socrates did not make the abstract concrete. Socrates' concern was to make the abstract *visible* through the immediate. Socrates was not ignorant, but the very point is that he had knowledge of his ignorance. And by this, he destroyed every bit of knowledge and left nothing, not a stone upon a stone, not even a stone. That is the work of irony.

Kierkegaard wrote in praise of this Socrates and said that we could divide time as before and after Socrates: the man was a turning point in history. Hellenism was then dangerously eroded, and all values were wearing thin. The Sophists had introduced reflection, but it had been improperly used. It provided "information" instead of knowledge. Therefore it leveled rather than contradicted, and it deceived itself by using quantitative measures instead of qualitative ones. Everything was true. Though the age was very rich, it also became greatly impoverished. The Sophists never took the next step by saying that nothing was true.

Socrates became "the next step." This moment is irony. After that something new must come, but something of another quality altogether. In Kierkegaard's opinion, Socrates was the last Classical figure, who destroyed Classicism singlehandedly. It was his own grounding in Classicism that made it possible for him to "hover," to remain in this position of irony.

Socrates did not proceed from a good beyond. He arrived at "the good," and that was as far as he went. The movement was toward the good. All his life Socrates started people on that journey.

Kierkegaard drew parallels between what happened to Classicism at this point in history and what happened to Judaism at the time of the birth of Jesus. He argued that what the Sophists did to Classicism was similar to what, in Judaism, the Pharisees did to the Law. There John the Baptist is the turning point of irony; he knew that he was not the one who should come, yet he did not know what would have to come, or who. He destroyed Judaism not with the new but with the old, by commanding that it give what it professed it already had: Righteousness. He allowed the Law to remain, and therefore it perished because righteousness it could not deliver. The building stood empty.[16]

In the second part of the book on irony, Kierkegaard dealt with the contemporary movement of German Romanticism, which he saw as a reaction against the Age of Reason. But the question that he puts to Romantic poets is: What do they offer? Socrates was a gift to humanity. His person marks a watershed in human history. The Romantic poets, though their position is ironic, seem not to be able to bring out any new quality. Instead of living for the true ideal, they oscillate between actuality and dream. But:

The true ideal is not in any way beyond: it is *behind* us in so far that it is a driving force, *in front* of us insofar as it is an inspiring goal, but through all this it is *within* us and this is the truth.[17]

Irony is a *via negativa*. The individual separates himself from others beginning a personal life. Irony is not the truth, but a way to the truth. In every person's life, there is so much that has to be sorted out. Irony is a surgeon, said Kierkegaard. When irony has been mastered, it will function for the individual in a manner to acquire health.

What true irony teaches is that people should realize actuality, what happens, and not flee from it in dreams. The content in life must become meaningful through "action."

When irony has been mastered it no longer believes, as do certain clever people in daily life, that something must always be concealed behind the phenomenon. Yet it also prevents all idolatry with the phenomenon, for it teaches us to esteem contemplation, so it rescues us from the prolixity which holds that to give an account of world history for example would require as much time as the world has taken to live through it.[18]

Ideality and actuality; and in between lies the sober significance of irony. Thus armed, Kierkegaard was prepared to criticize the Romantic movement severely. For his purposes, he chose to scrutinize Schlegel, Tieck, and Solger, three very popular and influential authors. The Romantic poets were serious and doctrinaire, which Kierkegaard found "melancholy." Their irony was negative, as it must be, but nothing developed out of it. Nothing of another quality. This was so because they neglected the ethical commitment.

For example, Schlegel's *Lucinde* "seeks to abrogate all ethics, not simply in the sense of custom and usage, but that ethical totality which is the validity of mind, the dominion of the spirit over the flesh."[19] *Lucinde* was a very popular novel, much talked and written about. Some were shocked by its portrayal of nakedness. It ridicules exactly these people who are unable to tolerate nudity. But Kierkegaard annihilates the whole discussion by remarking:

However, I shall not concern myself any further whether this is a narrowmindedness, or whether the veil of attire is still not a beautiful image of how all sensuality ought to be, since when sensuality is intellectually mastered it is never naked. Instead, I shall merely call attention to the fact that the world still forgives Archimedes for running stark naked through the streets of Syracuse, and this surely not because of the mild southern climate, but because his spiritual exaltation, his "eureka, eureka" was a sufficient attire.[20]

What made Goethe so infinitely superior a poet is that he had a view of life, a "place to stand," which he constantly brought out in his poetry. According to Kierkegaard, this is what should be required of a poet: "The poet lives only poetically when oriented and thus assimilated into the age in which he lives, when he is positively free within the actuality to which he belongs."[21] To live poetically in this manner is not restricted to "poets" but is a desirable mode of living.

However, Kierkegaard had not finished. He hinted at something superior to irony, and that is humor:

Humor contains a much deeper scepticism than irony, here it is not finitude but sinfulness that everything turns upon. The scepticism of humor relates to the scepticism of irony as ignorance relates to the old thesis: *credo quia absurdum*, but humor also contains a much deeper positivity than irony, for it does not move itself in humanistic determinations but in the anthropic determinations; it does not find repose in making man human, but in making man God-man.[22]

Irony turns upon finitude and humor upon sinfulness. Socrates eviscerated the established values of Classicism. John the Baptist hollowed out the established rules of Judaism. What is *behind* us is also *before* us because it is *within* us. Here we have *in nuce* some of the most important statements that came to guide what Kierkegaard wrote as well as the way in which he lived.

For the student of Kierkegaard, none of his books are unimportant or in-between or preparatory. They are all valid parts of a consistent whole; that is true about all great writers because that is precisely what makes them great. Nobody saw this more clearly than Kierkegaard, who stated it from the very beginning of his authorship. The fact that he later did not include *Papers of One Still Living* and *The Concept of Irony* in what he called "his authorship" clearly indicates that when he wrote *Papers,* he considered himself "still living" and thus not worthy of being a poet; and *The Concept of Irony* was not a "book" but a dissertation. Yet, it is all there in readiness, waiting for the occasion, the experience.

CHAPTER 3

The Experience: Four Crises

THE decisive experience that made Kierkegaard a poet was a love affair. Much has been written about it, though in fact we know rather little. The effects, however, were profound. The experience changed the direction of his life; it radicalized his thinking and revolutionized his life.

Why do we have to bother with the "actual" Kierkegaard? Because his work on Socrates gave him the idea. His inclination had always been to hide himself behind his wit and satire, and in Socrates he found a model who did the same with a purpose in mind. The body of writing that Socrates inspired Kierkegaard to produce proceeds on three levels, and in order to grasp what is going on in the creative process, we must use "integral calculus."[1]

Kierkegaard's life eludes the common manipulations of a biographer: Father's family, mother's family, siblings, friends, a picture of the town, a background in the round of social conditions and politics, and then the events, the color of which has spilled over into the works of the author. Most of Kierkegaard's biographers have concluded that his life was uneventful. This is not so. But he cleverly organized his material so that it came to look that way. Four crises are singled out, and to them, his journals return again and again. In his published works we meet them meticulously set and polished. Biographers therefore often make the mistake of considering the journals and papers to be "the real Kierkegaard." But it is not quite that simple.

Kierkegaard came to suspect that, in the future, people would begin to look for a master key to his writing, and he has taken pains to hide it for good. In his youth, when he was still wondering what to do with his life, he had begun a journal; but later when he had become an author, he started to write systematically in notebooks—believing that one day they too would be published. The entries are finger exercises in preparation for performances, or, as he expressed it, random thoughts: "Random thoughts, the fruit of the moment's more clear intuition are poetic in their aphoristic form, not scholarly. They are the culmination points of thinking."[2] The journals and the papers, then, are just the same as the public works: a kind of costume—more loose-fitting, more colorful at times, but tailored for a purpose. That purpose is not to elucidate his everyday life.

We know from various sources that Kierkegaard's life was not uneventful. His childhood might not have been the most cheerful, but it was filled with imagination and excitement. His weak constitution was compensated for by a brilliant mind that was richly fed by daily events in a big household with children and servants and in schools in which everybody was bigger and stronger than he. Later there came the usual stormy student days which, in his case, were prolonged to a decade. On the social scale, he went to the opera and the theater and visited burlesque shows. He met all sorts of people. There were short trips by carriage and long journeys by coach. He went abroad to Berlin, where he sat in crowded lecture halls to listen to the famous philosopher Schelling. He finished a brilliant dissertation and defended it before an unusually large crowd. He became known as a wit and was welcome in the most fashionable houses.

He was well-met at the aristocratic Heiberg family where he could count on laughter to follow his jokes.[3] He admired Professor Heiberg, who had been one of the first to introduce Hegelian thought to Denmark; and although Kierkegaard got mixed reviews from Heiberg, and he himself wrote satirical reviews of Heiberg's books in his *Prefaces,* he maintained a warm relationship with the family. He wrote a lengthy review (*The Present Age*) of a novel by Heiberg's mother, Madame Gyllembourg, and he adored Heiberg's actress wife, who served as the model for his book *The Crisis and A Crisis in the Life of an Actress.*

In his early youth Kierkegaard relished his conservative stance —making him an important figure in student politics, debating against the emerging liberals. He was also among the founders of the Danish Music Association. He was rich and lived in opulence and elegance with a personal valet at the most stylish address in town. On several occasions he met the king, who had read him and sought his advice.[4]

True, there was also the agony of being well known, written and gossiped about. There was personal sickness and exhaustion, deaths in the family, disappointments over reviews. Later in life came employment and money problems.

When we begin to read Kierkegaard, we wonder about his silences or near silence. Why does he not mention his mother and his sisters? Why don't we know more about Anders, his valet? Or Bishop Peter Kierkegaard, his brother? Or Pastor Boesen, his most faithful friend?

These questions are answered indirectly in our preceding chapter. As a writer, Kierkegaard transcended his life. There was nothing remarkable in these relationships. They were his own and without unusual complication. They might have been used in his writing, but they were not *collisions,* and they have for the most part remained in his private memory bank. This part of himself Kierkegaard considered "uninteresting" to the world. To record it would have been "gossip."

The four crises that he dwells upon are the "interesting" ones. They arose from conflicts with people and issues and they touched him deeply. Each time he acted polemically and disguised his innermost feelings, thus separating himself and alienating the others. It would all be unbelievably strange if we did not know the value that Kierkegaard placed upon the power of indirect communication to intensify inwardness. He acted this way maieutically. This was not fiction; it was life. In each case, the birth process was agonizing. When he had set it in motion, he was no longer in command, and each time he suffered.[5]

I   *The Father, Inheritance, and Upbringing*

When Søren was born in 1813, his father, Michael Kierkegaard, was fifty-six years old. In that year his wealth had tripled, and he had just decided to retire. Søren was the youngest of seven children, and he became the father's companion and delight in the leisurely days of his old age.

The father had not always been in fortunate circumstances. He was raised in a poor family living in the western part of

Denmark on the barren Jutland heath. To help out, he tended sheep. He often walked for days, cold and hungry, wet from the rain, with no other company than the bleating sheep. We are told of one particular day when he was eleven years old: Michael felt miserable. He had been miserable before, but on that day his misery engulfed him. His resentment grew to such a passion that he climbed to the top of a hill and shook his fist, cursing God in Heaven for taking such poor care of his creatures. God ought to help, to feed and warm them. God was a cheat!

The experience was both profound and unforgettable.

What happened? Michael's ill luck changed. A relative from Copenhagen arrived, and from the plentiful brood, he singled out this Michael to bring back with him to the capital, making him an apprentice in a little shop, feeding him, clothing him, and keeping him warm.

Michael developed a considerable talent for business. He took over the store and expanded the haberdashery, making it into a profitable business. He became a wholesale dealer in wool and then in spices. He invested heavily in Royal Bonds, and in the year 1813—the same year that Søren was born—the stock market crashed. Nothing held but Royal Bonds. Michael Kierkegaard was a winner again.

Now a rich man indeed, he purchased a patrician home at Nytorv next to the city hall. He had arrived at the pinnacle, with the riches and the power that follow. At this point he retired.

Michael Kierkegaard had no formal schooling. He had learned how to read, write, and count, but his basic education came from Luther's small *Cathecism* and from reading the Bible. He was an intelligent man with a gift for catching the significant detail. There is the oft-told story of his taking little Søren on indoor walks that were filled with imaginary outdoor noises, smells, and touches that wonderfully conjured up the contemporary, congested Copenhagen or its peaceful environs.

But basically Michael was neither cheerful nor gregarious. He was serious and troubled. As a true Lutheran, he worried: not about God's existence, but about God's judgment and what God had in store for him. All had gone well. Maybe too well. Was God building him up in order to wreak enormous revenge? That little lonely figure out on the heath cursing God was but a fly for God to quash. But now his position was different; Michael was responsible for a large family and a great fortune.

Michael Kierkegaard had married twice. His first marriage was brief and childless. After only two years, his wife died. The prudent year of mourning had no sooner lapsed than he married his housekeeper, Anne, who was already pregnant with their first child. The terms of the marriage contract that was signed were harsh and unfavorable to her—a fact which might suggest that he felt trapped and revengeful: at least she is not going to get my money!

At any rate, the marriage seemed to function well. She bore him seven children, and she was reported to have been a good, cheerful woman. She was ten years younger than he, and their respective roles in the household were clearly defined and separated. They both came from a poor and unschooled background; while Anne grew busy bearing and rearing the children, Michael settled down to educate himself. It was unthinkable that they could have shared in this latter enterprise—not only because it was still a rare phenomenon for women to be educated together with men, but specifically because this education represented for Michael his personal search for meaning.

Michael became a highly motivated student of philosophy and theology. His position as a wealthy man made it possible for him to invite prominent teachers in these fields to his home. Søren was present at these occasions, as we know from his account at age thirty in a book that he never published. The story is called "Johannes Climacus or *De Omnibus Dubitandum Est.*" It followed his own development through the young student, Johannes:

When for any reason his father engaged in argument with anyone, Johannes was all ears, all the more so because everything was conducted with an almost festive orderliness. His father always allowed his opponent to state his whole case, and then as a precaution asked him if he had nothing more to say before he began his reply. Johannes had followed the opponent's speech with strained attention, and in his way shared an interest in the outcome. A pause intervened. The father's rejoinder followed, and behold! in a trice the tables were turned. How that came about was a riddle to Johannes, but his soul delighted in the show. The opponent spoke again. Johannes could almost hear his heart beat, so impatiently did he await what was to happen.—It happened; in the twinkling of an eye everything was inverted, the explicable became inexplicable, the certain doubtful, the contrary evident. When the shark wishes to seize its prey it has to turn over upon its back, for its mouth is on its underside; its back is dark, its belly is silver-white. It must be a magnificent sight to witness that alternation of colour; it must sometimes glitter so brightly as to hurt the eyes, and yet it is a delight to look upon. Johannes witnessed a similar alternation when he heard his father engage in argument. He forgot again what was said, both what his father and what the opponent said, but that shudder of soul he did not forget.[6]

Just as it is obvious that the father is the central figure, this story also reveals that the mother is not present. She was out of sight and literally out of mind on such occasions. But the account gives a wonderful picture of trust and unbounded admiration for the father.

Michael Kierkegaard was educated simultaneously with his children, and therefore he became an important part of their education. He taught them order in thought as well as in habit. He impressed piety upon them and reverence for authority. He treated them like grown-ups and did not shrink from difficult and painful subjects. It made an everlasting impression on Søren when he found a picture of the crucified Christ among his playthings; his father gave him a direct and pointed explanation of its ugliness and terror.

What Michael Kierkegaard learned from books did not quiet his heart. The black thoughts of the melancholy hours, the despair, gnawed at his happiness with his home and his pride in his children. The fear of God's judgment was not to be explained away by professors and bishops.

During the years between 1831 and 1835, four members of his immediate family died. Two children had died earlier in infancy. The aging father was by then left with only two sons and with the indescribable grief of realizing that his once thriving family was almost gone. His secret question was: God, will you have your revenge now? Will you smother me like Job, take everything away, leaving me alone? Did I commit the only unforgivable sin? The memory of the curse on the heath returned.

Was he guilty? In his agony, he became increasingly sure that
none of his sons would survive him—or the age of thirty-four,
the age Jesus is presumed to have been when he was killed.
Michael finally had to tell his sons about the curse.

At that time, Søren Kierkegaard was a student and a very
peculiar one compared to his exemplary brother. Peter had taken
the straight and narrow scholastic road pleasing to the father,
venturing into theology as a pupil of Professor Martensen and
getting his doctorate at Kiel, Germany; he had then proceeded
through the ranks of the church to become a bishop. He too,
however, was a deeply disturbed and melancholy person. At the
time of his death in 1870, Peter Kierkegaard was considered
insane: for several years he had been unable to hold his position
in the church. In 1865, he read in Søren's journal a rendering of
the story of the curse. Deeply moved, he burst out in tears:
"This is my father's story and ours too!"

In an entry in his journal in 1835, Søren calls this episode
"the great earthquake." It gave him immediate and frightening
insights into family history and into personally experienced
dread of the realities hidden behind the concept of "original sin":

Then it was that the great earthquake occurred, the terrible revolution which suddenly forced upon me a new and infallible law of
interpretation of all the facts. Then I suspected that my father's
great age was not a divine blessing but rather a curse; that the
outstanding intellectual gifts of our family were only given to us
in order that we should rend each other to pieces: then I felt the
stillness of death grow around me when I saw my father, an unhappy
man who was to outlive us all, a cross on the tomb of all his hopes.
There must be a guilt upon the whole family, the punishment of
God must be on it; it was to disappear, wiped out by the powerful
hand of God, obliterated like an unsuccessful attempt, and only at
times did I find a little alleviation in the thought that my father
had been allotted the heavy task of calming us with the consolation
of religion, of ministering to us so that a better world should be
open to us even though we lost everything in this world, even though
we were overtaken by the punishment which the Jews always called
down upon their enemies: that all recollection of us should be
utterly wiped out, that we should no longer be found.[7]

But Søren Kierkegaard acted. He wanted to undo the curse,
to challenge it.

He did not act with repentance, piety, and prayer as we might anticipate. He did exactly the opposite. Had he before been a procrastinating student, he now became the talk of the town, a flaneur, strolling down Main Street, frequenting the best coffee-houses, the most expensive restaurants. He threw parties and ran up bills with the tailor, the baker, and the bookseller. He was seen every night at the theater or at the opera. He was the life of the party wherever he showed up. He took an active part in student life, which meant not merely debating and politicking but drinking a great deal as well. Once he visited a brothel after such a drinking spree.

All this was playacting. Meanwhile, by himself, he was miserable. This life gave him no lasting satisfaction. The visit to the brothel, for instance, was a fiasco. His studies were a shambles, and all his wit and learning seemed nothing but froth.

His behavior served a purpose. Having left his father's house, Søren was in effect telling his father (indirectly through rumors and bills): "Don't think that I am your son! I am not like you." This was something very real for his father to worry about, and he was shaken.

Separately, both father and son were seeking new ways to God. A reconciliation between them eventually took place, which resulted in Søren's moving back home. The pressure of the curse eased. Only a few months later Michael Kierkegaard died.

However, he knew then that the father had left his indelible mark on the son. Søren had encountered a faith of a very different quality. He did not, by any means, possess that faith, but he had come to know something that most professors and ministers did not seem to surmise even existed. He wrote:

My father died on Wednesday (the 9th) at 2 A.M. I had so very much wished that he might live a few years longer, and I look upon his death as the last sacrifice which he made to his love for me; for he did not die from me but *died for me* in order that if possible I might still turn into something. Of all that I have inherited from him, the recollection of him, his transfigured portrait, not transfigured by the poetry of my imagination (ror it did not require that) but explained by many an individual trait which I can now take account of—is dearest to me, and I will be careful to preserve it safely hidden from the world.[8]

Now Søren could no longer put the old man off with endless arguments. He had lost his mentor and his opponent in dialogue. He had lost his shield against eternity. He was his own. He now belonged to the older generation. So he became his father's son. He applied himself to his studies, finishing his theological degree in two years and straightening out his dissertation on irony.

"We understand our lives backwards," as Socrates had said. It was only after his father's death that Søren came to understand him: what a remarkable person this strong, stern, self-taught man had been. It was only after his death that the son actually met his father. In meeting other people, Søren began to grasp the image of his father and began to wonder what had been transferred in their relationship.

The heaths of Jutland must of all places be suited to develop the spirit powerfully; here everything lies naked and uncovered before God, and there is no room for the many distractions, the many little crevices where consciousness can hide and where seriousness has such difficulty in running down one's scattered thoughts. Here consciousness must firmly and scrupulously close itself around itself. And on the heaths one may say with truth: "Whither shall I flee from thy presence?"[9]

He was keenly aware that he had inherited his father's intelligence and also his melancholy. He also knew that his upbringing had been extraordinary. After defending his dissertation and thus being set free from the academic life, Søren Kierkegaard undertook as his first act a pilgrimage to Jutland, his father's birthplace.

II *Regine and Indirect Communication*

It was not until after the pilgrimage to Jutland that Kierkegaard began to make advances to the girl who had already been his heart's secret delight for several years. In May of 1837 he had met her, a girl of fourteen, very young, but he fell in love with her nevertheless. She became his Beatrice, but his love story was even stranger than Dante's.

In those days it was of course improper for young men and women of the upper classes to be together without chaperons.

They were educated separately for their separate stations. They came together for divertissements, for making music, for dancing, for walks in the park, for a visit to the theater, or for a cup of tea. We are reminded of the world of Jane Austen's novels. Matchmaking served not merely as a favorite pastime but was, sure enough, the savage purpose behind many family gatherings. Property and prestige added much to desirability; and after his father's death, Kierkegaard had come into a good deal of money, which heightened his value on the marriage market.

Little in Kierkegaard's papers and books hints that the Kierkegaard household was anything but traditional when it came to the role of women. Women, felt the males, moved in different, mysterious, attractive, and repulsive ways. The world of power, influence, and action, they believed, properly belonged to men.

Kierkegaard never departed from the masculine attitudes to which he was accustomed. Though in *Either/Or* he attempts to intuit what it is like to be an abandoned woman, he never deliberately exposed social injustices committed against women. On the contrary, he found the growing feminist movement comical. The first article he ever wrote for a paper satirized Eve, revealing that he had adopted the view of women that had been prevalent for centuries. The fact that women differed from men (and not vice versa) relegated them—and not men—to an inferior position, he believed. And the "superior" male stayed well out of their reach.

Kierkegaard easily managed to maintain that sense of superiority until he met Regine.

Regine! charming, outgoing, and friendly, was singled out by Kierkegaard the first time he saw her. He observed her secretly and became more and more involved. He idealized her and—dreaming about her—gradually made up his mind to marry her. The thought of other young women faded, and the memory of other infatuations vanished. His feeling grew deeper and stronger and was finally self-sustained. The Romantics would call it "first love."[10]

Søren and Regine saw each other rather often on the street, in coffeehouses, or at social gatherings. They belonged to the same social class and, accordingly, moved in the same circles.

For three years, however, Kierkegaard kept his feelings secret.

Finally, he decided that the time had come to declare himself.
It did not bother him that Regine already had a suitor. Søren
knew that he was older, richer, and far more fascinating than
this Mr. Fritz Schlegel. Besides, he knew the art of being
dazzling at a party, and he proceeded to do so as soon as Regine
was present; he was careful, however, to pay her no special
attention, though he secretly watched her out of the corner of
his eye, well aware he was making an impression. Progress was
rapid, and her reaction excited him. The idea of telling the
world about his secret dream infatuated him. He wanted to
declare that she was his and he, hers. He decided to propose
and get engaged. We read the painful story in Kierkegaard's
recollections:

In August I returned. The period from August 9 till the beginning
of September I used in the strict sense to approach her.
   On September 8 I left my house with the firm purpose of deciding
the matter. We met each other in the street outside their house. She
said there was nobody at home. I was foolhardy enough to look
upon that as an invitation, just the opportunity I wanted. I went
in with her. We stood alone in the living room. She was a little
uneasy. I asked her to play me something as she usually did. She
did so; but that did not help me. Then suddenly I took the music
away and closed it, not without a certain violence, threw it down
on the piano and said: "Oh, what do I care about music now! It is
you I am searching for, it is you whom I have sought after for two
years." She was silent. I did nothing else to make an impression
upon her; I even warned her against myself, against my melancholy.
When, however, she spoke about Schlegel I said: "Let that relationship be a parenthesis; after all the priority is mine." (N.B. It was
only on the 10th that she spoke of Schlegel; on the 8th she did
not say a word.)
   She remained quite silent. At last I left, for I was anxious lest
someone should come and find both of us, and she so disturbed.
I went immediately to Etatsraad Olsen. I know that I was terribly
concerned that I had made too great an impression upon her. I also
feared that my visit might lead to a misunderstanding and even
harm her reputation.
   Her father said neither yes nor no, but he was willing enough
as I could see. I asked for a meeting: it was granted to me for the
afternoon of the 10th. I did not say a single word to persuade her.
She said, Yes.

I immediately assumed a relation to the whole family, and turned
all my virtuosity upon her father whom, moreover, I have always
loved.
But inwardly; the next day I saw that I had made a false step.
A penitent such as I was, my *vita ante acta,* my melancholy, that
was enough.
I suffered unspeakably at that time.
She seemed to notice nothing.[11]

Already "the next day" he knew he had made a mistake.
Here, hidden in the midst of this tragicomedy, lies a clue to
Kierkegaard's enigmatic personality. His intellectuality was in-
separable from his actions; its negative capability checked every
move. His brain worked at full speed, all-calculating, rearranging the dream, swooning, regretting, longing, shifting forward
and backward again. He had dreamed of the ideal marriage.
He now saw himself as he had been and what he must become
if he stayed with her.
No longer could he see her ideally as the picture constructed
in his mind during the lonesome, dreamy hours. Rather, he now
saw her as lovely and young, to be sure, but as a person who
had an underdeveloped mind, a child with no religious in-
clinations.
They became engaged. He had given away his command.
Or had he? He considered the possibility of breaking off the
engagement. The joy of letting go and of relegating his other
cares to God was not a possibility for him. He had never
developed the courage to accept the challenge of an uncertain
future but had trained himself to predict every next move.
He concluded that exposing Regine to his brain-steered existence with all this "hysteria of the spirit" would constitute
plain and simple cruelty.[12] Inevitably there would be daily, even
hourly, collisions between actuality, the things to be done, and
his melancholy, hovering personality. Inwardly, he screamed
because he wanted so badly to hold onto the dream that he
soberly and realistically knew could never be anything but a
dream.
Sending back the ring, he asked her to release him.
The opposite occurred. She felt more closely tied to him now;
seeing him suffer, she wanted to rescue him from his suffering.

Full of trust and courage, Regine made him do all the things that engaged couples were supposed to do. They went visiting, took promenades; they went to church and to the theater. They were seen and greeted like any engaged couple. She enjoyed it. She smiled and kissed and encouraged him with an inquisitive glance: Isn't this just wonderful?

To please her, he played the part while telling himself: This must end.

Again, the Kierkegaardian strategy employed in the relationship to the father came into play. This time Kierkegaard was much more knowledgeable and aware of his actions. Just as he once had acted to demonstrate to his father, "I am not your son, you cannot arrange my world," so now he acted to force Regine to reflect upon their engagement. In both instances he hoped that such communication would produce an expanded awareness on the part of the other person, resulting in a rebirth of personality and a more spiritual relationship.

Consequently he stopped acting the part of the devoted fiancé and began playing the cold, detached, bored, and superior bachelor who might or might not marry her. If he could coerce her to reflect, she would discover herself. Through this inward movement, he reasoned, she would choose herself, and so develop to the point at which she was dependent neither upon her family nor upon him. The final result, he prayed, would make her relationship with God one of mature faith.

It was a cruel struggle. But there it was:

It was a time of terrible suffering: to have to be so cruel and at the same time to love as I did. She fought like a tigress. If I had not believed that God had lodged a veto she would have been victorious.

And so about two months later it broke. She grew desperate. For the first time in my life I scolded. It was the only thing to do.

When I left her I went immediately to the Theatre because I wanted to meet Emil Boesen. (That gave rise to what was then said in Copenhagen, that I had looked at my watch and said to the family that if they had anything more in their minds would they please hurry up as I had to go to the theatre.) The act was over. As I left the stalls Etatsraad Olsen came up to me and said "May I speak to you?" We went together to his house. "It will be her death, she is in absolute despair." I said "I shall calm her down; but everything is settled." He said, "I am a proud man and I find it difficult to say, but I beg you, do not break with her." He was indeed a noble-hearted man; I was deeply moved. But I did not let myself be persuaded. I remained with the family to dinner. I spoke to her as I left. The following morning I received a letter from him saying she had not slept all night, and asking me to go and see her. I went and tried to persuade her. She asked me: "Are you never going to marry?" I answered, "Yes, perhaps in ten years time when I have sown my wild oats; then I shall need some young blood to rejuvenate me." That was a necessary cruelty. Then she said, "Forgive me for the pain I have caused you." I answered: "It is for me to ask forgiveness." She said: "Promise to think of me." I did so. "Kiss me," she said. I did so but without passion. Merciful God![13]

On October 11 the engagement was broken. Two weeks later Kierkegaard went to Berlin. He fled the scene of the crime—if it was a crime: a thought that occupied him constantly. Guilty? Not guilty? He felt he had done what had to be done.

Now he had also become free from every conceivable tie. The engagement was broken; he had fulfilled his father's wish that he finish his studies and defend his dissertation. He was neither planning a teaching career nor contemplating becoming a minister of the Church.

He was free. True, he had a *"vita ante acta"* that weighed heavily upon him and that was part of his secret life—so different from the Kierkegaard people knew and talked about. He was free to act for himself, exploring himself as an object; the Regine affair had killed him as a subject, or so he thought. The experience had given him fundamental insight and a new outlook on the world.

So Kierkegaard arrived in Berlin and began to work. His responsibility from now on was to write. He worked furiously. His letters home consisted of reports from lectures and theater performances, but he occupied himself mainly with writing *Either/Or*. At the end of the winter semester he returned to Copenhagen and continued writing while trying to give an impression that he was idly enjoying this leisure time:

Then I employed another means [of making people believe I was an idler]. Every evening when I left home completely fagged out and had dined at Mimi's I was for ten minutes at the theatre—not a minute more. Being so generally known as I was, I reckoned that there would be several talebearers at the theatre who would report: "Every night he is at the theatre, he doesn't do anything else." Oh, you dear gossips, how I thank you! Without you I would not have attained my purpose. In fact it was for the sake of my former fiancée I did this. It was my melancholy wish to be as much derided as possible, merely to serve her, merely in order that she might be able to put up a resistance.[14]

In February of the following year *Either/Or* was published. Instantly it became the talk of the town—especially the part called "Diary of the Seducer." At Easter Kierkegaard went to church, and Regine nodded to him. Incredible! Instead of receiving a cold stare, he got a friendly nod. Not a word, just a nod and a smile, but it so upset Kierkegaard that he again took off for Berlin to resume his hectic work pattern from the previous year. Regine's nod had thrown him back to the original point from which he had first left Copenhagen.

As a poet living in his imaginative world, he had resolved the problem by solemnly regarding himself as bound to her by a marriage vow. But she had nodded. Which brought back the whole struggle with its possibility of marriage again.

But this was impossible. Daily he prayed for her, hoping that she, too, would find herself by accepting a life of inwardness and solitude. In this way the two of them might reach happiness and spiritual communion. Or could a miracle happen, a total change? During these days Kierkegaard wrote *Repetition* and *Fear and Trembling*, which strongly reflect the religious depth of his problem.

When he returned from Berlin, news reached him that Regine had become engaged to her former suitor, Mr. Schlegel. From that moment Kierkegaard hardened his views about women with regard to their ability to develop inwardly.

With all his strength, Kierkegaard remained faithful to Regine throughout his life. Now and then, at a distance, they saw each other. They met in church and greeted each other silently in the street. He sent her all his books which, in a sense, were written for her. He willed his possessions to her. In 1850 he wrote in his journal: "As a matter of fact, it was she, my relationship to her, which taught me indirect communication."

Regine survived Kierkegaard by nearly fifty years, dying in 1904. But just a few years before her death she made arrangements to have their correspondence published posthumously, a most urgent issue for her. She had known Kierkegaard for six short years. She married, had children, and later moved to the Danish West Indies where her husband became governor. But all through her life, Kierkegaard figuratively stood at her side. She has become immortal in history: not for herself or as Madame Schlegel, but as Regine, Kierkegaard's fiancé, the woman to whom his whole life's work was dedicated.

The experience with her provided the catalyst in Kierkegaard's life that turned him into a religious poet. It marked a decisive point, making him aware that his life was an exception.[15]

III   *The Corsair—Speaking "Without Authority"*

The affair with Regine closed many doors to Kierkegaard. It was considered scandalous and became the subject for much gossip. Public opinion took Regine's side. When *Either/Or* was then published (and "Diary of the Seducer" was the part that attracted the most attention), it elicited both admiration and detest, and Kierkegaard's name became associated with the worldly and risqué.

Although Kierkegaard took notice of this he was not offended. On the contrary, he cultivated the image of the aesthete, idle and superior, because that stance was so alien to the manner in which he actually lived his life, and the confusion this caused pleased him. Actually, he lived according to monastic discipline, in solitude, bringing forth books along two lines, the aesthetic and the religious. The work excited and exhausted him, and for relaxation he took rides in the forest or walks in the streets. During these walks he systematized his thoughts, reworking them until the patterns cleared and the argument was tight. Schemes and arguments presented themselves in such abundance that he had to fight them off at times. Since this was a lonely pursuit, never bringing him face to face with an adversary, he became severely polemical, questioning all that came his way. Nothing escaped his observing eye. During the span of four years he wrote fourteen books: seven aesthetic works under pseudonyms and seven religious or edifying books under his own name. And his journals and papers were piling up at home.

He had really intended the *Concluding Unscientific Post-script* to be his last major work: and in it he had consequently taken pains to acknowledge his responsibility for his earlier pseudonymous writing and to give a short guide as to how they should be understood. But now that he had finished it, he began to look around and to assess his position in the world. What should he do next? The old alternative of becoming a country parson had tempted him when he began to write *Either/Or*, and it introduced itself anew. He seriously contemplated this possibility and made some practical arrangements for such a move.[16] He was stopped in a curious manner.

Five or six years earlier a bright young Jewish writer and journalist named Meir A. Goldschmidt had founded a weekly called *The Corsair*.[17] It was now very successful and, though few openly admitted that they read it, literary Copenhagen was well aware of its new kind of journalism: a piquant blend of gossip, satire, and brilliant criticism. A liberal paper, it gladly attacked the new monarch, Christian VIII, and jeered at his attempts to reform. But *The Corsair* happily snapped at just about everybody. And Copenhagen loved it.

Kierkegaard remained one of the few who had not been attacked by the journal—an honor he did not appreciate. Goldschmidt respected and admired Kierkegaard's intellect; after the publication of *Either/Or*, he had even arranged a banquet in his honor. Kierkegaard, characteristically, did not attend. He abhorred the sleazy superficiality of *The Corsair* and found it a shame that anyone so gifted as Goldschmidt might so readily contribute to the leveling process. In no way did he want his name to be associated with the journal.

However, other intellectuals gladly, if secretly, contributed pieces, one of whom was Paul L. Møller, who aspired to the chair in aesthetics at the university. Believing that Kierkegaard had unfairly exposed Regine, Møller wrote a review in another journal, *Gæa*, in which he severely criticized Kierkegaard's "Guilty/Not Guilty," a section in *Stages on Life's Way*. In this, he touched upon Kierkegaard's sore point. Here was the occasion on which to dissociate himself publicly from that kind of frothy journalism.

Retaliating, Kierkegaard replied in *Fædrelandet* (*The Fatherland*) that his detractor, Møller, was indeed an associate of Goldschmidt.[18] This meant the end of Møller's chances for the position at the university. So Kierkegaard found himself again in the midst of a scandal. By openly challenging Goldschmidt, Kierkegaard begged to be attacked; yet Goldschmidt hesitated. But the challenge was finally too blatant to ignore.

On New Year's Day, 1846, it broke loose. Poor Kierkegaard! Whatever he had anticipated, it had not been this. The *Corsair* attack rendered him speechless. The journal caricaturist, Klæstrup, had drawn a character with stooped frame, uneven pantlegs, umbrella in hand, top hat and all—the Kierkegaard that Copenhagen knew so well from his daily walks. This Kierkegaard character appeared again and again in ridiculous situations. Kierkegaard could hardly show his face in the streets before people recognized him and began to snicker. Children would shout after him, "Either–or! Either–or!" "Søren" became a nickname synonymous to "clumsy" and "clownish." Kierkegaard, who had aspired to fight the noble fight, felt this as a bitter blow. Copenhagen was a small town, and word of such things spread quickly. Kierkegaard had again lost command.

Andersen can tell the fairy tale of "The Lucky Galoshes," but I can tell the tale of the shoes that pinch.

. . . I know my exterior well, and indeed few men have so often been the object of good-natured raillery, or a little witticism, or a little banter, or a smile in passing, as I have been. And truly I have no objection to that: it is the expression of an instantaneous impression. The person in question cannot help it, and that is the atoning factor, and perhaps many who have thought too much of my talents have, as a set-off to this, got a little joy out of my legs— many a maiden who perhaps set me up too high by reason of my mental gifts has found herself reconciled to me by reason of my thin legs. And all this I find in the highest degree innocent, pardonable, and indeed enjoyable. But it is another thing when an abusive person takes the liberty of egging on the crowd to observe them.

In proportion as enlightenment and culture increase and requirements become greater and greater, it naturally becomes more and more difficult as a philosopher to satisfy the requirements of the age. In old times what was required was mental talent, spiritual freedom, intellectual passion. Compare the present age—now in Copenhagen it is required that a philosopher shall also have thick or at least well-shaped legs and that his clothes shall be in the fashion. It is becoming more and more difficult—unless people will be content with the last requisite alone and will assume that every one who has thick or at least well-shaped legs and whose clothes are in the fashion is a philosopher.[19]

The attacks lasted for about half a year. Kierkegaard suffered and raged at times, but wisely realized that nothing could be done. He hardly noticed that one of his initial ambitions of "raising consciousness" actually took place. Goldschmidt resigned from *The Corsair,* later on founded a serious publication, *North and South,* and became a highly respected author. Paul Møller, on the other hand, disappeared from Denmark and did not publish any more poetry. Some years later he died in Germany.

The *Corsair* episode pushed Kierkegaard by blocking him, just as the Regine affair had five years earlier. There was no conceivable possibility that he could now abandon Copenhagen and disappear into a country parsonage. He felt too scandalized. No position would be open to anyone with his reputation. But the main reason he felt he could not go away was that he was undergoing a Christian development. Suffering and sacrifice, experiences that now took on strong personal coloring, had to be thought through and transcended. He was waiting for his own "metamorphosis."[20]

The years 1847–1848 were a time of tremendous productivity for Kierkegaard in regard to Christian concepts. Christ had to be confronted, not as "the Christian alternative," as the pseudonymous writer Climacus had done in *Fragments* and *Postscript,* but as the pattern, the example and prototype. Kierkegaard's investigations proved to be so revelatory for him and the goal so high that he again decided to write under a pseudonym, so that nobody would confuse him and his person with the content of these books, *The Sickness unto Death* and *Training in Christianity.* He chose the pseudonym Anti-Climacus.[21]

Of the year 1848, Kierkegaard wrote in his journal the following year:

> 1848 potentiated me in one sense, in another sense it broke me, that is to say, religiously it broke me, or, as I put it in my language, God had run me to a standstill. He has suffered me to undertake a task which even in reliance upon Him I could not lift in a higher form, I must take it up in a lower form. And hence this thing has become really my own religious or more inwardly religious education in an inverse fashion. In a certain sense I would be so glad to venture; my imagination lures and incites me; but I must just learn to be good enough to venture in a lower form, i.e., pseudonymously. It [*The Sickness unto Death*] is certainly the truest and most perfect thing I have written; but my relation to it must not be such as to make it seem as if it is I that come down upon all the others with an almost damning judgement—no, I must myself first of all be educated by it; there is perhaps no one that has a right to be so deeply humbled by it as I before I have a right to publish it.[22]

Kierkegaard did not, however, completely abandon aesthetic writing during this time. For Heiberg's wife he wrote *The Crisis and A Crisis in the Life of an Actress*. Characteristically, he signed this *"Inter et Inter."* He experienced endless qualms about publishing it in between his religious works. With his self-image so intensely in mind, he was reticent to publish yet another aesthetic work. In the end he decided to do so mainly because he did not want people to say that he was getting religious in his old age. Afterward he was happy that he had published it because, in his opinion, it effectively hindered people from confusing his personality with his books. Serialized as a feuilleton in *The Fatherland*, it was later published as a complete book only after Kierkegaard's death, and then by Heiberg himself. As Kierkegaard's last work on aesthetics, it formed a divertissement *inter et inter*.

How curious, we might think, that a brush with a frivolous paper would force Kierkegaard to give up the dream of taking on holy orders. But he had to face the reality of his position as an author and as a Christian:

> For originally I conceived of authorship as an escape from, a temporary postponement of, this thing of going out into the country

as a priest. But is not my position here essentially changed in the
fact that I as an author reach the point of working for a religious
aim? First I intended to desist immediately after *Either/Or.* That
was really the original thought. But productivity laid hold of me.
Then I would have left off with the *Concluding Postscript.* But
what happened? I was involved in all the persecution of vulgarity,
and just this brought it about that I remained on the spot. Now,
said I to myself, now there can be no question of a glittering career;
no, now the situation is appropriate for a penitent. Then I would
have ended with the *Christian Discourses* and gone on a journey,
but I did not make the journey after all—and in '48 I attained
my richest productivity. Thus has Governance held me in the saddle.
I put the question to myself: Do you believe that in a parsonage
you would have been in a condition to write three such religious
books as the three which followed the *Concluding Postscript?* And
I must answer, No! It was the tension of reality which put a new
string in my instrument. And so also in '48.[23]

Suddenly he can see "Governance" also in the *Corsair* episode.
It taught him what it means to be scandalized and considered a
fool by the masses. The blessing of it was that it changed his
image. It effectively killed the old image of a superior, dandyish
intellectual by substituting a new image of a foolish old man
in a big black hat and uneven, ill-fitting trousers. The costume
was correct for a religious writer. Indirect communication was
recaptured. His personal image had no authority. The possibility
of acquiring disciples was erased. The words "without authority," which appear on the title pages of his later religious works,
had gained their right to be there.[24] In his *The Point of View*
and *On My Work as an Author,* Kierkegaard tells us how he
saw the situation in retrospect:

I had now reckoned out that dialectically the situation would be appropriate for recovering the use of indirect communication. While
I was occupied solely with religious productions I could count upon
the negative support of these daily douches of vulgarity, which
would be cooling enough in its effect to ensure that the religious
communication would not be too direct, or too directly create for
me adherents. The reader could not relate himself directly to me;
for now, instead of the incognito of the aesthetical, I had erected
the danger of laughter and grins, by which most people are scared

away. And he even who was not scared by this would be upset by the next obstacle, by the thought that I had voluntarily exposed myself to all this, giving proof of a sort of lunacy.[25]

However, there are so many signs during his later years that Kierkegaard wanted "to venture," that he longed to abandon the indirect, the cocoon, and wished to speak out "in character." He waited and prepared for "the moment."

IV *The Church and "That Individual"*

After the publication of Kierkegaard's enormous works of the year 1848, he found himself in a strenuous position. His money was running out. He had never really thought about money before, partly because he had always *had* money, and he received some income from his books. But also, he had never expected to live very long. He found, to his amazement, that he survived the thirty-four year life span of Christ only to arrive at that point as a poor man. He had to give up his large apartment for one much smaller and less elegant. He considered himself unemployable, and his books provided no secure source of income. How could he possibly live out his remaining years? The lilies of the field and the birds of the air? The unclear picture gave him no immediate answers; he watched and waited. Something was brewing:

The best in me will not be understood. I toil so slavishly, soon with fear for my livelihood, and yet people reproach me for not taking a living. What I understand—that to take a living means giving up the best of which I'm capable—nobody can or will understand. People imagine that one can achieve more if one takes a living. That's a fine story! No, once one has taken a living one's activities become caught up in that hallucination that one is teaching Christianity because it is one's means of livelihood. That that is the case is clear enough—but what then was to become of all the salaried people? And as these are legion they have turned things upside down: *they* are serious because of their salaries and I am frivolous because I work as hard as anyone else but don't earn one.[26]

All his life, Kierkegaard maintained close contact with official Christendom. His father had been a friend of Bishop Mynster, and his brother had become a minister. His studies had brought him together with many theologians, and his best friend, Boeson, was a pastor. While continuing his investigation of Christianity, he watched these people very closely as well as others related to the Church. He waited for a reaction, a response that would signal to him, a sign of life in their faith. He particularly respected one person, and yet at the same time he suspected him: Bishop Mynster.[27]

Mynster, the primate of the Danish Church, was an aristocratic and reserved man. Kierkegaard often went to listen to his sermons, later reading them carefully when they were published. How did words and actions fit together? From what source did Bishop Mynster derive his authority? Kierkegaard pondered such questions a long time before he finally made an open attack on the Church.

It had all begun with a country parson, Magister Adler, who had been a disciple of Hegel but had turned against him. Adler claimed himself a Christian, stating that he wrote on direct dictation from Christ. The established Church did not accept that; Bishop Mynster dismissed Adler.

Kierkegaard became immensely interested. He bought Adler's books, and they sparked his creative genius to write *The Book on Adler*, which, however, he did not publish. He rewrote the book twice, and it occupied him long after Adler had retracted his statement. The confusion in people's minds concerning authority and the difference between civic and religious authority sparked his fury. He writes about the irony of the incident:

So Mag. Adler was born, brought up and confirmed as a native in geographical Christendom—thus he was a Christian (just as all the others are Christians); he became a theological licentiate—and was a Christian (just as all the others are Christians); he became a Christian priest and then for the first time the curious chance befell him that through a profound impression made upon his life he came into serious touch with the decisive experience of what it means to become a Christian. Just at this point, when by being religiously moved he undeniably comes nearer to the experience of what it means to become a Christian than he had come during all the time he was a Christian—just at this point he is deposed. And his deposition is quite justified because the State Church only now has the opportunity to ascertain how the matter stands with regard to his Christianity. But all the same the epigrammatical application still remains—that as a heathen he became a Christian priest, and when he had got somewhere nearer to the experience of becoming a Christian he was deposed.[28]

The book investigates the probability of revelation today and the meaning of speaking with divine authority. Who can do that? Answer: the exception. *The Book on Adler* is the background to the Anti-Climacus works in which he sharpens the position of the Christian to mean imitation of Christ and absolute dependence on God. To be "a witness to the truth" is to become a martyr (Kierkegaard wants to reestablish the original relationship between those two words), to suffer and to be accountable to God alone. An "established" church, he felt, brought horrible confusion since it compromised with this world. The harlot of Babylon.

This did not sit well with Bishop Mynster. The relationship between them faded although it never came to an absolute, open breach. This came only when Mynster died and was eulogized by Professor Martensen, Kirkegaard's old teacher, who was calling Mynster a "witness to the truth."

This marked the breach. For many years, Kierkegaard had reverently and expectantly listened to Mynster. Kierkegaard's later writings had been penned with the edification of Mynster specifically in mind. In 1854 he wrote in his journal:

March 1, 1854. So now he is dead.
    If only it had been possible to persuade him to end his life with the admission that what he represented was not really Christianity, but a mitigation of it: that would have been most desirable, for he carried a whole age along with him.
    The possibility of this admission had therefore to be kept open to the last, to the very last, lest he should perhaps make it dying. Therefore he had never to be attacked.[29]

Now the situation was altered. When Martensen came out and called Mynster a "witness," using exactly the term that Kierkegaard had so carefully given the meaning of "martyr," Kierkegaard felt that Martensen had shamelessly lied, misusing his term on purpose. He went to work at his desk. But he published nothing. Despite his indignation, Kierkegaard did not want to harm Martensen's chances of becoming the next Primate, a position for which he was next in line. But the excitement built up within him, and he was prepared for a fight.

Mynster died in January of 1854. In December of that year, with Martensen finally installed with pomp and circumstance, Kierkegaard published the article against him. His surprise attack produced a weak answer.

The polemic went on through the spring of 1855 in the conservative paper *The Fatherland*. In May, Kierkegaard began to publish his own pamphlet, characteristically named *"Øjeblikket"* ("The Moment" or "The Instant"), which received a substantial number of subscribers because the attack had attracted enormous attention, not all of it unfavorable to Kierkegaard.

If he had suspected a lynch mob, he had misjudged the situation. Martensen, of course, had not been pleased. Many were angry that Kierkegaard had attacked Mynster personally. But people who had earlier never read a line of Kierkegaard (a few clergymen among them) now began to read him because of the many references he made in his attack to his own books. Among the people, he became popular.[30]

Kierkegaard apparently did not notice. In March, he published an article entitled "What I Want":

Quite simply: I want honesty. I am not, as one with the best intentions has wished to represent me, I am not Christian severity contrasted with Christian leniency.

By no means; I am neither severity nor leniency—I am: mere human honesty. . . .

I want honesty. If that is what this race and this generation wants, if it will uprightly, honestly, frankly, openly, directly rebel against Christianity and say to God, "We can but we will not subject ourselves to this authority"—but observe that it must be done uprightly, honestly, frankly, openly, directly—well then, strange as it may seem, I am for it; for honesty is what I want. And wherever there is honesty I can join in. An honest rebellion against Christianity can only be made when one honestly admits what Christianity is and how he himself is related to it.

And what have the clergy done for their part? They have (and I am sorry to be compelled to be so courteous, but it is true), they have preserved a significant silence. It is curious: if they had replied, something very fatuous was sure to come out, perhaps the whole of it would have been fatuous; now on the other hand how significant the whole thing has become by reason of this significant silence!

What then does this significant silence signify? It signifies that what concerns the clergy is their livings. In any case it signifies that the clergy are not witnesses for the truth, for in that case it would be inconceivable that the clergy as a whole—especially after the Right Reverend Bishop Martensen had made such a luckless attempt at speaking—could want to preserve silence while it was openly made obvious that official Christianity is both aesthetically and intellectually ludicrous and indecent, a scandal in the Christian sense.

Assuming on the other hand that a living is what concerns the clergy, this silence is perfectly understandable. For it was not the livings in a finite sense I was aiming at with my attack, and well known as I am to the clergy they must know very well that such a thing could never occur to me, that not only am I not a politician but I hate politics, indeed that I might even be disposed to fight for the clergy were any one to attack the livings in a finite sense.

Hence this complete silence—my attack did not really concern the clergy, i.e. it has nothing to do with what does concern them. Take an example from—I had almost by a slip of the tongue said, "another world"—take an example then from the same world, from the shopman's world. If it were possible to make an attack upon a merchant in such a way as to show that his wares were bad but without this having the least effect upon the usual turnover of his wares—then he will say: "Such an attack is perfectly indifferent to me; whether my wares are good or bad does not concern me at all in and for itself; remember that I am a merchant, what concerns me is the turnover. In fact I am a merchant to such a degree that if one could show, not only that the coffee I sell is damaged and spoiled, but that what I sell under the name of coffee is not coffee at all—if only one assures me that the attack will have no effect whatever upon the turnover, such an attack is perfectly indifferent to me. What does it matter to me what sort of thing it is people guzzle under the name of coffee? What concerns me is only the turnover."[31]

Something new has entered into Kierkegaard's style. No longer dialectical and difficult, it flows in plain, exhortative prose, un-

derstandable for the plain person. He writes not for the clique and
the initiated, but for the people he knew from his many walks.
The last issue of *The Instant* (number ten), which lay on his
desk at the time of his collapse, addresses common people
directly:

Thou plain man! I have not separated my life from thine; thou
knowest it, I have lived in the street, am known to all; moreover
I have not attained any importance, I do not belong to any class-
egoism, so if I belong anywhere, I must belong to thee, thou plain
man, thou who once (when one profiting by thy money pretended
to wish thee well), thou who once wast too willing to find me and
my existence ludicrous, thou who least of all hast reason to be
impatient over or ungrateful for the fact that I am of your company,
which the superior people rather have reason for, seeing that I have
never decisively united myself to them but merely maintained a
loose relationship to them.
Thou plain man! I do not hide from thee that, according to my
notion, the thing of being a Christian is endlessly high, that at no
time are there more than a few that attain it—as Christ's own life
attests when one considers the age in which He lived, and also
His preaching indicates if one takes it literally. Yet nevertheless
it is possible for all.[32]

After almost a year of intensive attack on "Christendom,"
Kierkegaard collapsed in the street one day and was taken to
the hospital. Having just withdrawn the last sum of money
from his inheritance, he had been returning home from the
bank. He recognized his end and welcomed it. He had no fight-
ing spirit left for himself. His collapse left him paralyzed from
the waist down.

Pastor Boesen visited him, talking anxiously to him about
reconciliation with the Church and accepting the sacrament.
But if he could not receive it from a layman, Kierkegaard had
no desire for it. The image that had taken so much pain to find
had developed fully. His life was consummated. He thanked
God for His grace.

Søren Kierkegaard died on November 4, 1855.

We have dwelt at length on the four crises of his life, and
we have done so because, to understand Kierkegaard's work,

it is necessary to consider what he made of his life. It was essential for him that his readers try their ability in "integral calculus." There is no doubt that Kierkegaard organized his spiritual history. But that is just the point that must be reckoned with. He was proud of having created the category of "the individual," which he considered the greatest, most important, and most necessary invention at a time when Hegelian philosophy gave priority to the race, the state, and the majority. "If the crowd is the Evil, if chaos is what threatens us, there is salvation only in one thing, in becoming a single individual, in the thought of 'the individual' as an essential category."[33] On his gravestone Kierkegaard wanted simply the inscription: the individual. As "the individual" he was polemical through and through, not leaving anything established standing. He carried out what he had learned from Socrates with the conviction that someday a reader would come along who would perceive that the religious author was concealed within the ironic author and that there was a Christian purpose in his productivity, for which he had been willing to change his life.

Kierkegaard has attracted two kinds of biographers.[34] Some interpret him positively. They scold a little at his rantings and repetitions, but on the whole they find so many wonderful qualities displayed in his works that they weave his life into a tapestry in which he stands out as a hero, a martyr, a Christian genius.

Naturally, others become irritated by this haloed picture, and they point out how difficult and unpleasant the man was. With the help of a little psychology, they reduce him to an immature, father-dominated, sex-frightened cripple, whose enormous ego perversely found the means to dominate others with the help of Christ.

Kierkegaard was neither beautiful nor nice, and certainly not a liberal. He did not champion any "good cause." Yet, after becoming acquainted with him, we cannot say that he was ugly, mean, or the champion of a bad cause.

At the end of that last sentence a tension arises, which would have pleased Kierkegaard. He, who planned everything minutely, knew that we would be out after him, and he certainly has supplied us with material. We learn how he thought, how he wrote, how he prayed, how he raged, how he laughed, how he loved, and how he suffered.

In the end, his life is insignificant in itself. Like the best teacher of criticism, he tells us: If there is something you want to know, you'll find it in my works. If your curiosity takes you outside, then all you find is curiosa. It is in my books that I have the relationship. If you feel the tension, well, so did I, and then you are my kind of reader. If you don't then there is nothing there.

CHAPTER 4

Either/Or

*E*ither/Or is the first book in the main body of Kierkegaard's
writing and the first of his pseudonymous works. It is immensely rich in form and content. It is written to confuse the
reader and to raise questions, rather than to answer them. How
can this book be introduced without destroying its structure and
denying it the tension it was so carefully planned to create?

Either/Or is one book. Should this chapter impart only this
one fact it will have made a good beginning. The overarching
theme of the book is *choice.* Simply expressed, *Either/Or* presents the reader with two ways of looking at life: Either you
look at what life does to you, or you turn around and look at
what you do to life. The characters in the book dramatize the
dire consequences for the personality in the choice of stance.
But, of course, nothing is simple in this highly sophisticated
book.

Critics now as well as then have often failed to see that the
greatness of the book lies in its wholeness. This failure has led
to grievous misuse and to misunderstandings. Some parts emerge
as more brilliant, moving, engaging, and fun for the reader
while others remain laborious, boring, didactic, and glum. The
brilliant pieces have been lifted out and anthologized, and, with
the help of such advertising, they are the better known. But this
practice has obscured the meaning of the whole work.

This is, of course, Kierkegaard's own fault. His constructive
mind built layer upon layer, and he took delight in seeing them
function and interact. When critics complained about the length
of the book, we can understand his frustration; any elimination
would disturb the total edifice. He knew he had accomplished
an extraordinary feat that went far beyond efforts by his contemporaries; but instead of attracting readers who followed what

he had written, he found admirers who picked out their favorite pieces.

Living more than a century, and hundreds of commentaries, later, readers today still have difficulties with the book, finding it hard to see the forest for the trees. In this excursion we shall try not to lose track of consistency but at the same time will make an attempt to live up to the challenge of Kierkegaard's style. After having read *Either/Or*, one should be aware, not only of a philosophical structure, but also of a gallery of characters who challenge us to think and feel.

What is in a name? The first character to emerge is Victor Eremita, the editor of the book. Victor is a gentleman scholar, a bachelor and something of a pedant. In a lengthy foreword he spells out all the precious arrangements concerning the publication of this extraordinary manuscript that by chance has fallen into his hands. First he relates the history of the manuscript, worthy of an eighteenth-century novel. He had fallen in love with an expensive piece of antique furniture, a secretary. When finally purchased, it became the pride of his household. However, once, as he was about to embark on a trip, he had placed his travel purse in a drawer of the secretary which— at the very moment his cab was waiting for him downstairs— refused to open. In his frustrated state, he sent for a hatchet and dealt the secretary a blow that revealed a secret drawer containing a manuscript. Exhilarated, he emptied the drawer and brought the manuscript with him, reading it alone while journeying through the woods.

The manuscript turned out to be two manuscripts, each very different from the other, each written on a different type of paper in a different hand, each different in style and quality.

Now Victor Eremita properly categorizes the material as "A" and "B." One of those two unknown writers, "B," reveals himself to be a judge by the name of William. Victor has a more difficult time trying to identify "A." Is he identical with the Seducer, Johannes, whom we learn about in the last essay among "A"'s papers? Bewildered, Victor wonders how to proceed: "Here we meet with new difficulties, since 'A' does not acknowledge himself as author, but only as editor. This is an old trick of the novelist, and I should not object to it, if it did not make my own position so complicated, as one author seems to be enclosed in another, like parts in a Chinese puzzle box."[1] Here Victor points out his ironic situation.

In his meticulous pedantry for options, Victor has considered the possibility that one person wrote both manuscripts. Recognizing the necessity of taking all possibilities into account, he nevertheless rules it out as "unhistorical, improbable, unreasonable that one man should be the author of both parts."[2]

Thus it is Victor Eremita who introduces us to "A" and "B." "A," the author of "Either" is a difficult character for us to grasp because it would be out of character for him to reveal himself. We must catch his aesthetic personality from the glimpses of himself he allows us. His trademarks are secrecy and mystification. "B," the author of "Or," however, comes across as an uncomplicated, straightforward person who works hard during the day and sleeps well at night. He is Judge William who fulfills his duties with gladness, a happily married man who worries in earnest over the meandering ways of his philandering friend, "A." Judge William endears us to him while his friend "A" fascinates us. In *Either/Or* Kierkegaard has performed a remarkable balancing act of indirect communication.

I *"Either"* (*Volume I*)

The motto "Are passions then the pagans of the soul? Reason only baptized?" is taken from Edward Young's *Night-Thoughts*. With it, Kierkegaard puts a significant question to the reader.[3] *Night-Thoughts* became a precursor of a genre that gained great popularity during the Romantic period. The feelings we have, the visions we see in flashes at night—are they not legitimate and true? The Romantic poets rushed to their defense.

At night, life takes on different proportions. Shadows soothe the edges of external reality. Thoughts come and go for the sleepless, as time slowly disappears. Ah, bittersweet hours! Lonely and melancholy! Everything in the present. The passions stir. When the bustle of the day has passed, night brings on meditation about the meaning of life. This moonlight mood, this suspension between the finite and the infinite—should it not be reckoned with?

A. "Diapsalmata"

The very first part consists of a collection of aphorisms called
"Diapsalmata," which means "refrains." These sayings all echo
the same melancholy mood: life's meaninglessness. The lack
of lust for life. The overbearing feeling of immobility. "My
melancholy is the most faithful mistress I have known."
Taken one by one, these aphorisms are markedly uneven in
quality. Some are striking, but the impact of the whole set of
aphorisms confuses us by its fragmentary nature. With whom
are we dealing? With the poet mentioned in the first diapsalm?

What is a poet? An unhappy man who in his heart harbors a deep
anguish, but whose lips are so fashioned that the moans and cries
which pass over them are transformed into ravishing music. His fate
is like that of the unfortunate victims whom the tyrant Phalaris
imprisoned in a brazen bull, and slowly tortured over a steady fire;
their cries could not reach the tyrant's ears so as to strike terror
into his heart; when they reached his ears they sounded like sweet
music. And men crowd about the poet and say to him, "Sing for us
soon again"—which is as much as to say, "May new sufferings
torment your soul, but may your lips be fashioned as before; for
the cries would only distress us, but the music, the music, is delightful." And the critics come forward and say, "That is perfectly
done—just as it should be, according to the rules of aesthetics."
Now it is understood that a critic resembles a poet to a hair; he
only lacks the anguish in his heart and the music upon his lips. I
tell you, I would rather be a swineherd, understood by the swine,
than a poet misunderstood by men.[4]

This aphorism first conjures up the picture of the suffering
poet who produces delightful music for the multitudes and then
the image of critics who praise the music yet remain unable to
perceive the suffering.

The disproportion in my build is that my forelegs are too short.
Like the kangaroo, I have very short forelegs, and tremendously
long hind legs. Ordinarily I sit quite still; but if I move, the tremendous leap that follows strikes terror in all to whom I am bound
by the tender ties of kinship and friendship.[5]

This mysterious aphorism unsettles and threatens us. What can this "tremendous leap" mean? But the next entry is a miniature lecture on the subject of choice. With an allusion to Socrates it begins: "If you marry you will regret it, if you don't marry you will regret both."[6] Here we see a person who weighs and plays with possibilities. Therefore he is immobile. Intellectually, he foresees only disadvantages in proceeding to act. Consequently, he prefers to keep all possibilities open for as long as possible. The result? Nothing happens! Nothing is pure joy and true sorrow. Life comes to him as a dream.

The last diapsalm again touches on the subject of the books: Choose, but only one thing. The poet, so admonished by the gods, finds himself at a loss, but chooses to have the last laugh. Then all the gods laughed. "I concluded that my wish was granted and found that the gods knew how to express themselves with taste." With a light stroke of the pen, the ironic author has erased the seriousness of the situation, and indeed, the situation itself is lost in good taste.

The "Diapsalmata" intentionally make us uneasy. Although they offer entertainment, they do not "say" anything. Nothing emerges. But they create the mood for the book.

B. "The Immediate Stages of the Erotic or the Musical Erotic"

We need only glance at the title of this essay to know that we are dealing with an intellectual, an art critic. Immediately, though, the subtitle jolts us from the security of that knowledge: "Insignificant Introduction." Should we skip it? Has the author intended irony? Is this a clue to the work?

The author offers an accolade to Mozart's opera *Don Juan*. (The translation calls it *Don Juan* but it is always called *Don Giovanni* otherwise. We follow the translator's usage, since it brings about the least confusion.) From all the delightful works of Mozart, he believes that *Don Juan* stands out as the masterpiece that, of itself, would make its creator immortal. Why, one wonders, does the author place *Don Juan* so far above *The Magic Flute*, for instance? The author answers by saying that *Don Juan* embodies perfect harmony between form and content. A happy coincidence may well have made Mozart choose *Don*

Juan, but the result in any case is a classic work. The subject matter penetrates the form, and the form penetrates the subject matter, blending in perfect union.

"A" argues that no other art medium but music could serve the subject and the idea of *Don Juan*. No mere accompaniment, the music is fused with the idea. The erotic is the subject for this essay. The sensuous attraction to the female, the wish to seduce occurs commonly enough, but the idea of "a sensuous genius," an abstract concept, would elude such a concrete medium as language. Only music can express it, and "A" wants to explain why he thinks it is so.

His first thesis is startling: "Christianity brought sensuousness into the world. This came about exactly because Christianity wanted to drive sensuousness out of the world."[7] The sensuous did not threaten beauty as its enemy for the Greek personality. On the contrary, the sensuous was physical, a natural ally to the soul. It was Christianity that introduced the idea of the "sensuous-erotic," the flare-up of instant passion as something dangerous, leading to swift perdition, an enemy to the soul. Thus Christianity spiritualized the sensuous. Music alone among the arts can communicate this immediacy, insists the author. Although music can naturally communicate other things, "A" points to the sensuous-erotic as its most "proper object." Sculpture and painting are sensuous arts that address themselves to the eye. Music, however, speaks when the other arts remain mute. In this manner, music may be viewed as a language. Language has time as its element while the other media have space. Music, a crossbreed among the arts, qualifies itself spatially in that it exists only in the moment of its performance; it carries us along:

Language has time as its element; all other media have space as their element. Music is the only other one that takes place in time. But the fact that it does take place in time is again a negation of the sensuous. What the other arts produce indicates their sensuousness precisely by reason of the fact that it has its continuance in space. Now there is, of course, much in nature that takes place in time. Thus when a brook ripples and continues to ripple, there seems to be in it a qualification of time. However, this is not so, and in so far as one may wish to insist that we have here a qualification of time, one would have to say that time is indeed present, but present as if spatially qualified. Music exists only in the moment of its performance, for if one were ever so skillful in reading notes and had ever so lively an imagination, it cannot be denied that it is only in an unreal sense that music exists when it is read. It really exists only in being performed. This might seem to be an imperfection in this art as compared with the others whose productions remain, because they have their existence in the sensuous. Yet this is not so. It is rather a proof of the fact that music is a higher, a more spiritual art.[8]

In language, prose stands farthest removed from music while poetry comes closest to it. This does not single out music, however, as a higher or better medium than language. On the contrary, music limits language. The use of language involves reflection and thereby the loss of immediacy. To interpret and spiritualize an event, we must use language. But to express a spiritualized moment, we must use music. Thus, the author maintains that sublime music cannot dispense with words.

Music seduces. "A" points out that the Church has instinctively felt its demonic power and at first tried to prevent the building of organs for churches; later it tried to convert the use of music to its own glory. However, because of its seductive powers, music finds its proper object in "the sensuous genius." "A" proceeds to demonstrate this thesis by stages.

First, he presents the Page in *Figaro*. This melancholy figure is dreaming, longing, wanting, without knowing what he desires. He has not focused his attention on any object outside himself. Neuter or androgynous, he rests within himself. A high-pitched, almost feminine, voice is most suitable for the part.

The second stage is represented by Papageno in *The Magic Flute*. Papageno's heart beats joyously because he has discovered an object for his desire—outside himself, to be sure! He pursues, cheerful and confident of his power to conquer. According to "A," however, *The Magic Flute* has a flaw, because in the end it extols married life. And that is definitely unmusical. Prose. Church bells mingle in the music.

Don Juan represents the third stage. Don Juan desires the particular, i.e., intercourse with a woman, "absolutely, triumphantly, irresistibly and demonically." The author clarifies what

he means by "sensuous genius qualified as seduction" by in-
forming us that *Don Juan* is a medieval legend. It was during
the Middle Ages that the spiritualization of the sensuous took
place and the tension grew. The interest in pornography intensified. Fear became part of the attraction:

There the sensuous has its home, there it has its own wild pleasures,
for it is a kingdom, a state. In this kingdom, language has no place,
nor sober-minded thought, nor the toilsome business of reflection.
There sound only the voice of elemental passion, the play of ap-
petites, the wild shouts of intoxication; it exists only for pleasure
in eternal tumult.[9]

Don Juan personifies "the principle of the erotic." He *is* the
seductive music. The moment we try to regard him as an
individual, he becomes ridiculous with his 1,003 seductions. In
the waves of the music, we enjoy him. But as a focus for
reflection, he becomes comical. When the music dies down and
reflection enters upon the theme of seduction, we discover
despair, guilt, and sin—considerations that were lost during the
performance.

The Greeks totally lacked this idea of the erotic as seduction.
Greek love was physical, not sensuous. "Chivalrous love," the
ideal during the Middle Ages, was faithful. But sensuous love
is faithless, catching the moment. Greek love and chivalrous
love can be portrayed beautifully in language. But sensuous
love, like a force of nature, is best expressed through music.

In order to clarify his point further, the author juxtaposes
Don Juan with another legendary seducer from the Middle
Ages, Faust. Don Juan seduced women by the hundreds. Faust
seduced only one, but he crushed her totally. Faust is an intellectual seducer; he needs the woman's innocence as a sounding
board for his own experiment with himself. Faust is reflection
personified. His medium is language.

Mozart's Don Juan brims like a glass of wine, always filled and
tempting by his very essence. How did he look? We don't recall
very well because we close our eyes and listen to the music.
Through hearing, we get a conception of him. The Don Juans
of Byron and Molière failed because they depicted him epically,
and that alters everything. We see him walk and talk, and we

smile at him. No; the power of seduction lies in an inward category. Only Mozart's music makes us "understand," i.e., *feel* Don Juan.

When writing drama, authors sometimes develop a mood, rather than an idea. While this can be disastrous in drama, it is commendable in opera. Drama requires unity of idea; opera, unity of mood. Mozart found the perfect medium in *Don Juan*.

In his "Insignificant Postlude," "A" rejoices over Mozart's happiness that is so transparent in the work. Humbly and significantly, he adds: "I, at least, feel myself indescribably happy in having even remotely understood Mozart and in having suspected his happiness. How much more then—those who have perfectly understood him—how much more must they not feel themselves happy with the happy."

This first essay compliments "Diapsalmata," and we get a better picture of "A." No doubt intelligent and perceptive, he is well read in aesthetics and has even done some significant thinking on his own. Best of all, his eagerness to clarify what he enjoys, proves that he enjoys.

Here the well-argued essay style has replaced the fragmentary style of the "Diapsalmata." The bold statement that Christianity introduced sensuousness and a new form of conscience is interesting, enjoyable, and profound. However, the tone, meaning, and direction of the book leave us uncertain. What kind of a book is this? Where is it going?

C. "The Ancient Tragical Motif as Reflected in the Modern"

This next essay deals with tragedy. Were it not for the setting, our anxieties about the author's intent would turn completely to admiration.

"A" belongs to a club, a men's club of course, where the elected and selected members come together to read papers to each other on aesthetic subjects. They call themselves "*Symparanekromenoi*," a "homemade" Greek word meaning something like "the fellowship of those who live buried lives." This name, as well as the ludicrous requirements of the papers (they must be fragmentary in an attempt to simulate posthumous papers) produce an eerie effect. They hold as a dogma that a finished product should bear no relation to the poetic personality. Each single meeting of the club must be different. As a rule, they allow nothing to become routine.

This essay was delivered as a paper before these "*Symparane-kromenoi.*" It deals with the essential difference between ancient and modern tragedy. The author warns us not to believe that Aristotelian determinations and requirements exhaust the concept of drama. The world has changed fundamentally since Aristotle's day, and we would be naïve to believe that the qualifications in his *Poetics,* general as they are, suffice for modern times. Aristotle's main requirement is plot, and ancient drama includes characters for plot's sake. Action is the epical event, and action does not spring solely from subjective decision. In modern drama the emphasis falls instead on character. The heroes stand or fall on their own acts, not according to epic heritage.

Aristotle requires that heroes have guilt.[10] Guiltless individuals spur no dramatic interest. On the other hand, absolutely guilty individuals are not tragic either: they are merely criminals. Ancient drama dealt with inherited guilt and unchangeable fate, *moïra.* The heroes could not be wholly responsible for their own fate as a result of their own acts. In modern drama, however, they are singularly responsible for their own acts. But modern drama has come up with a strong replacement for fate that similarly can arouse "fear and pity" in a spectator: namely, despair, self-inflicted guilt.

"A" makes the point that mankind has grown up since those ancient times which were childlike in their compassion, their piety, and their sorrow. Ancient drama unfolds with transparent clarity. Fate strikes the family, and, because of the clarity of the relationships, family members have no questions with regard to one another and act outwardly from the core of their relationship. A modern, "adult" tragedy requires deceptive characters who grieve over some hidden deed in their past. In ancient drama, people sorrow together over their fate. In modern drama, there is less sorrow and crying together but more individual pain and self-inflicted punishment. With "sorrow," the whole drama stands transparent; we understand why we cry.

With "pain," we guess the suffering and remorse of the characters in the modern drama.

To illustrate this difference, the author conjures up his own modern Antigone whom he contrasts with the ancient Antigone. This modern Antigone knows that something is wrong in her family, but she does not know what. Her anxiety drives her to discovery, but she cannot tell what it is. This modern Antigone turns inward, living with a secret. Proudly, she keeps her painful secret to herself. Dedicated, she mourns over her father's destiny. In order not to betray herself, she takes pains at festivals to seem gayer than anyone else. She falls in love passionately, but dares not confess her secret to her lover. He beseeches her, but she withdraws in insufferable pain. As long as she remains silent, she can live with her pain. But the moment she acts by talking, she must then die because she has betrayed herself.

We applaud. The sensitivity with which "A" has brought out a fundamental difference between two types of drama and two types of consciousness betrays his empathy with piety and his understanding of guilt.

D. "Shadowgraphs: Psychological Pastime"

The second paper delivered before the "*Symparanekromenoi*" begins with an "Improvised Salutatory" to the victory of darkness, hailing the coming doom and the destruction of everything. This and the title, "Shadowgraphs," coupled strangely to the subtitle "Psychological Pastime," shows us how "A" seems to be living up to the standards of the club. Yet we find it difficult to take him seriously. Rather, we tend to think of it all as a satire on the custom among scholars of enjoying each other's company on a level at which all feel comfortably elevated.

But "A"'s lecture is a continuation of the discussion of his beloved Antigone. With the exception of some ludicrous asides to the fellows present, both papers make a serious joint effort to penetrate the problem of artistic portrayal of inward upheaval. The author names as subject for this second paper a mental state that he refers to as "reflective grief." The destruction of the equilibrium between the inner and the outer world of people stricken with reflective grief makes this state extremely difficult to represent artistically. Such people can find neither peace within themselves, nor encouragement from their environment. The author proposes to portray this inward destruction by means of what he calls "shadowgraphs," inward pictures perceptible through external behavior.

He has chosen three women for his subject: women because he feels that in them more than in men "energy works up anxiety." These three women have one thing in common. All have been deceived by the man they trusted. Now they are in a state of grief.

First, Marie Beaumarchais in Goethe's *Clavigo*. She contemplates her broken engagement to Clavigo. He has just left her. She lives with the unanswered question: Did he deceive her? The people around her find it easy to say "yes." They have never loved Clavigo, and they will not miss him. She loved, and she misses him grievously. This "buries her alive," because these people, her environment, want her to forget while she wants to remember. She has nobody who will listen to her empathetically. Hence, Marie carries on a secret inquiry within herself. She reviews the case: he loved me/loved me not, he deceived me/deceived me not. This continues ceaselessly and without verdict. Her suffering allows her no peace. Just when she had opened herself to a wonderful future, it was cut off without explanation. Over and over, she returns to that moment. What happened? To help us understand "A" inserts a lyrical example concerning this grief and its object, telling a story of a man with a letter:

If a man possessed a letter which he knew, or believed, contained information bearing upon what he must regard as his life's happiness, but the writing was pale and fine, almost illegible—then would he read it with restless anxiety and with all possible passion, in one moment getting one meaning, in the next another, depending on his belief that, having made out one word with certainty, he could interpret the rest thereby; but he would never arrive at anything except the same uncertainty with which he began. He would stare more and more anxiously, but the more he stared, the less he would see. His eyes would sometimes fill with tears; but the oftener this happened the less he would see. In the course of time, the writing would become fainter and more illegible, until at last the paper itself would crumble away, and nothing would be left to him except the tears in his eyes.[11]

Those tearful eyes belong to Marie Beaumarchais.

For his second example, the author uses Donna Elvira from *Don Juan*. This is a woman who has been seduced and then abandoned. She is brought up by nuns in a cloister, where erotic passion has been suppressed to the point of eradication. Don Juan snatches her away from this setting, and when he does, her suppressed passion bursts forth, all-encompassing. She leaves the cloister with absolute faith in this one person. When he seduces and leaves her, her hatred breaks out with all the force of the passion she had given in her love. He deceived her. At this moment, she becomes "visible."

The author "A" transports us to Spain to encounter Donna Elvira rushing down the hill from the convent in pursuit of Don Juan. He has her confront him a second time. As a magnificent woman, this time Donna Elvira wants revenge. She has left the convent. She has thrown away everything for this man— even her eternal happiness.

Now Don Juan's passion reawakens. He has met here a "new" woman. As soon as Elvira senses this, she is beside herself. Her moral indignation and religious fervor vanish. For her own sake, she must love him. But can she love him despite his deception? Did he understand what he had done to a woman? Her struggle with love and hate brings her to no conclusion. Like a shipwreck, she is thrown back and forth on violent waves. Who is there to ask for advice? No one but herself.

In the third "shadowgraph," we meet Margaret, a pure child-like soul, unfortunate enough to meet Faust. As a seducer, Faust differs from Don Juan because, as we have learned already, Faust reflects.[12] His mind is in constant motion, probing and doubting. He does not want a woman like himself; he wants one who is as unlike him as possible. He wants innocence from a woman. He demands purity, trust, and piety. Sensually, not spiritually, he desires the immediacy of her simple, innocent person. Take away that simplicity, and she would mean nothing to him. She does not understand this, of course. In his tremendous superiority, he becomes her hero and her god. He becomes everything, and

she nothing. When Faust senses that her love for him has grown
too much for her and too much for both of them, he abandons
her. Her god gone, she is left with nothing. She prays to him,
and she curses him. Left alone, she cannot grieve alone. She is
utterly desolate.

At the end, "A" unites the three women and leaves them like a
group of priestesses consecrated to their grief. There is no
development. "Only he who has been bitten by a serpent knows
the suffering of one who has been bitten by a serpent."[13]

E.   "The Unhappiest Man"

By this point, our admiration for "A" 's sensitivity and imagination has risen high. His goal, however, remains enigmatic. Our
irritation with his evasiveness increases when we find that the
next piece of writing forms yet another address before the
precious *Symparanekromenoi*, a piece entitled "The Unhappiest
Man," subtitled "Peroration Presented at the Friday Meeting."

But perhaps we find here a key to the evasiveness. The unhappiest man is one who is never completely present in himself,
who exists outside himself, absent from the present and constantly identifying himself with something else: a divided
personality.

"A" seems quite familiar with the unhappiness of not being
able to live in the present. First he analyzes what happens to a
man who lives in hope with nothing but expectations, if he then
loses faith in that future. Then he becomes unhappy because
his life has no grasp on reality. Similarly distressed is the man
who has been living for his memories. The present can never
please him as much as the past. Or worse, consider the person
who never had much of a childhood, who suddenly discovers
the beauty of youth and looks back longingly, unable to recover
that past forever lost to him. There is no memory that can satisfy
his longing.

Then "A" combines the two types to enable us to imagine
unhappiness in its highest degree: A person who cannot find
himself in memory, and this seeking for memory prevents him
from finding himself in hope. He hopes that something will
happen to him that will be worthwhile remembering. Such

vanishing visions throw him back and forth, pending between past and future, making it impossible for him to act in the present. He becomes a poet poeticizing himself out of existence. The poet is then the unhappiest because he lives totally in imagination. But at the same time he is the happiest because he is therefore also able to live in all ages. Time for the poet does not exist. His tomb is empty. He is not there. He is in the future or in the past. Transfigured, he moves over time, and people in all ages identify with him in everlasting repetition. The essay flows rapidly and seems at times clear, but then a paragraph obscures its meaning. It enjoys paradoxical language:

So live well, then, unhappiest of men! But what do I say: the unhappiest, the happiest, I ought to say, for this is indeed a gift of the gods which no one can give himself. Language fails, and thought is confounded; for who is the happiest, except the unhappiest, and who the unhappiest, except the happiest, and what is life but madness, and faith but folly, and hope but the briefest respite, and love but vinegar in the wound.

He vanished, and we again stand before the empty tomb. Let us then wish him peace and rest and healing, and all possible happiness, and an early death, and an eternal forgetfulness, and no remembrance, lest even the memory of him should make another unhappy.[14]

The style of "now you see it now you don't," of hide-and-seek with the reader is most prevalent in this piece. Who is the unhappy happy, dead and transfigured poet? Or is it all a play with words?

F. "The First Love"

This chapter deals with comedy. Hegel in his *Aestetik* ranks comedy higher than tragedy. Is this a sign here that "A" agrees with Hegel and follows his pattern? It is not clear because "A" has chosen to review an insignificant play by Scribe (1791–1861), the French writer who produced plays by the hundreds.[15] The play's title, *The First Love*, a comedy in one act, serves as the chapter's title.

The long review tests our patience. Discussion first focuses on the subject of "first love." "A" admits that this subject has special interest for him because of his own life story and a certain coincidence that both he and his mistress went separately to the same performance of *The First Love*. Keenly aware of each other, they listened and laughed at the action in a heightened manner. When they met the following day, they understood each other, thanks to Scribe, who gave them a common ground. "A" thinks that Scribe must have foreseen this kind of meeting, and his foresight must have given him the occasion to write.

"A" argues for the category of *the occasion* as something accidental yet necessary for the creative process to start—the nothing from which everything arises. He marks it as *the moment* when a writer becomes an inspired prophet, pressured by a vision to sit down and write.

The First Love is a comedy of errors.[16] The main character misunderstands the play's theme, first love. From that awkward center, the whole plot spins out in endless webs of ironic situations through mistaken identity. The main character, Emmeline, lives with the illusion of first love taken most literally. She is so rigidly faithful to that illusion that she does not comprehend what is happening around her. Because she does not waver, her part proves most difficult to play. She must be attractive enough to hold the spectators' attention, and at the same time, unattractive enough to underscore the point of the play.

Emmeline reminds us of Jane Austen's *Emma*, irony's darling. The memory of that novel helps us to understand the importance of what "A" wants to say: irony erases! Reading the book or seeing the play, we do not identify ourselves with a single character:

... the destruction which irony, straight from the beginning, has been preparing for everything and everybody in it. When the curtain falls, then everything is forgotten, only nothing remains, and that is the only thing one gets to see; and the only thing one gets to hear is a laughter, which like a sound in nature, does not issue from a single human being, but is the language of a world force, and this force is irony.[17]

This little much-ado-about-nothing comedy then becomes the occasion for our author to write laboriously on the importance of divertissements and the difficulty of handling them skillfully. To

bring across the point of irony requires experience and reflection.
Nothing is more difficult than to be entertaining about nothing.
A fine point! But our infatuated "A" does not notice how long-
winded and boring he becomes in praising every turn of Scribe's
imagination. And what should follow at the heels of this review
but an essay on boredom!

G.   "The Rotation Method"

"A" frankly declares that "boredom is the root of all evil."
If we did not get bored, we would not try to change our
environment, manipulate our relatives, and mystify our friends.
Take a look at children. As long as they are satisfied, they play
beautifully in happiness and harmony according to the rules.
But the moment they tire, they want to change the rules. They
get angry and frustrated, and they begin to throw things around.
They misbehave. They cry. They scream. And they derive satisfaction from the turmoil they create. Boredom, the word whose
very sound suggests the staid and stolid, sets demons into motion.
"A" warns that boredom should not be confused with idleness.
Idleness constitutes a great art for which some have great
talent—Englishmen, for example, of breeding and wealth.

When it dawns on us that we are doing something of no
consequence, we become bored. Boredom originates in a certain
flash of insight into our own existence. The nothingness of our
existence! Suddenly, all that we touch turns to ashes, and we
grow restless, even dizzy, from the colossal proportions of
enterprise and the absolute meaninglessness of the results.

"A" now proposes a remedy for boredom in what he calls
"the rotation method." He has modeled the idea after the agricultural concept of crop rotation. Never cultivate anything for
too long, keep changing subjects, balance your mind to such
a degree that you master the art of forgetting and remembering.
Pick your pleasant memories and drop the burden of the
unpleasant ones. If these latter should appear, quickly plow
another furrow.

Guard yourself from developing tedious ties with other people.
Do not form friendships. And above all, never marry if you
want to live an interesting life. Nothing threatens freedom more
than proximity to others and the obligations that go with close

ties. If you want to lead a beautiful life full of possibilities, then you must defend yourself against the onslaught of other peoples' demands on your time, your capacities, and your emotions.

The secret of success in the rotation method lies in its application of "arbitrariness." No easy task, this requires work! "A" states the rule: Transform something totally accidental into something absolute and then stare at this arbitrary point until the world takes on new proportions, a new face, and thereby becomes interesting again, at least for a while. When you feel boredom coming on, quickly change your object of admiration. Concentrate again, and the arbitrary and the accidental will continue to amuse you.

"The Rotation Method" flows at a rapid pace. As teasing as ever, "A" reels off advice: be arbitrary; be elusive; be secretive; conceal your motives; avoid showing who you are: next time you might choose to be someone else. If you can stay on top of the situation and manipulate others like marionettes, you might have an interesting time. Be clever, and you'll find out how easily people will fall for rather simple tricks; you can start them dancing, and you can enjoy yourself immensely by just watching them move. But don't become involved yourself. Remember: boredom lurks around the corner. Move on. Master the art of forgetting. Remember only the delicious things.

All through the essays we have heard echoes from *The Concept of Irony,* and the voice of the Romantic poet seems to come through particularly clearly in the "Rotation Method." Our author, "A," whoever he is, is obviously of that ilk, and by overstressing the arbitrary element in the "Rotation Method," he turns the piece into a satire on his own working methods and their results.

Turning to the "Diary of the Seducer," we are particularly reminded of Kierkegaard's criticism of Schlegel's *Lucinde,* which was destructive, he said, and without a hold on reality.

H. "Diary of the Seducer"

"Either" 's last chapter is yet another of "A" 's clever exercises in pastiche. This time it is the diary novel. The diary, like the letter, provides the form in which to introduce the goings-on in a person's head. With the advice from "The Rotation Method" freshly in mind, we are not startled to find a person who actually plays by those rules. Suddenly, though, all the disparate essays and discourses in "Either" fuse, functioning in one character, the Seducer. "Diary of the Seducer" makes a devilishly clever finale, the logical destination of everything going before it in the book.

For this grand exercise, "A" needs an alter ego apart from the essays, and he christens him Johannes. He pretends he has broken into Johannes's secretary drawer, thus finding the journal, and confesses to a bit of bad conscience on this account, yet "a bad conscience can still make life interesting."

The motto for the diary comes from Mozart's *Don Juan*: "His ruling passion is a fresh girl."

Not quite a young man, Johannes seeks what is interesting in life and tries to reproduce it poetically. Other than recreating an experience, he has no ulterior motive in writing a diary: by means of the document he can enjoy the experiences twice, savoring the pleasant memories. Through his poetic skill, he creates a mood. Far too intellectual to be an ordinary seducer, Johannes arranges his relationships so that they flatter his mind as well as his senses. The diary centers on a certain young woman selected for her beauty and intelligence. The Seducer takes pleasure in creating a state of anxiety in her at the close of the affair. Terribly involved, she struggles with the doubt that perhaps the whole thing had been simply a figment of her imagination. Having nothing to confide, she cannot confide in anyone. The Seducer has succeeded in making her believe that it was all her doing. Hence, neither a Don Juan nor a Faust, he has seduced the whole person, pushing the event into infinity and myth. Clearly, he is the cleverest, most cunning seducer that ever was. Watch!

The diary opens in April and closes in October, thus including spring, summer, and fall. Johannes, a flaneur and girl-watcher, tends to focus his attention on young girls in particular. Affairs with mature women, he feels, remain merely piquant while true beauty is possible in an affair with a young woman. Forever an aesthete, he seeks out the beautiful. One day, a green cloak worn by a young woman catches his eye. The beautiful combina-

tion interests him passionately, and he keeps on the lookout
for the cloak.

Normally, he never lifts a finger to find out where a woman
lives, letting chance arrange an occasion; that way, life takes
on an extra flavor. This time, however, he tries to find her whereabouts, and makes an effort to meet her. When he finally does,
this innocent creature charms him utterly. Completely enchanted,
he watches her walk, her neck, her bosom, her nose, her laugh.
How beautiful to be in love, and how interesting to know that
one is! Even her name, neither ordinary nor unpoetic, offers
him a definite bonus. Cordelia! Cordelia, King Lear's daughter.

Cordelia lives a secluded life with her aunt. Her parents are
deceased. Johannes sets to scheming about how to get access
to her so he might observe her at close quarters. Obviously, she
possesses imagination and passion, he decides: however, she
simply doesn't know it yet. He laments that she does not play
an instrument. Music provides a perfect means of communication
with women. Never having been in love before, she has a free
spirit, living her life without a care. Johannes decides that she
is ideal. Like Galatea, she will become the object of an interesting
experiment. He will change her personality. He maps out a
strategy.

As a first step, he must provide her with a suitor—necessarily
a respectable and dull one. This suitor's prosaic nature will fail
to respond to her femininity, which in turn will be insulted and
neutralized. Edward Baxter, the son of a businessman, has
already appeared on the scene, very much in love with Cordelia.
Johannes decides that Edward suits his purposes, and they
become fast friends. Edward, unsuspecting and trusting, confides
in Johannes that he plans to invite Cordelia out. Johannes offers
to come along to entertain the aunt. Edward expresses his
gratitude. Johannes cleverly foresees that Edward will blurt
out everything by confessing his love at once, and after such
a confession, what else can be said?

Everything happens exactly as Johannes predicted. While
Edward and Cordelia sit mute and embarrassed, Johannes carries
on a spirited conversation with the aunt about agricultural
matters that interest her. The two lovers cannot help over-
hearing. Cordelia becomes more and more curious and enraged.

Johannes himself presents an enigma to her. There she sits, a beautiful young woman with her lover, at the most marvelous moment of her life. And there sits Johannes discussing milk prices. Her feelings for him verge on hate: this seemingly secure, utterly confirmed bachelor has insulted her femininity. She longs to confide in someone other than Edward, who sits at her side, so unsuspecting and undeviating in his devotion, so boringly honest and open.

Johannes has managed to create a conflict in Cordelia's soul. His next step is to get rid of Edward and—to everyone's surprise—take his place in Cordelia's life. A leaked rumor alleges that Johannes is in love and about to be engaged. The story creates the desired effect, arousing great curiosity in the aunt and consternation and bewilderment in Cordelia. The moment for a proposal approaches, and Johannes decides to make it as insignificant as possible, so that she must one day confess that in retrospect she does not know how it came about.

Johannes surprises her one day alone at home, and they become engaged. This delights the aunt, but Edward is beside himself with rage, feeling betrayed by the whole world. He makes a fool of himself and then drops out of the story for good.

Now comes a delicate moment. Cordelia still has no real conception of the erotic. She wishes to please Johannes. As part of his plan, he tries to convince her how common, low, and unbeautiful engagements in reality are. To this end, he takes her to a party for engaged couples where she can see for herself how ridiculous such people seem and how uniformly disgusting their behavior is. They hear sounds of kissing from every corner and from behind every door, as if someone were going around with a fly swatter. This upsets Cordelia, who now shares his taste. Their relationship must be rare and beautiful. The weak give in to engagements, but she daringly begins to think of herself as different. Her thoughts turn toward a more individual and free style of love, strong and poetic.

Meanwhile Johannes realizes that she is becoming attracted to his body as well as being entranced by his exceptional soul. Conversation will not suffice to arouse greater erotic attraction. Silences, long pauses, and mystification must season the relationship. Johannes speaks in ambiguous ways. Cordelia notices the change. Johannes constantly sends her letters and notes. In the long letters he aims at improving her mentally and in the short notes, at developing her erotically.

Then something changes. Cordelia becomes more daring, interested now in seeking out the marvelous. Johannes must take care that she does not fall into the same pattern as Faust's unfortunate Margaret, who uncritically worshiped Faust. He must make sure that she develops within herself, so that the strong feelings she harbors will imbue her every act, all that she sees and hears. He hovers about her every move. She must live her dream. She sits on his lap, stands at his side, and rests her head upon his chest. He drops his notes on her table, in her knitting bag, and surprises her wherever she goes. Passionately in love with him, she is his, and he knows it.

Now comes the moment to withdraw in order to help her "naïve passion" develop into "reflective passion." Erotically aroused and aware of him at all times, she will refuse to give him up. Like Don Juan's Elvira, she will pursue him. As he commences with his withdrawal tactics, she, in turn, applies tactics of her own. Decided against pursuing him openly, she also begins to withdraw, in the hope that he will pursue her. She hints that she has become tired of the engagement and its crude external bonds. To her aunt's dismay, she breaks off the engagement, and to Johannes's delight, the world feels sorry for him. People reproach her, and she goes to the country to avoid their criticism.

The moment for the final phase of the seduction has arrived, as all lies in readiness. Johannes sends Cordelia notes, making erotic references to their beautiful relationship. Now, as two free persons, they can belong to each other in earnest. He selects the perfect meeting place and arranges for the night of seduction, knowing that she will come eagerly. He will have her, body, soul, and spirit. She will be completely his.

After that night, Johannes hopes never to see her again. "Now all resistance is impossible, and only as long as that is present is it beautiful to love; when it is ended there is only weakness and habit."

So ends the "Diary of the Seducer." All through his journal, Johannes has mentioned (seventeen times, no less) other interesting objects for manipulation, prospective future possibilities. The finished chapter on Cordelia pleases him. She progressed beyond the stages of Elvira and Margareta. Cordelia is left with nothing. In her words, she has "embraced a cloud."[18] We find nothing and yet everything in her story. She sought out the marvelous. Miraculously, she found nothing but herself.

II *"Or"* (*Volume II*)

Kierkegaard has stated that he wrote volume two before volume one. He may have started out with the idea that a series of letters to an aesthete from a person firmly placed within the ethical would illustrate the difference between the two points of view and the crucial importance of the choice involved. "A"'s papers might have taken shape as Kierkegaard wrote these long, didactic letters. He wrote the answer before he formulated the question. With volume two down on paper, Kierkegaard felt free to pick and choose from all the material he had collected, all the studies he had made since he had started work on *The Concept of Irony*. This provides one explanation for the fact that "B"'s letters answer "A"'s papers rather indirectly. Both deal with the same material and confront each other dialectically. But Kierkegaard does not exploit the advantage that "B" might have had in quoting "A" verbatim to refute his position. Sometimes "B" refers to points never mentioned in "A"'s papers. The other explanation is, of course, that it is more clever not to be direct.[19]

"B," the author of volume two, is a judge named William. He comes across as a solid character, with a bourgeois family background and conventional upbringing. He lives with his wife—a woman with common sense, lovely manners, and a cute little nose—in a home surrounded by a garden. They entertain friends modestly. On the whole, their circumstances resemble those of a thousand others, a fact that does not distress them in the least.

Sucking at his pipe, the Judge sits down at his desk and begins patiently to answer the fragments of writing (the papers just reviewed) that he has received from his young friend, "A." Neither brilliantly witty nor desperately daring, Judge William does not pretend to be a poet. He has neither the time nor the patience for that kind of exercise. Busy during the day, he sleeps soundly at night. Obviously, his young friend is headed for perdition, and so he considers it his duty to take the time to warn him. His answer is patient and thorough.

A. "Aesthetic Validity of Marriage"

In his first letter-essay, Judge William presents his answer to the three essays in "Either": "First Love," "The Unhappiest Man," and "The Rotation Method." He begins by adducing all the attributes: the interesting and the accidental, chance, observation and manipulation, mystification, illusion, and the possibility of the imagination, etc. If his young friend wants to restrict himself, lose himself in these, he should be aware of two inevitable results.

First, he will become synonymous with the Seducer, a playboy who in his eagerness to play the role of fate poses a danger to others: The Judge would certainly warn his own daughter against such a fellow. And, secondly, a danger to himself, since he will inevitably suffer increasingly from frequent bouts of melancholy when his spirit despairs and he feels sorry for himself, yet is unable to make a single move.

The Judge believes he has glimpsed his friend's nothingness and despair at a decisive point. He sympathizes because he remembers that he has had some of the same experiences. He wants to tell the story of his own salvation, how he found the courage to act and find meaning again. What happened in his case?

Nothing spectacular. He fell in love and got married. But it was and still is a revelation to him. He now wants to teach, using his own marriage as the example of the difference between their respective points of view:

. . . but the point with me is to renew constantly the first love, and this again in such a way that for me it has just as much religious as aesthetic significance; for to me God has not become so supermundane that He might not concern Himself about the covenant He himself has established betwixt man and woman, and I have not become too spiritual to feel also the significance of the worldly side of life. And all the beauty inherent in the pagan erotic has validity also in Christianity, in so far as it can be combined with marriage. This renewal of our first love is not merely a sad reflection or a poetic recollection of something that has been experienced whereby one at length deludes oneself—that sort of thing produces fatigue, but this is action. Generally, the moment comes soon enough when one has to be content with recollection. One ought as long as possible to keep life's fresh spring open.[20]

"First love" means not only to remember an occasion in the past but to live it into the future. A romantic, the Judge believes that heaven gives birth to marriages. Man and woman form two parts of a whole, designed *a priori*. When the right partners meet, they experience a blissful moment of discovery, a marvelous attraction. This moment of discovery constitutes an aesthetic experience, but the full beauty of first love lies in seizing this moment, capturing it, and developing it by living it over and over in fresh, new situations of discovery—of oneself, of the other, and of the whole. Marriage has this function. Marriage rescues the moment of first love by distributing it throughout life. Marriage does not dilute it. Indeed, it capitalizes on the essential quality of the first experience, namely, its eternal aspect. Only marriage has the tools to make that which is given in eternity concrete in time.

The primary objective of marriage is to renew first love. Contrary to what the young man had taken for granted, huffs the Judge, absolutely no cleavage exists between love and marriage. Marriage presupposes love, not in the past, but in the present, for the future and all eternity. Christian marriage is higher than pagan love because it perfects love:

That marriage belongs essentially to Christianity, that the pagan nations have not brought it to perfection, in spite of the sensuousness of the Orient and all the beauty of Greece, that not even Judaism has been capable of this, in spite of the truly idyllic elements to be found in it—all this you will be ready to concede without compelling me to argue the matter, and this all the more because it is sufficient to remember that the contrast between the sexes has nowhere been made a subject for such deep reflection that the other sex has complete justice. But within Christianity also love has had to encounter many fates before we learned to see the deep, the

beautiful and the true implications of marriage. Since, however, the
immediately preceding age was an age of reflection, as is ours also
to a certain degree, it is not so easy a matter to prove this, and
since in you I have found so great a virtuoso in bringing the weaker
sides into prominence, the task of convincing you of the side
which I have undertaken to defend is doubly difficult. I owe you,
however, the admission that I am much indebted to you for your
polemic. When I think of the multifarious expressions of it which
I possess in their dispersion, and imagine them gathered into a
unity, your polemic is so talented and inventive that it is a good
guide for one who would defend the other side. For your attacks
are not so superficial that (if only you or another would think
them through) they might not contain the truth, even though neither
you nor your adversary observe this in the moment of conflict.[21]

The Judge demonstrates that he has formed a view of history
and has found his place within it. For the benefit of the young
man and his ethical development, Judge William makes a
conscious effort not to sweeten the requirements of marriage.
Rather, he tries to elevate such requirements and bind them
firmly to the religious. He believes that experimental love can
have nothing to do with the eternal. Marriages are concerned
with the eternal, states the Judge, precisely because they are
based on "resignation." That startles us. Why should that be
so, we wonder?

Because love can be destroyed, answers the Judge. Either one
can romanticize it out of existence (love, love, love, love ...),
beating it to certain death. Or one can doubt it from the beginning, believing that such a good thing certainly cannot last.
Reflection questions the reality of love. Marriage provides the
necessary relief from such reasoning.

The young man had looked at first love by staring himself
blind on the word "first." To him, the "first" meant only "first"
in a series of repetitions, instead of containing a promise that
held the future. This mistake appalls the Judge. It saddens him
to have to stress the lack of dreaminess in first love. Since it is
directed toward one person, first love stays awake and alert.
Sensuous but not reflective, first love acts. Persons in love are
not schemers: they feel wonderfully free and in possession of
all their powers, confident about what they must do. A unity of

freedom and necessity is the hallmark of such love. Persons in love feel drawn with irresistible power to the ones they love, and within this attraction they feel their freedom. The more they love, the more they feel religiously in tune with the world. Irresistible themselves, they can do anything they want, and they want only one thing: to be with the beloved.

The Judge anxiously emphasizes that marriage in no way changes the quality we have in first love. The religious impetus also prompts first love in marriage:

Already I have indicated above that even the illusory eternity in first love makes it moral. Now when the lovers refer their love to God this act of thanksgiving imparts to it an absolute stamp of eternity, as does also resolute purpose and the sense of obligation; and this eternity will not be founded upon obscure forces but upon the eternal itself. Purpose has at the same time another significance. That is, it implies the possibility of a movement in love, and hence, also, the possibility of liberation from the difficulty attendant upon first love as such, that it is incapable of budging from the spot. The aesthetical aspect of it consists in its infinity, but the unaesthetical in the fact that this infinity cannot be finitized. I will elucidate by a more figurative expression the fact that the addition of religion cannot disturb first love. Indeed, the religious is properly the expression for the conviction that man by God's help is lighter than the whole world, the very same faith which accounts for the fact that a man is able to swim. If, then, there were a swimming belt which could hold one up, one might suppose that a man who had been in mortal danger would always carry it; but one might also suppose that a man who had never been in mortal danger would likewise carry it. The latter supposition corresponds to the relation between first love and the religious. First love girds itself with the religious, even though no painful experience or alarming reflection has gone before. Only I must beg you not to press this analogy too far, as if religion stood in a merely external relation to first love. I have shown in the foregoing that such is not the case.[22]

The Judge believes that a person loves only once in life. He allows for the possibility of infatuations, but the kind of love he describes partakes of eternity and by definition can happen only once. Some writers have no clear idea of the relationship between the sensuous and the eternal, and this perturbs the

Judge. He feels that they lead people astray by making them wish for "more." Instead of pointing to the relationship between love and marriage, they cast a shadow over marriage. But marriage concretely encompasses those elements only abstractly present in the first love. The unity between the universal and the particular can be expressed only by marital love.

If we have not understood that marriages are "made in heaven," then we have not touched first base. The commonly given worldly reasons for marriage lack true substance. Something has gone fundamentally wrong if we have to give reasons "why." The less "why," Judge William argues, the more love. The couple knows "why." Simply: they have come together forever.

When one attaches finite reasons to marriage, the bottom falls out. Marriage as a school for character? False. Marriage liberates? Wrong. Ah—then one marries to have children. Horrors! One marries to acquire a home? Total misunderstanding! "All such marriages suffer from the defect that they treat one single factor in marriage as the purpose of marriage."

Then what is the relevance of the marriage ceremony? The Judge writes that the wedding ceremony is not the first thing that the couple thinks of when they discover each other. Rather as a force from the surrounding environment, the marriage ceremony comes upon them when their love affair is already in motion. By accepting the ceremony and taking part in it, they come out in the open, telling the world about themselves and their intention of doing what others have done. A wedding is a community event. The ceremony links this particular couple with history, from the first parents down to the people in a particular congregation in a particular place. It brings out the universally human. Most significantly, it takes place before God. The greatness of the vows lies in the fact that—contrary to expectation—they do not bind the couple. Although possibly stronger than anything else, first love remains constantly on the lookout; the couple involved anxiously watch each other's moves and weigh each other's faithfulness. But through the vows, the resolution before God, the couple is freed from gnawing worry:

Marital love is armed; for by the resolution the attention is not directed merely towards the environment, but the will is directed towards itself, towards the inward man. And now I invert everything and say: the aesthetic does not lie in the immediate but in the acquired—but marriage is precisely the immediacy which has mediacy in itself, the infinity which has finiteness in itself, the eternal which has the temporal in itself. Thus marriage proves to be the ideal in a double sense, both in the classical and in the romantic understanding of the word.[23]

After having repulsed the commonly given reasons for marriage, the Judge, a tireless debater, tackles the commonly expressed reasons against marriage by trying to show their inadequacy: the necessity to work in order to support a wife and family, the prospect of boredom, the fear of suffering and death, and above all the fear of loss of freedom. All these reasons he refutes. All these reasons for *not* marrying seem to him as inadequate as the reasons for doing it. They are finite. They are external. Married or not, no one can avoid external trials. Besides, "he who has the courage to transform an external trial into an internal one has already as good as overcome it."[24] Man and woman become genuine human beings, fully developed people for the first time, writes the Judge, when they are married.

The true reason to marry then lies in the individuals themselves and in their personalities. Just as a growing person vaguely longs for something that seems to be missing, so must he or she come to terms with this vague longing through inward awareness. At the crucial moment, two people meet and recognize each other as the object of their longing. In their unity, the two develop their own particularity over the years and become unique. By so recognizing each other, they find the image they have been missing and develop their own history together from that moment.

Judge William tells his young friend that in the course of his adventures he could very well have run into the real thing: love. But because of his egotism and his fears of revealing himself to others, he found himself trapped in a dreadful impasse which made him unable to experience and understand love. The Judge argues that when experimenting with girls and exalting the beauty of conquest, his friend has completely overlooked a higher beauty, that of possession. Affirming that "true art will exhibit itself by possessing, not by conquering," the

Judge puts the two ways of thinking and acting squarely over against each other:

I return again, however, to the consideration of your whole spiritual make-up. You say that yours is a nature designed for conquest and not capable of possessing. In saying this you certainly do not think you have said anything to your own disparagement; on the contrary, you are inclined rather to think yourself greater than others. Let us consider this a little more closely. Which requires greater strength, to go uphill or to go downhill? Evidently more strength is required for the latter, if the grade is a steep one. The disposition to go uphill is inborn in almost every man, whereas most people have a certain dread of going down a steep grade. So, too, I believe that there are far more natures formed for conquest than for possession; and when you feel your superiority over a host of married people and "their stupid animal satisfaction," that may be true to a certain degree, but then you feel that you have nothing to learn from those who are beneath you. True art generally takes the opposite direction to the course which nature follows, though without annihilating the process of nature; and so true art will exhibit itself by possessing, not by conquering. The fact is that possession is conquest in an inverse direction. In this expression you can already see how art and nature strive against one another. The man who possesses has also something which results from conquest; indeed, if one were to be strict in the use of terms, one might say that only the man who possesses really conquers. You likely have the notion that you too possess, for in fact you have the instant of possession. But this is no possession, for there is no deeper appropriation. Thus, when I think of a conqueror who has subdued kingdoms and lands, he was also in possession of these oppressed provinces, he had great possessions, and yet such a prince is called a conqueror, not a possessor. Only when by wisdom he governed them to their own best interest did he really possess them. Now this is very rare in a conquering nature; generally he will lack the humility, the religious-ness, the true humanity, required for possession. It was for this reason, you see, that in my exposition of the relation of marriage to first love I emphasized especially the religious factor, because this will dethrone the conqueror and let the possessor come to evidence. Therefore, I commended marriage for the fact that it was precisely designed for the highest end, for lasting possession. Here I may remind you of a saying you often utter with a flourish: "The great thing is not the original, but the acquired." Now the passion for conquest and the fact that one makes conquests is the original, the primitive factor, but the fact that one possesses and wills to possess is the acquired. Pride is required for conquest, humility for possession; violence is required for conquest, patience for possession; cupidity for conquest, contentment for possession; food and drink for conquest, fasting and prayer for possession. But all the predicates I have used here, and surely have used rightly, to characterize the conquering nature may be applied with absolute propriety to the natural man; but the natural man is not the highest. Possession is not a spiritually inert and invalid "appearance" even though it has legal force, but it is a steady acquisition.[25]

Thus, the Judge concludes that possession surpasses conquest and marriage overtakes first love. He sees that such a thorough aesthete as his young friend must necessarily have difficulties. Aesthetics always has difficulties with that which is not instantaneous, momentary, and external, as is conquest. Magnificent paintings, great statues of the conqueror, celebrate the moment of victory; on the other hand, possession takes place in history and takes time, and in order to understand it, we need to understand something of the inner movements of heart and mind. We must also learn to observe how these inner movements reveal their manifestations in outer details. A person's virtues become visible with time in that person's actions:

For example, everything I am talking about here can of course be presented aesthetically, not, however, in the form of poetic reproduction, but in the fact that one lives it, puts it into effect in real life. It is in this way aesthetics is neutralized and reconciled with life; for though in one sense poetry and art are a reconciliation with life, yet in another sense they are at enmity with it because they reconcile only one side of the soul. Here I have reached the highest concept of the aesthetic. And truly he who has enough humility and courage to let himself be transfigured to this degree; who feels that he is, as it were, a character in the drama which the Deity composes, where the poet and the prompter are not different persons, where the individual, like a practiced actor who has lived himself into his part and into his lines, is not disturbed by the prompter but feels that what is whispered to him is what he himself would say, so that it almost becomes doubtful whether he puts words in the prompter's mouth or the prompter in his; he who in the deepest sense feels that he is poet and poetized, who

at the moment he feels himself to be the poet possesses the primitive
pathos of the lines, at the moment he feels himself poetized has
the erotic ear which picks up every sound—that man, and that
man alone, has realized the highest ideal of aesthetics. But this
history which proves to be incommensurable even with poetry is
internal history. It has the idea in itself and precisely for this reason
it is aesthetic. It begins, therefore, with possession, as I expressed it,
and its progress is the acquisition of this possession. It is an eternity
in which the temporal has not vanished like an ideal moment, but
in which it is constantly present as a real moment. When patience thus
acquires itself in patience we have inward or interior history.[26]

Abiding by his rules, Judge William can describe "The
Unhappiest Man" as creating an unhealthy situation, because in
this essay people are divided between those who live in memory
and those who live in hope. He asserts that one should be able
to grasp both at once. To engage in such either/or-type divisions
simply constitutes the thinking of a single person. A married
couple can look back upon a long row of anniversaries with
pleasure; yet, at the same time, they look to the future with
just as much anticipation as they had on their wedding day.
They don't live moment by moment. They become; they blos-
som; they bear fruit. They solve the riddle from the "Diapsalmata" of living in eternity and yet hearing the hall clock strike.
The Judge realizes that this might sound frightening to a bachelor, who clings to his own order and command of applying the
rule from "The Rotation Method." For a married man, this
exhaustive search for change proves unnecessary. Living with
and being committed to one another means constant change.
With commitment, a metamorphosis takes place.[27] All the fear,
reasoning and despair which the single person has nurtured
before the commitment disappear when he takes that step into
sharing everything with the other.

Hence, duty—a dull word to the aesthete—becomes a beautiful
reality for the committed person who realizes that there is
essentially only one duty, and that is to love. The Judge truly
believes that love and duty cannot be separated. Should we do
so, we doom love and head for perdition. We give up the task
of living and fill with resentment, bitterness, and doubt. Despair
separates. Duty unifies.

The main fault of "A"'s papers, according to Judge William, is that they pose the aesthetic, the ethical, and the religious categories as enemies. Judge William's parting shot in his first letter aims exactly at his friend's incapacity to see these three categories as mutual allies. The Judge feels that this failure lies at the heart of what is destroying his friend:

> You see, this again is despair, whether you feel the pain of it or seek in despair to forget it. If you cannot reach the point of seeing the aesthetical, the ethical and the religious as three great allies, if you do not know how to conserve the unity of the diverse appearances which everything assumes in diverse spheres, then life is devoid of meaning, then one must grant that you are justified in maintaining your pet theory that one can say of everything, "Do it or don't do it—you will regret both."[28]

It is a great mistake to separate the categories and try to single out just one as the only valid one. If we have a blind spot, the Judge warns, we'll miss the most important thing in life—living it. If we try to construct a house in just one of the categories, then it will not be livable and subsequently cannot be a model for others. The ethical will recapture the aesthetic in a higher sphere, and the religious, in turn, is what gives the ethical eternal validity. It is this interdependence that lends immense aesthetic validity to marriage, making it a beautiful and joyous form of sharing life.

B.   "Equilibrium Between the Aesthetical and the Ethical
      in the Composition of Personality"

When the Judge picks up his pen again to write a second letter to his friend "A," he has in mind something that was present all through the first letter but was never spelled out—namely, the importance of choice for the individual's inner development.[29] The second letter is an expansion of the discussion of love and marriage previously described. There the base of the argument was the apriority of the eternal in the marriage relationship. Marriages are "made in heaven"; two people who are made for each other recognize each other, fall in love, and marry, thus fulfilling their common destiny. In the second letter

the presupposition is the apriority of freedom within the individual. If we overlook that crucial point that the individual is at
all times free to decide for himself, then none of the Judge's
concepts of despair, choice, repentance, and the like, make
sense. Opposing freedom to necessity, however, brings him back
to the view of time and history that he had touched upon in
the first letter.

The theme of this second letter is choice. But before establish-
ing choice as a category, the Judge tells us what such choice
does *not* involve. It is not deliberating over contrasting alternatives. Neither is it preferring good to bad.

The choice of either/or transposes into the choice of "to
will/not to will oneself." This means that either we take responsibility for willing, or we do not take this responsibility. Only
after this first either/or—the decision for or against freedom of
self—only after this choice is made does the choice between
good and evil emerge.

The young friend had said his "either/or" like "abracadabra!"
—a snap of the fingers and "you'll regret both!" This betrayed
the emptines of his character. If we do not overcome choice by
decision and action, then we amount to nothing. Choosing decisively structures the personality. Through choice the personality grows. Without choice, the personality withers. What we
choose depends on who we are and what we want to become.
If we postpone choosing, then others begin to choose for us, and
we lose our personalities. By choosing for ourselves, we affirm
our inborn character. By choosing, we become ourselves. In
the hour of decision, the soul matures. In that hour, we stand
alone.

Something much deeper than knowledge and reason takes
place in this process. Neither history nor philosophy can tell us
how to choose. These disciplines can mediate the past, but
they cannot foresee the future. If we concede to history or logic,
a true either/or situation cannot function; giving in to systems,
we abdicate freedom. But each individual has his or her own
inner history, and in that world, an either/or exists. There the
individual chooses for the future. When choosing to act on one's
own accord, one becomes not another person, but oneself, con-
firming one's own *character indelebilis*.

From birth, we each have our own given personality. At the beginning, each personality is merely potentiality. Many strains run through our genes. The many voices that people the world within each personality request a ruler. All of us must choose a ruler for himself. Only after accomplishing this task do we become "our own selves." It is by "choosing absolutely" that we become free to rule ourselves. An act of the will, this choice poses many difficulties. The Judge concedes that many people never reach that particular choice, which stands as the true watershed between the aesthetic and the ethical.

"The aesthetical in a man is that by which he is immediately what he is; the ethical is that by which he becomes what he is." The aesthetical individuals live for the moment and in the moment. Their goal? To enjoy themselves. They reach out for pleasure, and when the moment passes, they must think up a way to enjoy themselves anew. Cleverness stores up more possibilities for new pleasures. Talented people often linger at this stage because they enjoy their cleverness. However, within them "darkens a cloud," melancholy. Occasionally, such people have happy childhoods, but eventually they waste more and more of their time brooding. Their innate spirits languish, rebelling quietly but insistently against their lack of clear command. Judge William calls melancholy "the hysteria of the spirit."

The Judge is not offering any fancy anthropology. According to his way of thinking, a human being is made up of body, soul, and spirit. The body is the sensuous; the soul is the mind. The spirit brings the two together. The spirit craves harmony and equilibrium. The spirit knows what a person wants to become, and a spirit rebuked will take revenge. Melancholy is the ambush of the spirit; its low hum of discontent deprives pleasure of its tempting quality. Nothing can divert one for any length of time from this inner toothache. Despair gauges its degree of danger. To understand choice and to appreciate the true beauty of the ethical, a person must first have tasted despair, this state of supreme imbalance within the ego. To will oneself, to choose, means to free the spirit and restore equilibrium within the personality. Hence, despair differs greatly from doubt, which has to do only with mind and intellect. Judge William coins the chiasmatic saying: "Doubt is the despair of thought; despair is the doubt of personality."

We have arrived at a point at which the Judge lays his young friend out on the couch, so to speak, and the diagnosis seems very clear to the analyst. As a result of his brilliance and vast intellect—and the pleasure he takes in manipulating others— the young friend's personality is heading in a dangerous direction, and in his despair, moments of crisis will arise with increasing frequency.

As the Judge sees it, "A" has two alternatives. Either he can continue to vacillate between spurts of energy and attacks of passivity, both "puppeteer and puppet." In this case, the Judge would fear for him. Or he can choose despair, willing it by accepting it as "a thorn in the flesh," thereby freeing his spirit. This latter choice will transform him, the Judge affirms. It will free him to act and stop him from feeling sorry for himself. Liberated from narcissistic self-love, he can dedicate himself to loving others as much as he has loved himself. In this way, he can enter the human race, refuting his former precarious position.

Personality arises from choice. Only when we have decided to "will ourselves" can we know the difference between good and evil and choose for ourselves. This ability to perceive what one must do does not come from outside, from philosophy and theology; it comes from within. We begin to act on what we discern as good and evil. By so acting, we further choose ourselves, thus forming a unity between action and choice. This unity begins to act upon what we come to know as good and chooses it over and over again. This whole process can be described by one word, says the Judge: repentance. Why can repentance be understood in this light? Because it conquers memory.

When we choose ourselves, then we see our past lives in the context of good and evil. We wish that parts of our lives would go away—because we feel guilty about them. But these parts and pieces cling to us, and the only way we can shake them loose and thereby act freely is by repenting, which means coming to terms with these flaws. Repentance has an enormous liberating force, and—bound up in it—we find the joy of being *with* others, *for* others, and *like* others.

Monks and mystics upset the Judge very much. They withdrew from the world in order to find themselves. Fine! But they did not return to the world, and he feels that they developed no civic virtues. They turned inward. The Judge wonders what right they have to live solitary lives, loving God and leaving the world behind them. To him, this means setting the immediate before the universal. They try to bypass the ethical. They do not understand repentance in its proper meaning.

We repent for the mistakes we make, and in his love God forgives us and gives us strength to reenter the world "repentantly," able to work for others. The temporal exists for human beings. It gives them a place, a history, and an occupation in cooperation with God. This is what is meant by the term "calling." Persons are called from within. They choose themselves concretely, in continuity with the past. The choice of ethical persons makes them visible to themselves and predictable to their surroundings.

Aesthetical persons think of the ethical as a negative. But no! insists the Judge. Universal law is not negative, but positive. It develops within as a conscience that shapes personality. We see what we want to become. The *telos* is no longer something accidental and external, but it has merged internally with the composition of the personality. A unity has been created between the particular and the universal. Duty takes the place of aimless activity. We know what we must do. Certainty replaces doubt. The "personhood" one thus achieves effects a balance between freedom and dependence.

With a clear image of the *telos* follows a new relationship among ways of spending time. The aesthete as presented by "A" had no perception of the continuity of time. For him there were moments of pleasure and moments of boredom and a great need to "kill time." This is no longer true from the point of view of the ethical. Persons who have chosen themselves know their past and know what they must do in the present in order to gain the future. There are no longer any empty spots because time takes on the dimension of continuity. The ethical gives direction. It marks the end of wallowing in feeling and hovering in thought, by adding responsibility for what happens. Responsibility prompts to action and participation.

This is a higher view of beauty, and, according to Judge William, it is only when the ethical is reached that life grows rich; its point of view penetrates every experience.

For example: An aesthete may find a life of leisure beautiful. But leisure requires money, as every reflective person understands. The ethical personality realistically sees beauty in work because work brings daily bread. Employment then is what gladdens the heart. Thus, the Judge is able to explain his phrase, "the truly extraordinary man is the ordinary man" who has found his self and achieved universal humanity.

So the Judge urges his young friend to go to work on himself, to find out who he is and make a decision about his future, to develop a conscience for the sake of his salvation, and to recognize not merely immediate beauty, but the beauty that has everlasting qualities. He encourages him to grow up and come to terms with his relationship to the world.

Judge William has his friend's whole condition very much on his conscience. Before ending his correspondence, he adds this remarkable note:

If, then, a man who is desirous of realizing the task which is assigned to every man, the task of expressing the universal-human in his individual life, were to stumble upon difficulties, if it seems that there is something of the universal which he is not able to take up into his life—what then does he do?[30]

If human beings examine themselves in this way, honestly and repentantly with a true desire to accomplish the universal, it may happen that individuals must confess to themselves that they are "exceptions."[31] Then they must go their lonely way as outsiders, not proud but knowing that they are deprived.

"Exceptions" exist. Some people cannot marry. Some people are unable to reveal themselves. Some cannot open themselves to friends. Outsiders exist, solitary persons who, for the sake of their conscience, must go it alone.

The Judge bids farewell to his friend in a peculiar manner that could obliterate his plea for adaptation to society. He sends along a sermon that wraps his own message in a package labeled "contents ignite when close to fire."

C. "Ultimatum"

"Ultimatum" forms the last segment of volume two. We might have guessed that the ultimatum would be a demand to choose the ethical way of life, thus summing up the hundreds of pages of Judge William's admonitions and teachings. But this is not so. The voice has again changed. A new character is introduced: ". . . a little man with a squarely built figure, merry, lighthearted and uncommonly jovial. Although in the depths his soul was serious, his outward life seemed gaily inconsequent."[32] The Judge remembered from their student days that he had a loud voice and an intellectual originality that set him apart from other friends. He became a parson in a country parish on Jutland, and there he would go out alone on the heath to prepare his sermons. It is one of these sermons that the Judge is sending along to his friend "A."

The sermon, on the text of the fall of Jerusalem (Luke 19:41 ff.), deals with the problem of theodicy (theós=God, díke= justice). If God is almighty and wills the good, how is it, then, that the righteous suffer and the unrighteous prosper, or why do the righteous perish with the unrighteous? Job's question. Do we dare believe in a moral order?

This question comes as a devastating counterpart to the equilibrium the Judge has just been advocating. It is not an ethical ultimatum, an either/or admonition to make a decision. The word ultimatum seems rather to mean exposure to the ultimate question.

This time, then, the love affair is with God and the conclusion is strikingly original: When a friend does what we cannot understand, or what we even suspect is wrong, then we want with all our hearts to be proven wrong, want him to be proven right. This, in summary, is the answer that the Jutland pastor gives to the problem of theodicy.

This thought is "edifying," which means that it builds up the inner person. The statement "Before God we are always in the wrong" is not a philosophical dictum, not true or false. It is an edifying thought that speaks to our love. Before God it is edifying to be in the wrong.[33]

III   Either/Or: *A Conclusion*

It is, of course, not possible to sum up a work as rich in substance as *Either/Or*. Kierkegaard has not merely given us an outline of his conception of the categories, the aesthetic, the ethical, and the religious; he has filled the first two with wondrously imaginative content and suggestive power. Here we have picked out many of the illustrations and illuminating details, in the hope that—even secondhand—they will convey some of the strength of the work. Reading *Either/Or* with care is an experience that furnishes us with measuring cups. Afterward, we listen both to ourselves and to others for nuances that reveal a point of view. When people speak, we wonder where they stand: when we read, we ponder the author's position. What choices have been made?

For the purpose of clarity, however, let us augment this introduction with a swift generalization. *Either/Or* presents three different approaches to the possibility of *change*. Aesthetes, though they manipulate changes and make arrangements, do not really believe that change can occur. Ethical persons, on the other hand, see the possibility of change in *commitment*. Their personalities converge in that commitment and gain "equilibrium," a balance between their person and the surrounding world. It is over against this equilibrium that, in the final sermon, we see the "ultimatum," the highest, and catch a glimpse of what change means in the religious sphere: *conversion*, a complete turnabout before God. This subject is merely touched upon in *Either/Or*. "Ultimatum" give us only a glimmer of what is to come.

CHAPTER 5

Fear and Trembling

NO sooner had the reviews begun to come in on *Either/Or* than Kierkegaard became irritated—as well as amused— by the public's inability to grasp that work's progression toward the religious. His own thoughts concentrated more and more on his deepening relationship to God while his other ties slackened. In an atmosphere of abandonment, isolation, and rugged discipline, he then wrote two pseudonymous works dealing principally with the religious: *Repetition* and *Fear and Trembling*. For Kierkegaard, the religious moved apart, becoming a separate category which he had to define against the background of the other two, the aesthetic and the ethical.

In *Fear and Trembling*, Kierkegaard chose to meditate on a myth well known in both church and synagogue. He examines the test that made Abraham the hero of faith, his sacrifice of Isaac, "The Akedah," a key legend in the Judeo-Christian tradition.[1] The interpretations of this story vary greatly. Biblical criticism has advanced the opinion that it originated as a protest against human sacrifice, a common practice among the Canaanites. In a modern landmark of literary criticism, Erich Auerbach juxtaposed this legend to the story of Odysseus' scar in Homer's *Odyssey*, thus extracting it from theological confinement.[2] In his rendering of the story, Kierkegaard wanted his readers to forget its familiar Sunday school lesson and wake up to its horrendous message.

Kierkegaard, too, had heard the story many times ever since childhood. His father must have told it to him. In the *Prelude*, we find an intriguing, private allusion: "—he saw no reason why the same thing might not have taken place on a barren heath in Denmark. . . ." Filled with such feeling for the story, Kierkegaard desperately wants us also to forget our higher criticism and knowledge. He makes fun of the belief that knowledge

115

perfects: "That man was not a learned exegete, he did not know Hebrew, if he had known Hebrew, he perhaps would have understood the story of Abraham." Having found a prototype for the religious category in Abraham, Kierkegaard forcefully presents him to us as one whom our eyes can see and our ears can hear, and as one to whom our hearts can bend.

We listen to a sermon, or read it, and wait for the "Amen." So be it. Kierkegaard, however, did not want to be reassuring about existence. He aimed at arresting and transforming his reader. He wished to expose the folly of optimistic belief in progress and a future that pushed God out onto the farthest edge of the unknown. If God is God, Kierkegaard believed, then he is always near. And the larger the universe grows for an individual, the larger God becomes. *Mutatis mutandis,* the same truth holds for evil. Good and bad gain such intense personal concern that they break down the boundaries of conventional ethics. Truth and justice disappear as principles and reappear in "God," and to this message there could be no collective "Amen." Hence, the sermon format that had served in the "Ultimatum" proved inadequate in *Fear and Trembling,* incapable of revealing the man of faith who confronts God, dreads him, loves him, obeys him, and expects from him the impossible.

In *Fear and Trembling,* Kierkegaard presents the hero of faith as greater than all men: "great by reason of his power whose strength is impotence, great by reason of his wisdom whose secret is foolishness, great by reason of his hope whose form is madness, great by reason of the love which is hatred of oneself."[3] Madness? Kierkegaard does not shrink from the expression. He thrusts us up against the wall of paradox, relying on us to find the unreasonable reality. If we cling to reason or wisdom, we are put in utter discomfort; then we might admire the hero of faith without following him. Kierkegaard wants us to see that there is no kinship that binds the believer and the person who turns back in resignation.

I *Johannes de Silentio*

With this purpose in mind, Kierkegaard found the earlier pseudonyms unsuitable. He had to develop a new character who admiringly and willingly observed the movements of faith from a border outpost. If he were to go farther and enter the land of faith, he would be lost to us as a guide because such an immediate relationship to God would place him "beyond words." Kierkegaard introduces Johannes de Silentio. (Johannes = the disciple Jesus loved the most; de Silentio = of silence.)

Johannes is a sensitive young man, thoroughly educated in Western literature and philosophy. He draws parallels from the Classics as from folklore with equal ease. His facility in quoting Shakespeare and Goethe, as well as Aristotle and Hegel, does not make him arrogant, however. Not merely interested in myth, he actively sympathizes with it. Well-trained in dialectics, he grasps a puzzling phenomenon whenever it occurs, setting it up as a problem and dissecting it neatly. But when dissection proves insufficient, he accepts that fact with a smile, marveling that the puzzle remains, that the explanation goes only as far as the explanation.

We do not learn many surface facts about Johannes. Is he short or tall? Plump or slender? Does he travel or spend his whole life in Copenhagen? Married? Confirmed bachelor? In this unusual novel such facts remain superfluous and unmentioned. We get to know that he is an amateur writer. Certainly not a professional philosopher, but he can apparently afford the luxury of writing for his own pleasure without having to please the public. He concedes that fewer and fewer people buy and read what he writes.

In his views on philosophers, Johannes holds special admiration for Descartes. He observes that Descartes modestly admitted that "his method had importance for him alone and was justified in part by the bungled knowledge of his earlier years."[4] He shows no mercy for the "Privatdocenten" of the Hegelian school. He finds himself impatient with their inability to make a connection between their actual experience and what they conjure up with such dialectical ease. Even when confronted by the chasm that separates faith and doubt, they lack the humility to stop and tremble. They want to go further. But, says Johannes, there is no "further." In *Fear and Trembling*, Johannes exhibits that ultimate chasm as it deepens within him.

"As God created man and woman so too He fashioned the hero and the poet." The story unfolds with Abraham as the hero and Johannes as the poet. The subtitle of the book, *A Dialectic Lyric,* specifies "lyric," as opposed to treatise, and calls attention to the book's emphasis on intensity of feeling in its meditation on Abraham. If we try to understand, then the mind bloodies its forehead. Johannes stands in awe of Abraham, admiring him. But will he be able to follow him?

Johannes has heard the Abraham story since his childhood, and it has always captured his imagination. Even though this sacrifice took place four thousand years ago, he senses the power of the event. The intervening millennia make no difference. His father, a man who knew no Hebrew, told it so vividly that Johannes and Abraham became contemporaries. Abraham rides for three days to Mount Moriah with Isaac, his son. Johannes gets to ride beside them. He recalls four attempts to break in on that scene and explain what happens during the ride, four attempts made by the man who knew no Hebrew.

These four pastiche vignettes are perhaps the most quoted and most beautiful of all Kirkegaard's writings. Each begins, "It was early in the morning," but soon the story veers away from the Biblical text, slipping into the details about Sarah in the window, Sarah kissing Isaac, Abraham thinking of Hagar and Ismael, or Eliazar, the faithful servant.

The poet who knew no Hebrew could not help himself. "Every time he returned home after wandering to Mount Moriah, he sank down with weariness, he folded his hands and said, No one is so great as Abraham! Who is capable of understanding him?"[5]

We can surmise that Johannes grew up close to his father and close to his mother, the Church. "When the child must be weaned, the mother blackens her breast, it would indeed be a shame that the breast should look delicious when the child must not have it."[6] Each vignette ends with the poetic words about the severing of mother from child in the child-rearing process. First: "Happy the person who had no need of more dreadful expedients for weaning the child!" Then the ominous: "Happy the child who did not in another way lose its mother." So then the flat: "Happy the person who has kept the child as near and needed not to sorrow any more!" And finally: "Happy the person who has stronger food in readiness!"

Johannes is now on his own. These four vignettes seem to tell us that we are helpless in terms of understanding the Abraham story if we add our own experiences, our own details, our own psychological insights, our ethical standards; they bounce off the story or ruin it. Yet we must come to grips with what happened. Johannes tries another approach, a panegyric, a eulogy of Abraham in which he pledges faithful service. He will do nothing but praise the greatness of Abraham.

II   "The Panegyric"

The truly great in this world are never forgotten. But Johannes reminds us that the word "great" means different things in each of the three categories: The persons who love themselves become great by themselves. Those who love others become great by their selflessness. But those who love God become greatest of all. All become great in relation to their expectations. The first expect the possible, the second expect the eternal, but the third, like Abraham, expect the impossible and are therefore the greatest of all.[7]

Hence, the task that Johannes has now assumed is to become a poet of the greatest of them all. A worthy cause, but is it not also impossible? How can that which defies divination lend itself to description without contradictions and absurdities? Johannes makes a courageous decision. He will not shrink from paradox. He will use it, emphasizing it, and calling it by its right name, the absurd.

Johannes goes to work by retelling the life of Abraham, who once received a promise that in his seed all races of the world would be blessed. Abraham believed it, fully expecting it to happen. Time passed. As years went by, he grew old as did Sarah, his wife. One would imagine, says Johannes, that they would sorrow. But Abraham left us no lamentations. If he had not believed, Sarah probably would have died from the sorrow of being barren; believing, they kept young. And in the fullness of time came the fulfillment of the promise. Their joy over Isaac thus became complete and was undimmed by bitterness rooted in disbelief and grief.

And then the test came again for Abraham. God claimed Isaac back, and suddenly in an instant everything seemed lost, their whole life meaningless.

Johannes, with his lively imagination, conjures up alternative ways in which Abraham could have met this threat from God. Feeling cheated, he might have gotten angry and defied God's command, retaining Isaac, but losing God. Or, in the misery of his doubt, he could have made some glamorous, heroic gesture such as plunging the knife into his own breast. Instead, he believed for his life, and he did something *holy*, something totally inexplicable.

Johannes knows at this point that he has again fallen into feeble attempts at explanation, when all he should do is to praise and uplift that holy passion, that faith, and to hold it so high that all can see its immensity. That he must do, so that people will not dismiss faith as something one gets over or goes beyond.

III *"Problemata"*

After his laudatory ejaculation, Johannes's orderly dialectical mind starts backtracking. This extraordinary faith! One cannot simply stand beholden to it in its magnificence; it requires scrutiny. This phenomenon begs the test of familiar categories to become divided up in scholarly fashion into a series of problemata.

These problemata are concerned with the essential difference between the ethical and the religious categories, between our duty to humanity and our duty to God. When these two seem to agree, then there is no problem; but when, as in the case of Abraham, they do not agree, there comes the terrifying dilemma to which there is no direct answer. The answer is hidden in Abraham's silence.

The ethical is the universal. It applies always and has no *telos* outside itself. When individuals have chosen to subordinate themselves for the good of others, they have entered the ethical realm. After that commitment, every time they feel a temptation to yield to their own personal need to the detriment of others, they also understand that this constitutes temptation to sin.

By doing our duty, we fulfill the requirements of state, church, and family. We pay our taxes, obey the laws, honor our family tradition, and keep the commandments. But in doing our duty, we do not get into a relationship with God. In faith, however, there exists a relationship between an individual and God that stretches beyond normal duties. In such a relationship, the individual is absolutely on his own—not the norm, but the exception. To illustrate the difference between the ethical and religious categories, Johannes picks out Agamemnon, the Greek king, who also sacrificed his child, Iphigenia. Agamemnon hated the act but acted according to the rules by following what the gods demanded of him. Ethically considered, Agamemnon did the right thing. Though our rules are different, we can understand him. We lament his dilemma. We sorrow for the girl. But we admire the strength of Agamemnon, who did not plead with the gods or make any compromises. As a tragic hero, he did his duty.

The difference between the tragic hero and Abraham is clearly evident. The tragic hero still remains within the ethical. He lets one expression of the ethical find its *telos* in a higher expression of the ethical; the ethical relation between father and son, or daughter and father, he reduces to a sentiment which has its dialectic in its relation to the idea of morality.[8]

If the religious category did not exist, the teachings of the Greeks would have to suffice. We would look up to the long line of larger-than-life heroes who reinforced the laws and the rules of human behavior by dedicating themselves to their implementation, thereby subordinating their own needs and wishes.

Not so with Abraham. If we apply ethical standards to what Abraham did when he took the cleaver and brought the boy out to Mount Moriah and tied him down to the firewood and raised his hand, then we must condemn his act. From the ethical point of view, Abraham was ready to commit murder. And in such light, we dread the man. Ethically, we condemn him.

But, says Johannes, in the religious category, it seems totally different. When it comes to faith, every particular situation gets higher priority than the universal. If not, Abraham would be lost, and with him the Judeo-Christian tradition. From the religious point of view, Abraham became a hero. His glory shines because he entered this dreadful situation and then came out of it *together with Isaac*. "Abraham" is a paradox.

I will not recall here the human distinction between loving and hating—not because I have much to object to in it (for after all it is passionate), but because it is egoistic and is not in place here. However, if I regard the problem as a paradox, then I understand it, that is, I understand it in such a way as one can a paradox. The absolute duty may cause one to do what ethics would forbid, but by no means can it cause the knight of faith to cease to love. This is shown by Abraham. The instant he is ready to sacrifice Isaac the ethical expression for what he does is this: he hates Isaac. But if he really hates Isaac, he can be sure that God does not require this, for Cain and Abraham are not identical. Isaac he must love with his whole soul; when God requires Isaac he must love him if possible even more dearly, and only on this condition can he *sacrifice* him; for in fact it is this love for Isaac which, by its paradoxical opposition to his love for God, makes his act a sacrifice.[9]

To illustrate the relationship between love and hate, Johannes uses the words of Jesus in Luke 14:26: "If any man cometh unto me and hateth not his own father and mother and wife and children and brethren and sisters, yea, and his own life also, he cannot be my disciple." These words make no sense at all, says Johannes, unless they are taken literally. He makes a satirical swipe at the exegetes who have tried to soften the impact by tastefully replacing *miseīn* (to hate) with *meísein* (not to love).[10] No! Precisely in the word "hate" do we find the clue to what Jesus is speaking about: namely, the paradoxical relationship between love—hate, the nearness in passion, the tension that holds them both inseparably together.

Acting in such a passionate manner requires enormous courage. The individual leaves the race. We must not think, however, that encouraging such behavior would dangerously allow people to let themselves go. Becoming "a single individual," being separate and standing alone, is not the easiest, but the hardest, thing. The person who crosses that border with fear and trembling takes a leap over an abyss. Never enlisting a mass exodus, this "higher-than-the-universal" attracts only a few heroes. This transcendence of the universal is miraculously more human. By their lives these heroes bear witness to the faith in them. Thus, with the aid of Abraham, Johannes states that "there is such a thing as a teleological suspension of the ethical." There is "an absolute duty toward God."

Yet, what is faith? An enormous, overcoming passion? Johannes again lets his imagination run freely. How would he have acted, had he accompanied Abraham on that ride to Mount Moriah? Certainly he would have tried at every turn to persuade Abraham to go back. But after the trial, as they happily returned home, joyous and glad, Johannes would stand out as an embarrassment to the party, because he had given the wrong advice. The paradox of faith paralyzes Johannes personally. He does not deny its existence. He sees faith bursting forth—not as a small thing, but as lifelong, gigantic strife, which is capable of transforming a murder into a holy act. Faith can indeed move mountains.

As soon as we realize what a gulf separates Abraham and Johannes, the book becomes charged with suspense. Johannes again dramatizes the juxtaposition by introducing into the exposition another pair of contrasting figures, *the knight of faith* and *the knight of resignation*. Because he now wishes to focus upon the spiritual dimension of heroism, he changes Abraham and Agamemnon into medieval knights. Cleverly done, this transposition throws their two positions into relief. Not only do we gain a new perspective on the distance between these two figures, but we also learn more about the depth of Johannes's inwardness.

What is infinite resignation? A movement by the spirit, it stands as the last stage prior to faith. A decision to reconcile oneself with existence, it really effects this reconciliation, here and now in the realm of the temporal.

The knight of resignation is a young swain who has fallen in love with a princess, whose hand, he knows, he cannot win. In his dilemma, this intelligent, reflective man makes sure that love for the princess really is "the content of his life." He immerses himself in his love until it has completely absorbed him, so that the whole significance of reality is contained in one single wish. He concentrates his thoughts upon one act of consciousness. Then he is ready to move. He does not contradict himself; he does not forget himself. But how can he move?

Love for that princess became for him the expression for an eternal love, assumed a religious character, was transfigured into a love for the Eternal Being, which did to be sure deny him the fulfillment

of his love, yet reconciled him again by the eternal consciousness
of its validity in the form of eternity, which no reality can take
from him.[11]

Thus the knight of resignation gets his wish, but only spiritually, since he is satisfied with having it that way, for in that
manner he can keep his love as young and wonderful as it was
in its first moment. He has come a long way toward understanding life and accepting it. But Johannes reminds us that this only
exemplifies human courage. This is not "Abraham," but "Socrates"; this is renunciation of the temporal in order to gain the
eternal.

But then there comes the second movement in which one
renounces the temporal and gains both the eternal and the temporal. Abraham *and* Isaac. This is the movement of faith. Johannes confesses that he had never met a "knight of faith." He
can only imagine how solidly such a knight must tread the
ground.

...I have not found any such person, but I can well think him.
Here he is. Acquaintance made, I am introduced to him. The moment
I set eyes on him I instantly push him from me, I myself leap
backwards, I clasp my hands and say half aloud, "Good Lord, is
this the man? Is it really he? Why, he looks like a tax-collector!"
However, it is the man after all. I draw closer to him, watching his
least movements to see whether there might not be visible a little
heterogeneous fractional telegraphic message from the infinite, a
glance, a look, a gesture, a note of sadness, a smile, which betrayed
the infinite in its heterogeneity with the finite. No! I examine his
figure from tip to toe to see if there might not be a cranny through
which the infinite was peeping. No! He is solid through and through.
His tread? It is vigorous, belonging entirely to finiteness; no smartly
dressed townsman who walks out to Fresberg on a Sunday afternoon treads the ground more firmly, he belongs entirely to the
world, no Philistine more so. One can discover nothing of that
aloof and superior nature whereby one recognizes the knight of
the infinite. He takes delight in everything, and whenever one
sees him taking part in a particular pleasure, he does it with the
persistence which is the mark of the earthly man whose soul is
absorbed in such things. He tends to his work. So when one looks
at him one might suppose that he was a clerk who had lost his soul

in an intricate system of book-keeping, so precise is he. He takes a holiday on Sunday. He goes to church. No heavenly glance or any other token of the incommensurable betrays him; if one did not know him, it would be impossible to distinguish him from the rest of the congregation, for his healthy and vigorous hymn-singing proves at the most that he has a good chest. In the afternoon he walks to the forest. He takes delight in everything he sees, in the human swarm, in the new omnibuses, in the water of the Sound; when one meets him on the Beach Road one might suppose he was a shopkeeper taking his fling, that's just the way he disports himself, for he is not a poet, and I have sought in vain to detect in him the poetic incommensurability. Toward evening he walks home, his gait is as indefatigable as that of the postman. On his way he reflects that his wife has surely a special little warm dish prepared for him, e.g. a calf's head roasted, garnished with vegetables. If he were to meet a man like-minded, he could continue as far as East Gate to discourse with him about that dish, with a passion befitting a hotel chef. As it happens, he hasn't four pence to his name, and yet he fully and firmly believes that his wife has that dainty dish for him. If she had it, it would then be an invidious sight for superior people and an inspiring one for the plain man, to see him eat; for his appetite is greater than Esau's. His wife hasn't it—strangely enough, it is quite the same to him. On the way he comes past a building site and runs across another man. They talk together for a moment. In the twinkling of an eye he erects a new building, he has at his disposition all the powers necessary for it. The stranger leaves him with the thought that he certainly was a capitalist, while my admired knight thinks, "Yes, if the money were needed, I dare say I could get it." He lounges at an open window and looks out on the square on which he lives; he is interested in everything that goes on, in a rat which slips under the curb, in the children's play, and this with the nonchalance of a girl of sixteen. And yet he is no genius, for in vain I have sought in him the incommensurability of genius. In the evening he smokes his pipe; to look at him one would swear that it was the grocer over the way vegetating in the twilight. He lives as carefree as a ne'er-do-well, and yet he buys up the acceptable time at the dearest price, for he does not do the least thing except by virtue of the absurd.[12]

The knight of faith treads heavily on reality, while the knight of resignation steps lightly, aware of the risk of stepping through.

While the knight of resignation renounces everything, the knight of faith acquires everything.

Abraham made the double movement from resignation to faith and thereby regained the temporal, the finite. He got Isaac back. By virtue of the absurd, everything turned around. How wonderful to live! God performed the miracle that Abraham sought out in his faith.

IV   *Dreadful Silence*

Abraham never told his family what he was about to do. He did not speak to those who for him had the highest ethical priority, his family. This I must try to understand, says Johannes; why did he keep silent? This is not ethically defensible. Or is it? To speak means inevitably to be heard and interpreted, not only by oneself, but by others. Had Abraham spoken, others would have translated him. What he heard within himself was in no way translatable to those he loved, and, even more important, it was also unintelligible to himself. That unknown, terrible voice! Abraham could not speak. But he moved; he acted. His spirit performed what Johannes calls "the double movement." First, he made the movement of resignation. He gave up all his dreams, all his love, all earthly hope. Thus far, Johannes can well understand him. But then he moved again, and in that moment, a chasm opened between them. Abraham moved forward in faith.

Instead of turning back to explain his position to himself and then to his family, Abraham struck out in silence and fear. For three days he traveled to Mount Moriah. Johannes finds the proof that he did not speak on that journey in Abraham's answer to Isaac's question where the offering was: "God will provide himself the lamb for the burnt offering, my son." Only our familiarity with the story hinders us from understanding the enormity of that answer. Abraham actually walks in another world. He listens inwardly. He knows what he must do. The Lord has commanded that Isaac be sacrificed. Abraham has resigned himself to obedience; once he had done this, it remains for the Lord to act, to return Isaac to him. When asked, he answers truthfully. As Johannes puts it: "He speaks another language."

Ethics abhors such an unintelligible and indefensible lack of clarity. Concealment goes counter to the rules of the teachings of ethics. In the aesthetic category, however, concealment fits in. Drama is based on concealment and recognition, hide and seek. Both the demonic and the divine build with silences. "Silence is the snare of the demon, and the more one keeps silent, the more terrifying the demon becomes; but silence is also the mutual understanding between the Deity and the individual."[13]

Abraham made the double movement and produced new speech. Every word meant something that sounded positively absurd, but was nevertheless full of meaning, to the last syllable. Abraham uses the language of the prophets and the apocalypse. It makes eminent sense for those who have ears to hear.

Silence before speech. Or just silence and no speech. Silence and its dreadful isolation. Such thoughts form the core of Johannes's further investigation. What happens in silence?

To point out the difference between the demonic and the divine silence, Johannes makes use of the medieval legend of "Agnes and the Merman":

The merman is a seducer who shoots up from his hiding-place in the abyss, with wild lust grasps and breaks the innocent flower which stood in all its grace on the seashore and pensively inclined its head to listen to the howling of the ocean. This is what the poets hitherto have meant by it. Let us make an alteration. The merman was a seducer. He had called to Agnes, had by his smooth speech enticed from her the hidden sentiments, she has found in the merman what she sought, what she was gazing after down at the bottom of the sea. Agnes would like to follow him. The merman has lifted her up in his arms, Agnes twines about his neck, with her whole soul she trustingly abandons herself to the stronger one; he already stands upon the brink, he leans over the sea, about to plunge into it with his prey—then Agnes looks at him once more, not timidly, not doubtingly, not proud of her good fortune, not intoxicated by pleasure, but with absolute faith in him, with absolute humility, like the lowly flower she conceived herself to be; by this look she entrusts to him with absolute confidence her whole fate. And, behold, the sea roars no more, its voice is mute, nature's passion which is the merman's strength leaves him in the lurch, a dead

calm ensues—and still Agnes continues to look at him thus. Then the
merman collapses, he is not able to resist the power of innocence,
his native element is unfaithful to him, he cannot seduce Agnes. He
leads her back again, he explains to her that he only wanted to show
her how beautiful the sea is when it is calm, and Agnes believes
him.—Then he turns back alone and the sea rages, but despair in
the merman rages more wildly.[14]

Now the merman and Agnes are both unhappy. He could talk
and make her happy, but that would mean playing tricks on her,
continuing to deceive her. He could remain concealed, but he
would still know that she was suffering. His conscience plagues
him. Although he has seduced innumerable Agneses before in
his life, he now becomes conscious of sin for the first time. "Sin
is not the first immediacy, sin is a later immediacy. By sin,
the individual is already higher than the universal!"

If he repents before God, that will mean the cloister, and
nobody but God will know because he cannot speak. Though
Agnes will be saved, he will be lost to the world.

The merman fascinates Johannes. He gives this legendary
demon a human consciousness and puts before him alternative
ways to deal with the situation. "The demonical element in
repentance" could tell him that it is right that he is unhappy,
because it is his punishment and the more he punishes himself
the better. This demonic element might force him to make some
attempt to save her by mocking her and studiously hiding his
torment from her.

As the counterpart to Abraham in this book, the merman is
of great importance. Johannes understands the merman's movements, while Abraham's faith remains unintelligible. For in
order to extricate himself, the merman would also have to
repent and speak "the foreign language."

The merman stands at the dialectical turning-point. If he is delivered
out of the demoniacal into repentance there are two paths open
to him. He may hold back, remain in his concealment, but not rely
upon his shrewdness. He does not come as the individual into an
absolute relationship with the demoniacal but finds repose in the
counter-paradox that the deity will save Agnes. (So it is the Middle
Ages would perform the movement, for according to its conception

the merman is absolutely dedicated to the cloister.) Or else he may be saved along with Agnes. Now this is not to be understood to mean that by the love of Agnes for him he might be saved from being henceforth a deceiver (this is the aesthetic way of performing a rescue, which always goes around the main point, which is the continuity of the merman's life); for so far as that goes he is already saved, he is saved inasmuch as he becomes revealed. Then he marries Agnes. But still he must have recourse to the paradox. For when the individual by his guilt has gone outside the universal he can return to it only by virtue of having come as the individual into an absolute relationship with the absolute.[15]

Johannes can understand a person whose guilt forces him outside the universal and thus make him into an exception.

The movements of the merman I can understand, whereas I cannot understand Abraham; for it is precisely through the paradox that the merman comes to the point of realizing the universal. For if he remains hidden and initiates himself into all the torments of repentance, then he becomes a demon and as such is brought to naught. If he remains concealed but does not think cunningly that being himself tormented in the bondage of repentance he could work Agnes loose, then he finds peace indeed but is lost for this world. If he becomes revealed and allows himself to be saved by Agnes, then he is the greatest man I can picture to myself; for it is only the aesthetic writer who thinks lightmindedly that he extols the power of love by letting the lost man be loved by an innocent girl and thereby saved, it is only the aesthetic writer who sees amiss and believes that the girl is the heroine, instead of the man being the hero. So the merman cannot belong to Agnes unless after having made the infinite movement, the movement of repentance, he makes still one more movement by virtue of the absurd.[16]

Ethics has its highest expression in repentance, but it is precisely at this point that it also contradicts itself, says Johannes in a footnote. For some reason this extremely bright writer has gotten very involved in the story of the merman, and it is here that the heart beats fastest. Johannes brings forward other characters: Sarah and Tobias from the book of Tobit, Richard III in Shakespeare's drama, Goethe's Faust, and he is able neatly to dissect their motives for silence. But none seems to catch his imagination as much as the merman. The demonic lurks in the silence of the merman who comes, ridden with guilt, from the murky depths.

Johannes can understand the merman, but he cannot understand Abraham. He can only admire him, as we do admire heroes—for their passion. Abraham achieved the highest passion, which is faith. Johannes's whole investigation comes to a halt before this miracle.

Fear and Trembling is a *tour de force*. Kierkegaard succeeds eminently in making us empathize—not with Abraham, but with Johannes de Silentio, this thinly drawn character who nonetheless possesses such seething inwardness that we find ourselves weeping one moment—for our cowed, disciplined minds and our lack of passion—and congratulating ourselves in the next that we do not let ourselves get carried away by unchecked emotions.

Most authors aspire to offer visions beyond their actual story, but Kierkegaard has undertaken something uncommon in the history of literature. He has chosen a well-known myth and used it as is, without bending or shaping it. Its essence makes it strong and phenomenal. He leaves it alone. The story of Abraham stands there as before, nothing added or amended, nothing explained. The hero Abraham is untouched.

But much is clarified. Moving on three levels, the aesthetic, the ethical, and the religious, Kierkegaard has produced a lyric, a form of literature that speaks to our feelings. But it is a dialectical lyric. Since the poet Johannes is a man of experience and learning, disciplined in choosing a point of view, we are offered an exposition of extraordinary excitement. The religious hero is the only subject that can really challenge Johannes as a person and as a poet. Over against the religious hero, he exhibits a gallery of other characters, whose choices he explains and juxtaposes to Abraham. The tragic hero, for example, offers him no difficulties whatever. That motif he presents with crystal clarity. Actually the ethical even seems to bore him when, in the "Problemata," he distinguishes between what belongs to the ethical and what constitutes the religious.

Out of the depths of his understanding of the ethical he seems

himself to have reached a point of resignation and crisis. Therefore the story of the merman is difficult and engaging to read.
It seems to illustrate his dilemma. The ethical has driven him
forward to a position in which he realizes he is losing touch with
the truly human. Only the model for the religious, Abraham and
his faith, can restore him, since neither aesthetic feeling nor eternal values are sufficient for him.

In *Fear and Trembling* Kierkegaard has mapped out the roads
to the religious category, and it is to his eternal merit that he
has in no way damaged Abraham. He has surrounded him with
silence. The book gives energy to the spirit. It stimulates our
imagination and cleanses our thoughts. Further, it prompts
self-examination and meditation. Rather than solving problems,
it points them out. It ends with the paradox, but the fear and
trembling lie not in the absurd but in the silence. Having read
the book we have made a long journey, frightening but also
alluring.

CHAPTER 6

Stages on Life's Way

I *Original Sin and* The Concept of Dread

THERE is another word for fear and trembling: dread. And there is the word, sin, which occurs in *Fear and Trembling* in relation to the religious category. Sin and dread became the subjects of a separate investigation, *The Concept of Dread,* that Kierkegaard published under the pseudonym of Vigilius Haufniensis (The Watchman of Copenhagen).[1] Vigilius presents himself as a psychologist who claims psychology as the proper science through which to approach dread and sin. Vigilius is a cool analyst and what he has to say about dread serves as a link between the earlier books and *Stages.*

"What is sin?" he asks. There is much confusion about that word, and Vigilius's aim is to clarify it: if we approach it sloppily from an aesthetic angle, viewing sin from the outside as a momentary event, then we are bound to end up with contradiction. Aesthetics has no tools that can properly be applied to sin. It can define it only insufficiently in terms of committing a more or less grave mistake, and this may appear either tragic or comic in the eyes of the aesthete. But sin is not merely a mistake.

The ethicist also has touble with the concept of sin. Ethics does not deal with reality as reality presents itself. Ethics structures reality and, by introducing ideals, tells us how things ought to be. Ethics tells us how we should behave and condemns us if we break the rules. We must correct the errors we commit, or else society falls apart. Ethics can deal with sin merely as an error against some legal or moral code. But sin in a Christian culture is more than breaking the rules.

When theology deals with sin, it goes about the business from the opposite direction.[2] It does not prescribe; it describes dog-
132

matically. It confronts reality in all its messiness. Theology's aim is to elevate this mess into universality, and precisely for this reason theology speaks about "original sin," thereby affirming the complexity of the human condition. Vigilius finds this solution ingenious, but as nobody seems to have more than an inkling of the meaning of the concept of original sin, he proposes to help, using his science—psychology—as a proper aid to come to terms with sin. After all, psychology has to do with what happens inside an individual who is on a collision course with rules and commandments.

Psychology is the science that examines the expressions of the psyche. It can illuminate concepts such as "ominous premonitions" and "anxiety about impending danger." All human beings share this anxiety or dread, says Vigilius, although in varying degree, and, according to Vigilius, dread is what causes sin. Dread is the fear that we will do what we should not. This indefinite and unspecified terror is rooted in our nature, our very being, as we are afraid of nonbeing, of nothingness and of annihilation. Sin, then, enters when individuals act in dread. Hence, dread in itself can become an instrument for either salvation or perdition.

Dread is always the background to "the leap." Through the dread that individuals suffer they are informed of a destiny that both attracts and repels them, and in dread they discover that they are free to act. Dread places individuals in a holding pattern of uncertainty. They can react in one of two ways: either to follow their *daimon,* their spirit's call to become themselves—which is the way to salvation; or they can frustrate their spirit by not acting at all, or not acting decisively—which is the way to perdition. In dread we discover our freedom to act. Sin is an act in despair of one's salvation, a striking out against oneself. As Vigilius puts it in his scholarly terminology, dread is "a sympathetic antipathy and an antipathetic sympathy."

II   Stages on Life's Way

Kierkegaard has shown us the categories, their prototypes and attributes, through different pseudonymous characters, each of whom lives and breathes in these books. These observers and interpreters differ from the heroes (Don Juan, the Seducer, Abra-

ham, etc.) in their various points of view. Only in the case of
the ethical sphere is there an open relationship between the
Judge and the readers. He speaks directly and openly, revealing
himself. However, his point of view, his long-winded yet heart-
warming direct communication, should make us wary of confusing the Judge with Kierkegaard.

Through brilliant mockery, these pseudonymous characters
nag us, challenging us to discover what they represent. Respec-
tively different, they require a more discerning investigation.
When we try to untangle the various attitudes unfolding, we find
that they do not all belong in the categories proper. Some only
brush the categories tangentially and remain forever outside in
the doldrums. Vigilius is very clever in defining the concepts, but
where does he stand?

In *Stages on Life's Way*, Kierkegaard brings in a raft of
pseudonymous characters to represent two new categories that
cover these "doldrums." At the time he composed this book,
Kierkegaard was moving fast. More and more, two in-between
categories, *irony* and *humor*, emerged and these fascinated him
both intellectually and emotionally—more so than the original
three. He wrote in order to clarify these positions for himself
as much as to communicate them to others. In *Stages*, he introduces "William Afham" (which means William "next to himself" as well as "by himself"). He also exhibits the long "Quidam's
Diary," in which he actually inserted unabridged parts from
his own journals.

Superficially and amusingly "collected, forwarded to the press
and published by Hilarius Bookbinder," *Stages on Life's Way*
starts out on a light note. Hilarius Bookbinder seems more
concerned with the binding of the book and its future appearance
on various bookshelves than with its content. As far as Mr.
Bookbinder is concerned, the middle part could be the first, and
the last the middle, and the first the last.

Contrary to the impression he gives us here, this solidly built
book has been carefully written. In *Stages*, Kierkegaard has
summoned some earlier pseudonymous characters, putting them
to a test. Where do they stand on their way to salvation? They
are tested by the ways in which they speak of women and love.
This will reveal them. This was what revealed him to himself.

A. *"The Banquet"*

Men's clubs, curious phenomena, had their heyday in the nine-teenth century. Our immediate associations with the term "men's club" might well bring to mind the English (Trollope, Conan Doyle) or the French (Jules Verne), and perhaps even Dorothy Sayers's surprising latecomer, Lord Peter Wimsey. Created in the wish for like-minded company, peace, and the comforts of association with peers, these clubs make us think of comfortable leather chairs, daily papers, small talk, business deals, and perhaps even conversation about marriage contracts— all to the accompaniment of fine food, exquisite drink, and superb service. The very old idea of fraternities may be inher-ently irresistible to many men. Plato's *Symposium*, which ends with the famous dialogue on love, provides us with the classic testimony to men's wish to imbibe together, while talking idealis-tically about life and love, undisturbed by the unpleasant realities of noisy children, nagging women, and jealous slaves. A flash of insight led Kierkegaard to open his *Stages* in the setting of such a club meeting.

All aesthetes in various stages of experience and conscious-ness, the participants arrive at the banquet, brought there by Constantine Constantius. Constantine wants to carry out suc-cessfully a suggestion they had entertained at an earlier meeting, when Victor Eremita had spoken extemporaneously and ec-statically about a perfect banquet:

A banquet in and for itself is a difficult business, for even though it be arranged with all possible taste and talent, there is still some-thing else essential to it, namely, luck. By this I do not mean what the anxious housewife might be most likely to think about, but something else which no one can absolutely make sure of: a happy concord of moods and of the subordinate features of the banquet, that fine ethereal touch upon the chords, that inward music, which one cannot bespeak in advance from the town band. Hence it is a risk to begin, for if the thing goes wrong, maybe from the very beginning, it is possible at one banquet to start off in such a way that it will take a long time to recover. Habit and thoughtlessness are the only fathers and godfathers of most banquets, and it is due to a lack of critical sense that the absence of idea is not noticed. For the first thing, there ought never to be women present at a banquet. Parenthetically be it said that I never have liked the word "ladies," and now since Grundtvig in his most Grundtvigian fiddle-faddle has *grundwichtiglich* employed this word—but that has nothing to do with this subject. Only in the Greek fashion can women be employed as a chorus of dancers. Since at a banquet the essential business is to eat and drink, woman ought not to be included in the company, for she cannot acquit herself properly, and if she does, it is exceedingly unaesthetic. Where a woman is present the business of eating and drinking ought to be reduced to insignificant proportions. At the very most the eating and drinking must be a little feminine occupation just to give the hands something to do. In the country more especially such a small repast (which may even be appointed at another hour than that of the important meals) may be extremely charming, and, if so, this is always attributable to the other sex. To do as the English do and let the other sex retire before the real drinking begins, is neither one thing nor the other, for every constructive plan ought to be a whole, and the very way I seat myself at the table and take hold of the knife and fork stands in relation to the totality. So too a political banquet is unaesthetic because of its ambiguity. One wants to reduce the essential elements of the banquet to an insignificance, and again one would not have it thought that the speeches are delivered *inter pocula*. So far we are doubtless in agreement, and our number —in case anything should come of the banquet—is well chosen, in accordance with the fine rule: neither more than the Muses, nor less than the Graces. I require now the richest abundance of everything that can be thought of. Even though not everything is actually present, the possibility of it, which is more seductive than the sight, must be immediately at hand, hovering over the table. From banqueting off matches, or, like the Dutch, off a loaf of sugar which all lick by turns, I beg to be excused. My requirement, on the other hand, is difficult to satisfy, for the meal itself must be calculated to awaken and incite that inexpressible desire which every worthy member of the party brings with him. I require that the fruitfulness of the earth shall be at our service, as though everything were sprouting the very instant when appetite desires it. I require a more exuberant abundance of wine than Mephistopheles procured by boring holes in the table. I require an illumination more voluptuous than that of the gnomes when they heave up the mountain upon pillars and dance in a sea of flame. I require what most excites the senses, I require that delicious refreshment of perfumes which is more glorious than anything in the Arabian Nights. I require a coolness which voluptuously kindles desire, and then appeases the desire already satisfied. I require the ceaseless animation of a fountain. If Maecenas could not sleep without hearing the splash of a fountain, I cannot eat without it. Do not misunderstand me: I can eat stockfish without it, but I cannot eat at a banquet without it; I can drink water without it, but I cannot drink wine at a banquet without it. I require a staff of servants, well chosen and good looking, as though I were seated at the table of the gods; I require chamber-music, strong and subdued, and I require that at every instant it shall be an accompaniment to me; and as for you, my friends, the requirements I make in this respect are incredible. Behold! By reason of all these requirements, which are just as many reasons against it, I hold that a banquet is a *pium desiderium*, and, regarding it in this light, I am so far from being inclined to talk about a repetition that I assume the thing cannot be achieved in the first instance.[3]

Everybody had agreed that a banquet such as that would certainly be a splendid thing, but nobody acted to make the idea a reality. For the most part, they felt that it would take too much thoughtful preparation to pull off without having something go wrong and break the spell. Almost everyone felt that the stakes had risen too high. Only Constantine, who had not spoken at that meeting and fully understood the risk involved, felt challenged to put it to work as an interesting event.

Late one evening, the participants, having received their respective invitations from Constantine, arrive at a place in the forest. A lovely room awaits them. Splendid music greets their ears, Mozart's *Don Juan,* no less. The banquet meal would delight a king: partridges, truffles, a vintage Margaux! And champagne!

"In vino veritas" is the password. Nobody may stay sober, and nobody may drink to the point of complete drunkenness. A high mood prevails to the end of the banquet when they all drink the last toast and fling their glasses against the wall, smashing them to pieces. When they walk out of the beautifully decorated banquet room, a demolition crew enters to remodel it; this keeps that tasteful moment of life singularly alive, retained like a unique event in memory for recollection, never again to be copied in the real world. Thus, they accomplish a feat.

The speeches mark the high points of the banquet. All speak on the subject of love. The first speaker, a young man, confesses that he has not yet been in love.[4] He simply observes what happens to his friends when they become lovers. He admits that he can only generalize on the subject, and yet that he would like to make a few comments.

For this youth, an observer as opposed to a participant, love seems comic. As a "third party" reflecting upon something generally indiscernible by its very nature, this young man thinks that love is a contradiction:

Sometimes indeed I feel as if there were something I had missed, but I cannot tell what it is, and on the other hand my reflection here again shows me at once the contradiction. So then, to my way of thinking, love is the greatest contradiction it is possible to think of, and at the same time it is comic. The one corresponds to the other. The comic is always implied in the category of contradiction—a theme which I cannot develop here. But what I would point out here is that love is comic.[5]

The idea of love between man and woman makes him feel like an uncomprehending outsider. The Greek erotic, with its platonic and intellectual aspects, a love between beautiful souls—that he can understand. But to fall in love with a woman and to kiss seems ridiculous. Such a relationship might bring pleasure, but that would constitute mere selfishness. The young man can understand filial love and piety, but he cannot find anything but comedy in love for a woman:

The lovers want to belong to one another for all eternity. They give expression to this in that strange way they have of embracing one another with the intensity of the instant, and all the pleasure of the bliss of love is supposed to consist in this. But all pleasure is selfish. The pleasure of the lover, to be sure, is not selfish with respect to the loved one, but in union they are both absolutely selfish, inasmuch as in union and in love they constitute one self. And yet they are deceived, for at the same instant the genus triumphs over the individual, the genus is victorious whereas the individuals are reduced to the position of being in its service. This I find is more ridiculous than what Aristophanes found so ridiculous. For the ludicrous aspect of the halving of man consists in the contradiction which Aristophanes does not sufficiently emphasize. In looking at a man one would surely think that he was a whole, all by himself, and that indeed is what one thinks, until one sees that under the obsession of love he is only a half which runs after its other half. There is nothing comic in half an apple, the comical would only emerge if a whole apple were a half apple; in the first case there is no contradiction, but surely there is in the latter.[6]

He must renounce this comic love because he as a person is thought and reflection through and through. He fears that abandonment of this reflection will mean the loss of himself. He stresses his ignorance and lack of experience, however, and feels that he should not speak.

Here, Constantine Constantius breaks in and takes over with a speech on the subject of woman. Woman is jest: "Jest is not an aesthetic but an imperfect ethical category." Women share this dilemma of falling in between. Constantine states that woman cannot take the really serious seriously because reality to her is sham. Already at merely sixteen years of age, she feels the flattering attention paid to her by those around her. People cater to her whims and wishes, blowing up her ego out of all proportion. She feels as if she were the star in the center of a big performance. She develops a false ideality. Woman is treated differently from man. Her treatment at times approaches reverence. A man can never dream of treating her as he treats a male adversary. Females constitute the weaker sex. "To shoot a woman, to challenge her to a duel, to show contempt for her, only makes the poor man more ridiculous, for woman is the weaker sex." We needn't wonder at her confusion. People judge her on a different scale. The best thing to do, concludes Constantine, is simply to consider women as pure jest. Entertainment, so ironic.

The more gifted the woman, the greater her potential to amuse. Led to believe that men respect what she does and reflect on what she says, she does not know that they only pretend to listen to her. Gladly they put her on a pedestal, but never, never do they treat her as an equal. When it comes to infidelity, for example, an amusing double standard exists; the unfaithful man gains respect from his peers while the unfaithful woman is considered fallen.

Constantine admits that he finds women aesthetically lovely, pleasant, and interesting, but he emphasizes that Plato and

Aristotle considered woman incomplete in form and of irrational quality. Nothing could be more ridiculous than an "emancipated" woman, according to Constantine, a woman trying to become that which she can never become, a man.

At this point, Victor Eremita picks up the thread, winding it, in his way, around the same theme. He believes that a woman encounters misfortune because at one moment she seems to have the utmost significance, and at the next moment she has none whatsoever. Her life becomes meaningless. Because of her limited intellectual ability, he believes, she cannot understand her situation. What happens to her lies beyond her comprehension. Her life has more to do with fantasy than with realism. As a growing child, she reigns as "Princess" and "Empress," and a year or so later, she becomes simply "Mrs. Peterson." For this reason, Victor Eremita prefers the treatment accorded to women in the Orient. Although their fathers there sell them as slaves, they at least know their place, and they don't get any confused ideas about their roles.

Victor Eremita praises women as most useful in one capacity, that of acting as the inspiration for men. Certain men fall in love but do not marry. Instead they become geniuses, heroes, poets, and saints, because they did not get the woman they wanted. In this negative way women make men productive, develop the intellects of men, and awaken man's consciousness of his own immortality.

"If I had become a woman and could understand what I now understand—how dreadful!" Victor, like Plato, thanks the gods that he was born a man. He views marriage as a strenuous institution, a situation brought about by default. Does Victor Eremita advocate the cloister? No, he answers. He feels that such withdrawal constitutes compromise with immediacy, and therefore, a fallacy. The trick, the beautiful performance, according to him, rests in our ability to remain hermits although we are riding a crowded bus.

After Victor Eremita has so roundly denounced women, the Ladies' Tailor leaps up to rave about them. A fashion tailor, he has observed women dressing and undressing, standing forever unable to make up their minds in front of the mirror and in front of him. He claims to understand women; "for I am a madman, and one must be mad in order to understand her, and if one was not mad before, he must be so when he has understood her."[7] The Ladies' Tailor identifies women with fashion, actually equating the two, and calling them both crazy and changeable. Fashion forms the logic of women. Fashion is their faith. Women love the Tailor's surprises and obey his every whim. In their world, the Tailor reigns as king.

For when a seducer boasts that the virtue of every woman is vendible to the right bidder, I don't believe him, but I do believe that before long, every woman will be satanized by the crazy and defiling self-reflection of fashion, which depraves her more thoroughly than if she were to be seduced.[8]

The Tailor laughs. He has observed that women even go to church to worship God as a matter of fashion. The Tailor feels very confident that he can seduce every woman alive through fashion, from queen to servant girl. He wills it and sees to it that it happens. He will have the world at his feet. He will baptize women, then celebrate communion with them in the name of fashion.

After the fashion tailor's sinister remarks, the man we know from "Either," Johannes the Seducer, takes his turn and speaks. According to him, women are tempting, lovely, and enjoyable, but only up to a point. His message to his brethren: don't change women, and look out that you don't get caught. Nothing could be more wonderful and delicious than a woman, but the gods have hidden her delightful mysteries even from herself. She does not recognize herself as a temptress. She lives unaware of what lies dormant within her. Awareness comes only when a seducer, a truly erotic man, arrives on the scene. A woman never becomes angry with a seducer. After the seduction she can become the most admirable housewife, because for one moment she participated in immortal, marvelous illusion. To retain that moment, she puts up with the temporal in an ordinary marriage. Johannes the Seducer describes a seducer as an artist who leads the woman through that marvelous moment. Thus it is that the accident called woman makes life great for a man.

When the five men have spoken, the banquet ends. *In vino veritas* was a most suitable password. But what about the sixth man, the one who wrote it all down? He was William Afham, who never spoke up, although he recorded what was said and done and also wrote the prefatory note on the difference between memory and recollection. Sitting around a table with a group of people, we can remember together what we did some time ago. But we cannot recollect together; that can take place only individually because recollection retains the essential and forgets everything incidental. Recollection picks up the idea of the event, and it does this in a reflective and idealistic way. "In recollection man draws a check upon eternity." Remembering something from the past comes easy for us. But to reflect upon an event and to lift it up, giving it meaning for the present and the future, that is recollection. The person who understands recollection also understands eternity.

The first article that Kierkegaard ever published was a short piece on woman in which he spoke to his peers, his student companions, in the same ironic vein conveyed in the banquet scenes. Clearly, Kierkegaard's piece reflected on its author rather than on the subject. In "The Banquet" the five speakers do not seem to recognize love as anything other than erotic experience. As individuals, they value that experience quite differently, but they are united in looking at women externally, as objects. All the banquet speakers have one thing in common: they dread a sustained relationship with a woman.

Kierkegaard here does some private recollection work, taking an attitude that was once his own and building around it, showing us how some people go through life holding onto an attitude that ultimately informs their style of living. William Afham describes the gift of recollection as something akin to pregnancy, "being in an interesting situation," carrying the future within it. The participants in the banquet appear now comic, now tragic, but they have neither guilt feelings nor knowledge of "sin." They manipulate others for their momentary pleasure, having justified themselves by reasoning themselves into this situation. They talk about women, but not one of them has allowed a woman to enter his life.

Early in the morning they leave the banquet hall and take a stroll, which accidentally brings them to the place where Judge William lives. We remember him from *Either/Or*. He and his wife are having an early breakfast in the arbor. Our drinking companions sneak up close, so that they can peek unobserved into this scene of marital bliss. They hear the Judge jokingly remind his wife, who is preparing his tea, that Danish law still permits a man to beat his wife on occasion. The Judge and his wife smile.

In a moment of exuberance, Victor dashes into their house and comes across some papers, a manuscript, lying on the Judge's desk. He steals it and rejoins his companions, where William Afham in turn steals the manuscript from Victor's pocket. Thus ends the first part of *Stages*.

B. *"Various Observations About Marriage"*

Judge William is said to have written this manuscript, an essay on woman and marriage, for his own edification, but it includes refutations of all the objections to marriage raised in the speeches at the banquet. Getting married represents the significant midpoint of life for the Judge. This step changes everything. If we fear deception and therefore do not take the step, then we might well be deceived by life itself because we avoid participation in an experience that is truly human. People are "designed for marriage," people can grasp the depth and significance of life only when they are married.

For the Judge, "getting married" compares with "getting religion," in that he believes we need one thing alone: faith in it. People may laugh, but this does not discourage the Judge because he has the faith. He also has experience. Married for eight years, he has become an expert who knows what he is talking about. A married man is a genuine man, and a married woman is a genuine woman. As partners, they coauthor their life together, present, past, and future.

The Judge considers erotic impulses pagan and marriage Christian. In between the two lie reflection and resolution. The impulses arise immediately, suddenly, on the spot. However, immediacy is not lost in marriage. Religion mediates a new immediacy. Both man and wife attain religious immediacy, but—and here comes a difference—man reaches it through ethical development, while woman can translate her love directly into the religious without reflection.

Pagan love filled the speeches of the banquet. Paganism has a love-god, Eros, but it provides no god for marriage, which it does not really recognize. Extremely important to the Judge is this distinction between paganism and Christianity. He emphasizes that in pagan love woman becomes a pleasure object to man while in Christianity woman stands equal to man. Married love is Christian. Marriage expresses a refinement of love. If we do not understand this, then we either remain unmarried (scoffers, seducers, hermits), or our marriages become merely happenstance. Pagan love demands immediacy. Marriage involves the concept of a *telos*. In the Christian concept there is longing for consummation in marriage.

The Judge's idea of equality apparently requires some explanation. He means equal but separate. He does not believe in emancipation in the modern sense. He does not even wish to talk about emancipation because he believes so deeply in the separate roles of the marriage partners. Confusing them pains him. He thinks that when people wed, they resolve to carry out those roles.

Naturally, the synthesis of marriage can run into difficulties. The Judge is very clear on that score. But if we could just sit down to enumerate the difficulties, we would come to the conclusion *not* to marry. The resolution not to marry is a negative one. Marriage, the positive resolution, concerns two people who freely choose their future together.

We recognize the Judge's argumentation from *Either/Or* but we also find he is emphasizing other perspectives. Now he talks little about "first love" and places great emphasis on will and on the resolution. This time, he focuses on woman rather than on marriage alone, discussing the young woman, the woman as mother, and the old woman. At every point, he berates the aesthetes for not understanding the beauty that comes from within and with development, with time:

Woman as a bride is more beautiful than as a young girl, as a mother she is more beautiful than as a bride, as wife and mother she is a good word spoken in due season, and with the years she becomes more beautiful. The beauty of the young girl is evident to many, it is more abstract, more extensive. Hence they flock around her, the pure and the impure. Then the deity brings him who is her lover. He sees indeed her beauty, for one loves the beautiful, and that is to be understood as identical with this, that loving is seeing the beautiful. Thus it is that the beautiful passes unnoticed under the nose of reflection. From now on her beauty becomes more intensive and concrete. The wife has no flock of adorers, she is not even beautiful, she is only beautiful in her husband's eyes. In the degree that this beauty becomes more and more concrete, she becomes less and less easy to appraise by the ordinary standards of gauging and sorting. Is she for this reason less beautiful? Is an author less rich in thought for the reason that an ordinary perusal of him discovers nothing, whereas a reader who has made him his sole study discovers greater and greater riches? Is it a perfection in a human work of art that it makes the best showing at a distance? Is it an imperfection in the flower of the field, as in all of the works of God, that for microscopic observation it becomes finer and finer, more and more delicate, more and more charming?[9]

The Judge chides those "third parties" to whom love and marriage seem ridiculous. From the outside, we understand very little of anything, and this is especially true concerning love, which must necessarily be experienced from within where its wonder and its miracles live. Judge William does not consider the kiss to be a true symbol of love; rather, he thinks a more meaningful symbol is the wedding itself, two equal partners before the altar who by free will consent to accept each other and pledge to live their lives together.

He picks up Constantine's argument of woman as jest:

After all, a young girl is a phantom, one scarcely knows whether she belongs to reality or is a vision. And is this to be the loftiest attainment? Yes, let phantoms believe it. On the other hand, as a mother she belongs completely to reality, and mother-love is not like the yearnings and forebodings of youth but is an inexhaustible well-spring of hearty sympathy. Neither is it true that all this was present as a possibility in the young girl. Even if this were so, a possibility is after all less than an actuality. But it is not so. No more than the mother's milk is present in the young girl's breast is this hearty sympathy there. This is a metamorphosis which has no analogy in man. If one can say jestingly that a man is not full-grown until he has his wisdom teeth, one can say seriously that a woman's development is only complete when she is a mother, for only then does she exist in all her beauty and in the beauty of reality.[10]

The Judge becomes a poet of sorts when he sympathizes with the woman as wife and mother. Of course, he has thereby refuted Victor Eremita's argument that a woman's highest capacity lies in her ability to inspire men to become heroes and poets instead of marrying. There is a beauty that passes unnoticed by the aesthetes.

The Judge then launches into an attack on Victor's argument that also hems in the Ladies' Tailor:

On the other hand, the objections raised against woman assume an aspect of profound irony, which is not without a tragic and comic effect when it is set forth with a certain good humor, yes, even with sympathy for the sad fate which is supposed to reduce her to sheer illusion. It sticks to the assumption that she is the weaker sex. The tragedy lies in the fact that this is concealed from her by illusion, and outwardly concealed from her by man's gallantry.[11]

Finally, the Judge advances an argument for "getting caught," which could put the Seducer in his place. The miracle of love, a divine gift, should be handled with care. This happens when the couple resolves to marry. They decide to handle this gift of love with care. Love has its critical moments, and then marriage gives aid by providing second chances and letting the couple relax. Lovers, on the other hand, do not believe in second chances:

But just here is the difficulty, here it is that the devil sows evil seed while the lovers are not thinking of it. Even the seducer allows love to stand as a thing he cannot bestow upon himself (and it is only very young apprentices and Münchausens who talk about making conquests), but the demoniacal spirit within him causes him with demoniacal resolution to resolve to make the enjoyment as short, and in this way, so he thinks, as intense as possible. By reason of this demoniacal resolution the seducer is actually great in an evil sense, and without this resolution he is not actually a seducer. He may for all that be harmful enough, and his life may be thoroughly ruined, even though it is more innocent than that of a real seducer, or acquires a more innocent appearance because the oblivion of time comes in between. Such a man insults love; he is not evil enough to form a demoniacal resolution, but neither is he good enough to form the good resolution—to express the case precisely, he is not good enough to be a husband in the noble sense in which I use that word, in the noble sense that a man is a husband only when he is worthy to receive the gift of the Deity.[12]

The Judge works himself up to a high pitch in praise of Christian marriage. It is the highest reach of human existence, the central thing in life. He finds all talk about each sex for itself confused and profane. He believes that God has designed men and women to live and think together. Not to marry would be inhuman. During medieval times, people put emphasis on the spirit and tried to forget the body. In modern times, people put emphasis on the body and forget the spirit. The Judge rejects both tendencies. "The inhumanity consists in the fact that one will not have any concrete comprehension of that which for the majority of men is their life's reality."[13]

But are there not exceptions? Must all people marry? Are there not some people who cannot conform? Yes, the Judge admits, but as a true judge, he wants the expression to be well-defined and relegated to small print. The exception should strengthen the rule and not weaken it. He sets up five requirements for the genuine exception:

First, he must be in love. If he is not in love, then he cannot be a justifiable exception.

Second, he must be a married man, he must have made the resolution.

Third, after he breaks away from married life, he must love life.

Fourth, he must suffer the break, knowing that he is a rebel.

Fifth, he must comprehend that no one can comprehend him, yet he cannot become bitter.

Thus, the only acceptable requirement for the exception is that he has passed through the ethical stage. The ethical life, no matter how good for the many, has lost its meaning for the exception. He can understand it and even live with it, but his spirit is not in it. Terrible nothingness threatens his spirit. Dread. Then the Judge points to God as his only hope. Nothing human has a hold on him any more. Only God can give him back his humanity.

It begins to dawn on us that this is not another *Either/Or,* and that what are developing before our eyes are the models and the definitions for the two new stages, or in-between plateaus with a high claim on the mind and a low thrust on will and action. Victor Eremita and Constantine Constantius, for instance, are highly reflective and knowledgeable people who are fully aware of the three categories, but because they are such cerebral people they are much too sophisticated to make a commitment. They can creep in and out of all the categories in words and minds, and it is precisely this ability that puts them in the "ironic" stage. They probe; they ask questions; they make experiments; but they are not willing to do the one thing necessary: namely, to commit themselves fully, to make a resolution to belong to something. Therefore everything they say has a double meaning that hides a question mark. When they speak about the ethical, they sound eerie because we realize that they do not fully adhere to what they proclaim. When they speak about the aesthetic, they sound tired, and we sense their boredom. When they speak about the religious, they sound blasphemous. The ironic characters have separated themselves, but they cannot genuinely speak for themselves in any other manner than questioning like a tired Pilate: What is truth? These ironic characters hover between the aesthetic and the ethical categories.

Judge William is squarely within the ethical stage, but by setting requirements for the exception he tells us again—as he did by sending along the sermon of the "Ultimatum"—that, although he is perfectly satisfied with the step he has taken in life—the commitments he has made and the increasing wisdom that he finds therein—he is aware of a possibility with which, thank God, he does not have to reckon, but which is yet a possibility. He himself finds the joy of living in living for others and like others. The ethical, human ideality, gives him great security. His way of living makes eminent sense both in terms of history and of eternity. He knows his responsibility, and he does all he possibly can to meet it.

Judge William's adjusted style of living, however, is not

sufficient for "the exception." It would have bored Johannes de
Silentio to tears, and it is not the object for the psychological
experiment carried out by Frater Taciturnus, whom we will
meet in the next section of *Stages*. These two brethren of silence
sense a reality that goes far beyond the world of Judge William.
His is a world they know to distraction. The world that has
their attention is the religious, but the leap required to get
there is impossible for them. They live in another border
category, humor, reconciled with the human, yet longing for
a new immediacy.

C.   *"Guilty?/Not Guilty? A Passion Narrative. A Psychological
Experiment by Frater Taciturnus"*

A young man, Quidam ("Somebody," or "X," as we would
say nowadays), has become engaged to a young woman who
loves him very much. Quidam, too, has fallen in love truly
and wholly. In intellectual maturity the woman does not
measure up to him, but he has elected her and dedicates himself
to her. Yet before their engagement he had premonitions of
anxiety, even though the possibility of becoming married to
her remained to his mind the highest goal. But when possibility
met actuality in the moment of engagement, he came to understand something about himself that catapulted him into chaos.
If he were to continue the engagement and bring it to fruition
in marriage, he would perish as the person he was; he would
lose his self. In order to keep my self, he reasons, I must break
the engagement. In so doing, I will act unethically. But I intend
to keep my promise. Now even though he makes the decision
to marry, realizing that the situation offers him no escape, he
nevertheless deceives the woman and makes her break the
engagement. He acts unethically in order to preserve his self.
God commands it of him, or is it only his demonic self that
prompts him?
      This is the question: Is he unable to go through with the
engagement because he is maimed by his yearning for God,
or is he using religion to cover up for self-centeredness, plain
selfishness, and self-aggrandizement?
      By far the longest section of *Stages*, "Quidam's Diary" intrigues

and yet bores us. The arrangement is very clever and effective.[14]
The diary is supposedly written one year after the engagement,
and it takes us through the affair by reliving it in memory and
recollection. The morning entries record what actually took
place, and in the night entries—when sleep does not relieve the
pain of the past—recollection churns the questions: Who was
responsible? Guilty? Not guilty? Apparently the woman is
suffering; will she take her life? Who will be the murderer?
Ethically, the guilt falls on Quidam. The night entries vacillate
on that critical question. The inner dialogue goes on and on.

On the fifth of every month, Quidam enters a story in his
diary. Taken together, these stories tend both to clarify and to
mystify. They hint at Quidam's special heritage and at private
events in his life that have left such a mark on him that he has
become "the exception." These entries offer us nothing more
than hints about his *vita ante acta,* his heritage and environment
that have marked him indelibly.

In "Quidam's Diary," Kierkegaard has certainly cut a pound
of flesh from himself. Some of the entries are taken verbatim
from his own diary. His contemporaries took for granted that
here he was publicly recounting the story of his engagement to
Regine. The cartoon in *The Corsair,* with Kierkegaard riding
astride the back of a Regine on all fours, chastising her with
a whip, provides a stark example of the more popular and
obvious interpretations at the time. In his introduction to *Stages,*
Walter Lowrie says more or less the same thing when he wishes
that Kierkegaard would abandon the subject.[15] Suffering from
a situation that festered, Kierkegaard does not present us with
a pretty picture of himself.

The stories on the fifth of each month are interpreted by
Lowrie as reflecting his relationship to his father, and there are of
course any number of possibilities for conjecture, linking the
stories to specified events in Kierkegaard's life.

We know Kierkegaard well enough to understand that he has
not gone to these lengths in order to tell us how he felt at a
certain time, but that he is using his own experience in order
to teach us something. Thus the stories indirectly communicate
the urgency of searching our own backgrounds for the indelible
marks on our character, to review our own experience of

"original sin." It is the concept of guilt that lies at the center of the diary.

How else could Kierkegaard acquire such a forceful grasp on such questions—if not through his own experience? He uses his experiences in many ways, building outward and expanding them. After the diary there is a commentary by "Frater Taciturnus." Taciturnus's analysis of the affair makes a major contribution to our understanding of the varied dimensions in the concepts of love, time, mediacy and immediacy, the religious and the limitations of poetry.

D. *"Epistle to the Reader"*

The character himself, Frater Taciturnus, differs from Quidam. We see in him an intellectually gifted person who fully comprehends the differences between the categories. In contrast to Quidam, who is moving inwardly, suffering from his existence at every moment, Frater Taciturnus is steady. He acknowledges that he does not live in the religious category like Quidam. Yet nothing in the world interests him more than the religious because something more real than anything else is going on there. He himself has gone beyond the ethical and is now resting in the humorous stage. Quidam has gone even further. Frater Taciturnus lives with the absurd, though on a lower plane. He can enjoy the city he lives in, the people he meets, the language he speaks—all that belongs to his existence. But this enjoyment has taken on an absurd quality, and that is why the experiment with Quidam interests him so deeply—because it deals with an immediacy, a suffering that he can observe, even though its reality is one step beyond him.

Frater Taciturnus becomes a valuable guide to understanding what happens to Quidam. He is the one who calls the story "A Passion Narrative," and in his epistle to the readers explains that it is "suffering," for want of a better word, that characterizes the religious category. Love as suffering. Through Taciturnus we get the explanation of that expression. This is how he sees the story develop. He footnotes it with an aesthetic commentary, taking issue with a known aesthetician, Börne.

As a young poet, Quidam met the woman. The relationship changed him. Poetry deals with the immediate; it cannot deal

with the kind of ambiguity found in Quidam's love. Taciturnus
uncovers a possible clue as to why we might find the diary
boring. It does not end on time. It just gets more complicated—
more than we, as observers, can stand.

Happy love? Fine. Unhappy love? Even better! Poetry thrives
on these. But what happens when love splits inside itself? In
poetry, love can take on any outside threats and come through
with flying colors. But how can it deal with the ambiguity of
love and passion after the lapse of that time of immediacy?
Poetry would call the whole affair merely a misunderstanding
and make it either comic or tragic. But "Quidam's Diary" emphasizes the simultaneous existence of both comedy and tragedy
in the relationship. Very much alive and serious, this misunderstanding remains unresolved. The poet Quidam recognizes the
comical element in his situation, only to have the tragic re-
affirmed in his consciousness.

The diary form pinpoints the duality of the situation. In the
mornings, Quidam remembers what actually happened between
him and the woman. At night, he reflects on the same events
transformed by the other side of his self, by his spirit, his ideality,
his God-relationship. No longer a poet, living before an event
in illusion, he has become a religious person, living with God
after the event. And—this is very important—this transforms both
him *and* her. No longer a silly-wonderful-little girl, she becomes
a person whom he must love as he loves himself even though
he feels that she is neither his partner nor his equal.

Something happens to his love. In the ethical stage, we saw
Judge William and his wife developing side by side, but in
"Quidam's Diary," we meet two characters who develop
unequally.

Frater Taciturnus eagerly stresses the "heterogeneousness"
of the two characters for us. We see the young man Quidam
as reserved, his fiancée as outgoing. Our restraint stems from the
ability to see the merit of both sides. In the fiancée we see openness and immediacy of action, and this contrasts with his reserve
and its silent language. He is a philosopher; she is not. She
adores him, and it would make no difference to her if he spoke
some cryptic language. Anxious to use the proper expression,
he investigates the meaning of knowledge and truth. How could

he handle such a situation except through indirect communication, except by forcing her to believe that he was what he was not? In other words, the two live in different stages, different categories. On his way into the religious category, he watches her with concern for her religious development. Wedded to her in human relationship and yet being in a different category, he lives in a situation necessarily "incognito" to her. Frater Taciturnus tries to shed some light on the nature of their dissimilarities:

When the heterogeneity is presented as I have presented it, both parties have a right to say that they love. Love has an ethical and an aesthetic side. She says that she loves, and she possesses that love aesthetically and understands it aesthetically; he says that he loves, and he understands it ethically. So both of them love, and they love one another, and yet it is a misunderstanding. The heterogeneous is kept apart from other species by category, and so the misunderstanding is not like that of novelistic barter and exchange or of reconsideration within the aesthetic categories.

The male figure in the experiment therefore sees the comic, but not as a hardened observer sees it. He sees the comic and is thereby confirmed in the tragic. That is what interests me especially, for thereby the religious is illuminated.[16]

In "Guilty/Not Guilty," we deal not with people who are peers but with people who are worlds apart though they sit in the same room. A true passion story, their love story begins where most love stories end: namely, after the breaking of the engagement. Indeed, the religious category entails a life of struggle and ongoing suffering, a story that has no end. And from the point of view of an outside observer, this story remains incomprehensible.

She thinks that he has insulted her by breaking off the affair, but for him the affair has just then really begun to move forward. It becomes a turning point in his life that pushes him toward a religious stance. The fact that the experiment lacks concrete results does not lessen its significance. On the contrary. That is what is significant.

The Quidam of Taciturnus's experiment becomes "a religious hero." An ethical tragic hero, we have learned, performs great deeds. Whether they are historical or mythical makes little difference. The greatness lies in the person who performs the great deeds. Poetry praises those deeds and the persons who perform them. Poetry exhibits the results. Frater Taciturnus comments that the religious hero has to go through an inward struggle and has no outward results to show for it. The ethical category inquires about the deeds and gives its snap judgment, good or bad. The task of the aesthetic and the religious is "to space" the ethical in order to achieve development. But religious development takes place wholly in the interior. It is outward reality that tests the faith. But faith itself, the religious result, we cannot see.

Frater Taciturnus ironically admits that it would have been so much nicer to deal with some kind of system in which paragraph 17 could have handled Repentance, paragraph 18 the Atonement, and paragraph 19 would have glorified the finish of a System. But, alas, he says, that is not how it is in the real world. According to a system, we go from one paragraph to the next. But reality has made Frater Taciturnus a behavioristic experimenter; we must observe that the experiment with Quidam shows exactly that he lingers. A system works beautifully on paper but seldom in reality. Time intervenes.

Repentance is especially difficult when we do not know whether we are guilty or not. Reality takes its time. By deceit, Quidam takes away from the woman the impression she might have had of him had he simply left her. He did not reckon that the method would backfire on him as it did. He persisted in his course no matter what the woman said. He misled her, leaving her with no impression that he suffered. Looking back on the whole situation, we can see that she thought that he just wanted to end the affair and did so successfully.

Externally, it was so. But internally, one year later, we see Quidam still in deep conflict with himself. Reality has caught up with him. He has set a chain reaction in motion, and now he doubts his actions and must wait for reality to inform him of the consequences and how wrong he has been. Time intervenes. With a mere word, "meanwhile," fiction so often dispenses with this waiting, this inward reality of despair, doubt, repentance, and suffering that Quidam now gives us through his diary. Quidam represents a new Kierkegaardian type of hero in literature. No positive knight of faith, he is a continuation of the merman model, a negative religious hero, difficult to grasp because of his silence and his continued suffering.

Frater Taciturnus comments that the aesthetic hero is great because he conquers. The religious hero is great because he suffers. Quidam could have argued: All that I hoped to do in this world, all that I have the ability to accomplish is now threatened because this woman has come into my life. What I must do is to get rid of her. She must vanish, so that I can fulfill myself and my destiny. Instead he suffers.

Suffering is not commensurate with the aesthetic category. Sicknesses, such as gout or toothache, carry little aesthetic weight. Only when suffering relates to an idea does it gain the added dimension that allows it aesthetic significance. As Frater Taciturnus so rightly points out, if we transfer such an idea from fiction into reality, it becomes despicable. Poetry cannot reconcile us to long-lasting suffering and cruelty. It is only the religious that is commensurable with every kind of suffering. Our ability or inability to fulfill our plans has nothing to do with the case. Suffering exists in the individual's core, the core of his relationship with God.

But if suffering moves inward with no outward results, as Quidam's Diary does, we might well wonder why the experiment ever took place. Who is to benefit? He who has ears to hear.

In an effort to explain and justify what happens in his experiment, Frater Taciturnus picks up Aristotle's two terms of "fear and pity," which purify the feelings of the spectators bringing about catharsis. He feels that something quite similar to what Aristotle talks about is happening in both the aesthetic and the religious spheres. He argues:

Aristotle's meaning is clear enough. He assumes emotional susceptibility on the part of the auditor, and tragedy stimulates this by fóbos and éleos, but this in turn takes the egoistic from the individual thus affected, so that he loses himself in the suffering of the hero, forgetting himself in him. Without fear and pity he would be sitting like a clod in the theater, but if he gets no further than to fear for himself, he sits there as an unworthy auditor. This is not difficult to understand, but it is already implied here that the fear and pity must be of a definite sort, and that not everyone who knows fear and pity is able to behold a tragedy. The purely "natural" man has no fear at all for that about which the poet is concerned, so he feels at the play neither fear nor sympathy. Let him see a man walk a tightrope between the towers of Rosenborg Castle, and then he will fear, or with a man who is hung he will feel sympathy. The spectator of tragedy must have an eye also for the idea, then he sees the poetic, and his fear and pity are purified of all egoistic ingredients.

But the religious man has a different conception of what awakens fear, and therefore his sympathy is in another place. The aesthetic man is not concerned with sickness and poverty, he has no sympathy for these sufferings, he feels no solidarity with them, as Börne somewhere says, he himself is in sound health and does not wish to hear about sickness. But all healing art, that of poetry as well as that of religion, is only for the sick, since it is exercised through fear and pity. The last clause Börne should not have uttered, for in this case the aesthetic is already qualified by relation to reality, and so it is narrow-mindedness or obduracy not to be willing to know anything of it. When the aesthetic is confined to its pure ideality, one has nothing to do with such things, that is true, and the poet offends no one. It is a mistake therefore on the part of the religious man to be angry with poetry, for poetry is and remains lovable. With the spectator the case is different when he is aware that such things exist. It is of course stupidity or cowardly obduracy to wish to be unaware that poverty and sickness exist because for one's own part one is in good health; for even if the poet does not point this out, yet anyone who has thought two healthy thoughts about existence knows that the next instant he may be in this case. It is not wrong of the spectator to want to lose himself in poetry, this is a joy which has its reward, but the spectator must not mistake the theater for reality, nor himself for a spectator who is nothing else but a spectator at a comedy.

Fear and pity again are operative in the religious sphere to purify these passions. But here the fear has become different, and so also has pity. The poet does not want the spectator to fear what vulgar men fear, and he teaches him to fear fate and to pity the man who suffers under it—yet the object of this pity must be great and quantitatively conspicuous.

The religious man begins at another place, he would teach the auditor not to fear fate, not to be absorbed in pity for him who falls before it. All such things have for him acquired less importance, and hence too he sees, as the aesthetic man does not, all men, great and small, equally exposed to the blows of fate. But then he says, "What thou art to fear is guilt, and thy pity must be for him who falls in this way, for only this is danger. Yet thy pity must not run wild, so that for concern about any other man thou dost forget thyself." He will teach the auditor to sorrow, as does the parish clerk, a lowly servitor under orders, a humbly proud right reverend high priest when with inward emotion he proclaims "that we should sorrow for our sins"—a thing which of course the parish clerk would not dare to say to his reverend superiors, the *Docents* in the pulpit. Fear and pity are to be aroused by the matter presented, and these passions also should be purified from egoism, not however by absorbing oneself in contemplation, but by finding within oneself a God-relationship. For the poet says, "This is egoism, that in seeing the tragic hero thou canst not forget the blow of fate which struck thee; this is egoism, that in seeing the hero thou dost become as timid as a tailor who dreads to go home."—"But to dwell upon thine own guilt," says the religious man, "to fear for thine own guilt, is not egoism, for precisely thereby is man in a God-relationship!" Fear and pity are for the religious man a different thing, and they are purified not by turning one's mind outward but by turning it inward. The aesthetic healing consists in the fact that the individual by gazing dizzily into the aesthetic disappears from his own eyes like an atom, like a mote, which is simply part and parcel of man's lot in general, the lot of all mankind, disappears like an infinitely small element of sound in the spherical harmony of existence. The religious healing consists on the contrary in transforming the world and the centuries and the successive generations and the millions of contemporary men to an evanescent distraction, in transforming jubilation and acclaim and aesthetic hero-worship to a disturbing distraction, the notion of being "finished," to a juggler's illusion, so that the only thing remaining is the individual himself, the single individual, placed in his God-relationship under the rubric: Guilty/Not guilty?[17]

This far in our reading we have directed our attention to listening and learning, but questions begin to form in our mind: What is there to find in this demonic self-love that Quidam pursues and Frater Taciturnus observes? According to them, self-love becomes purified before God.[18] The self brought to its highest potential stands before God alone. There is absolutely nobody who can listen or understand that inner language except God. It is to that God then that the individual gives himself totally. He disappears in his God.

The "story of suffering" leaves us "without result." Frater Taciturnus remarks that it bothers him that his experiment might seem to exemplify masochism, and we are grateful that he makes that remark, though he argues that he does not pursue the question seriously. He is only describing what happened in this actual case. He says that he could of course recommend repentance and the forgiveness of sins, but that would constitute mere speculation on his part. So he concludes with exactly what he has found: "The religious consists precisely in being religiously concerned about oneself infinitely." All other ways of defining religious concerns he has found to be various kinds of sophism.

Frater Taciturnus writes at great length, and we smile when we finally read on one of the very last lines: "Ah, what luck that there is no reader who reads the whole thing through." Many times—not least toward the end where he equates the author with a seducer—do we feel an urge to quit this ambiguous enterprise. What is right side out?

A poet may be such a seducer. This author of course does not possess powers of this sort, just as he does not aspire after women, but yet in another sphere he is a seducer. Essentially he has nothing to say, is far from being dangerous, it is not for this that I warn against him, for as a profound philosophical friend said to me, "He who regards him with a genuine speculative glance sees with half an eye that he, himself deceived by life from being merely an observer, has become not a deceiver but deceit itself, the objective deceit, the pure negation." Only at a time when men's spirits are so profoundly moved that the rule, "He that is not with is against," applies with double force, only in an age when the individuals, keyed up by the great crisis and the great decisions which confront them, might so easily be harmed, even by the most insignificant things, only in such an age could one be tempted to waste a word by giving warning against him, if that after all is necessary. He is in another sphere a seducer. Arrayed in jest, and by reason of that deceptive, he is inwardly a fanatic. So there he sits, close to the place where the company is assembled, so he prefers the quieter moment when the ear of the inexperienced youth eagerly drinks in the false teaching. Himself intoxicated by dreams and rendered strong by vain imaginations, as quiet as an observer, he would delude everyone into the belief that the individual possesses an infinite importance, and that this is the significance of life. Therefore do not listen to him, for he wishes, without any evil intention, to seduce you in a period of ferment to accept the undivided legacy of Quietism, with the idle notion that everyone should look after himself. He would induce you to shirk the great tasks which require united strength but also provide abundant reward for all. Behold, this he has not understood because he lacks objectivity and positivity. His existence is sheer optical illusion, his speech is as powerless and impotent as that of a ghost, and all his views are only, as the poet would say, "Pearly hues upon the ancient gate, and like snow at the end of summer." But ye who are alive and are the children of the age, do ye not observe that existence trembles, hear ye not the martial music which beckons, are ye not sensible of the haste of the instant such as the hand of the clock is unable to follow? Why this roaring, unless something is seething in the depths? Why this dreadful anguish, unless it is a sign of pregnancy? Therefore believe him not, nor listen to him, for I suppose that in his jesting and tiresome way which he takes to be Socratic he would say that from the anguish one cannot directly conclude that delivery is at hand, since it is with anguish as it is with nausea, which is worse with an empty stomach.[19]

So the *Stages* do include a "Diary of the Seducer." "Quidam's Diary" was allegedly found on the bottom of a lake and its content, brought forth from the murky depths, remind us of the merman. Both Johannes de Silentio and Frater Taciturnus speak of something that we fear: what is in ourselves.

III   Stages on Life's Way: *A Conclusion*

Stages on Life's Way is about the stages. At the time that Kierkegaard was finishing this monumental work, he was more anxious to illustrate the darker spheres between the three categories than again bringing the categories proper into view. He had already dealt in several books with the aesthetic, the ethical, and the religious, and now he turned his attention to what it is in human consciousness that drives people to decision and action, and what it is that makes them withhold decision and action.

In his continuing investigation of attitudes or points of view, he came to think of existence in a kind of ladder scheme in which the aesthetic is the lowest rung, the ethical the middle, and the religious the highest. These are solid rungs. But in between are spheres of thin air, so to speak, one before the ethical commitment and one before the religious conversion, where individuals, lost in reflection and inwardness, hover in a holding pattern. These two in-between categories Kierkegaard called irony and humor, and they are characterized by the high degree of dread that the individual experiences before choice and action.

To illustrate the attitudes and the behavior of characters situated in the various categories, Kierkegaard uses love as his major theme. In the aesthetic category, love equals "pagan eros." None of the five speakers at the banquet is of the unreflected immediate type of seducer that we encountered in Don Juan. All of the aesthetes present are well aware of the ethical. The choice is before them, but they prefer not to choose the ethical, for this would mean abandoning an attitude that they enjoy. They prefer to keep love and women on the aesthetic level because they dread the change in them that a commitment to one woman would entail. Except for the young man, they have all got accustomed to their reasoning and to change them would take a miracle, a surgery of their cast of mind.

In the second part we renew our acquaintance with Judge William, a militant defender of matrimony. He has faith in what he calls "Christian" marital love. Love comes to fruition in marriage, and wedlock is the highest human status. Man and woman do not merely play games with one another; they become partners, responsible for one another, and together they "coauthor" their life. The Judge's thesis that "a woman's beauty increases with the years" stands to tell that his commitment to his wife and hers to him has given their life a natural continuum. They live forward and upward and not for the isolated moment.

It is, however, Judge William who introduces "the exception," the person who for some reason, which he himself must test against stringent rules, cannot marry: A person who thus sets himself outside the universal.

In the third section we meet "the exception," and it is indicative that this portion of the book is by far the most extensive. Here is a case in which a conflict occurs between a man's love for a woman and his love of self. The commentator to "Quidam's Diary" is Frater Taciturnus, a man who has intellectual command over the significance of the various categories. Like Vigilius Haufniensis, the author of *The Concept of Dread*, he is a psychologist, and Quidam's case interests him immensely because he sees in Quidam a personality moving into the religious. He himself is not in the religious but stands outside, resting in the category of humor. He understands "fear and pity" on several levels but he does not "suffer."

What Kierkegaard has done in *The Concept of Dread* and in *Stages on Life's Way* is, in short, to depict from a psychological angle a theological doctrine. "Original sin" is illuminated by Vigilius Haufniensis in a straightforward scholarly manner, while in *Stages* we are invited to entangle ourselves in a more intricate web spun by Frater Taciturnus around the theme of "self-fulfillment and self-denial." Love is the test and the center of the investigation; love of self, of woman, of God. *Stages*, too, has its diary of a seducer, but this time the seduction is relegated to the religious sphere. *Stages* is enigmatic because there is no solution. But that is precisely what was planned to invoke "sympathetic antipathy and antipathetic sympathy."

CHAPTER 7

Climacus–S. Kierkegaard–Anti-Climacus

KIERKEGAARD is known as a Christian writer, but so far we have not seen a word about Christ. In the preceding chapters we have dealt with the religious category as the highest rung on the ladder, but we have not got much further than silence. *Stages* spoke about love on the religious level; Quidam struggled with self-fulfillment and self-denial, and Frater Taciturnus interprets this self-denial as having nothing to do with masochism. Yet from what has been presented, we can agree with Nietzsche who—a few decades later than Kierkegaard—put the label of masochism on the Judeo-Christian religion and wanted to turn the tables. But Kierkegaard does not go that way. In *Stages,* suffering is the mark of distinction for the religious. The moment individuals are forced to leave the universal ideal and go beyond, they must suffer. Suffering cannot be said to be characteristic of one or two religions. In the Kierkegaardian terminology it belongs to *religion,* and it stems from setting oneself apart and having nobody to consult but God. Hence Kierkegaard would point out that the Superman suffers because he has left the race.

The reason we have not read about Christ is that so far we have dealt with only one side of Kierkegaard's writing: the aesthetic pseudonymous; we have not looked at the books that were published under his own name. Furthermore, we have not yet been introduced to the pseudonym that is the most intellectual and delightful acquaintance of all Kierkegaard's characters. His name is Johannes Climacus, and his attention is singularly focused on truth and the truth of Christianity.

I *Johannes Climacus*

Johannes Climacus is the author of two books: *Philosophical Fragments or A Fragment of Philosophy* and *Concluding Un-*
162

scientific Postscript. Climacus has a marvelously clear mind, and he can clarify for us what has so far been enigmatic and ambiguous. He is thoroughly knowledgeable about all the works by Magister Kierkegaard and his underlings, and he gives us a comprehensive review from his perspective in "A Glance at a Contemporary Effort in Danish Literature," which is incorporated in *Postscript.* Thus he is able, for instance, to tell us in his review of *Stages* what is meant by "humor":

. . . humor is the concluding stage of the immanent within the immanent; it is still essentially a retirement out of existence into the eternal by way of recollection, and only after humor do we come upon faith and the paradoxes. Humor is the last stage of existential inwardness before faith. Hence it was, according to my ideas, necessary to bring this stage to view, lest any stage be left behind that afterwards might cause confusion. This has now been done through the "Story of Suffering." Humor is not faith but comes before faith—it is not after faith or a development of faith. From the Christian point of view there is no advance beyond faith, because faith is the highest stage—for an existing individual— as has been sufficiently developed in the preceding. Even when humor makes an attempt at the paradoxes, it is not faith. Humor does not absorb the suffering side of the paradox, nor the ethical side of faith, but merely the amusing aspect. For it is a species of suffering, a martyrdom even in peaceful times, to have the happiness of the soul tied to that which the understanding despairs about.[1]

Climacus declares his own position to be that of a humorist, "content with the situation at this moment, hoping that something higher may be granted him." He is content because he is not embroiled in scientific and philosophic discoveries and debates. Rather, he is a private man "without authority," who can go about his own most personal investigation:

In the aloofness of the experiment the whole work has to do with me myself, solely and simply with me. "I, Johannes Climacus, now thirty years of age, born in Copenhagen, a plain man like the common run of them, have heard tell of the highest good in prospect, which is called an eternal blessedness, and that Christianity will bestow this upon me on condition of adhering to it—now I ask how I am to become a Christian." I ask only for my own sake, yes,

certainly that I do, or rather I have asked this question, for that
indeed is the content of the whole work.[2]

The question revolves around truth. We see how logical it is
that we should arrive at that question after having spent considerable time with the beautiful and the good. We are now
prepared for an analysis of the true on which all else hinges. The
intellectual Climacus is to be our guide.

II Philosophical Fragments
or A Fragment of Philosophy

On these pages, the words "pagan" and "Christian" have often
occurred in juxtaposition, and it has become obvious that
Kierkegaard's mind was preoccupied with the relationship between the two heritages, the Classical and the Christian. In
Fragments, Climacus states that the relationship between the
two is one not of continuity but of contrast. *Fragments* stages
a dialogue between two different attitudes toward truth. There
are two unsurpassed teachers, Socrates and Christ. Both of
humble origin, being above no one, leaving no one out, they
were targets for much ridicule. Yet for those who have ears to
hear, these two elicit the highest truth. Their approach to truth
is fundamentally different because there exists a crucial difference
in historical conditions between these two teachers.

The title page of *Fragments* reads: "Is an historical point of
departure possible for an eternal consciousness; how can such
a point of departure have any other than a merely historical
interest; is it possible to base an eternal happiness upon historical
knowledge?"[3] This was a question that—since it was once
raised by Lessing—had generated an academic storm that was
raging still in Kierkegaard's day.

The participants in the dialogue are, besides the teachers, the
learner, the reader, and the author, Johannes Climacus.

The learner asks: Can truth be learned? Socrates' answer is
that truth exists from eternity. Being eternal, it is always the
same. Socrates' role as a teacher is to actualize it, to help draw
it out of the pupil. His famous midwifery is the art of getting the
learner to find the true in himself. However, what a teacher
knows of the truth at a certain time can never have a decisive

effect on the learner because the teacher and pupil are on the same level. The teacher might have understanding, but he cannot "have" truth. Socrates holds on with all his might to this uncertainty.

Climacus then considers the Christian alternative (*the Possibility*): that truth is not always the same but at a certain moment it entered history—Christ became man, "the God in Time," as he is called throughout the book. Thereby the teacher-learner situation changes radically. The teacher *is* the truth who comes to save the learner from untruth.

At a certain moment in history, a decisive change took place. Christ came in the fullness of time, *The Moment*, to give the learner a new possibility to choose a new life with the truth. The all-important moment in history is then the moment of Incarnation, when the God who is the eternal truth became man in order to teach the learner. In this proposition, there is no equality between teacher and learner. Christ sets the example of what it is to be fully human, and the learner is admonished to follow Christ.

Socrates tried to get to know himself, but in spite of lifelong pursuit, he had to admit that he could not do so. There is something that reason cannot understand even though it passionately wants to do so. But up against the miracle, reason is helpless. The miracle is beyond Socratic cognition.

Christianity, on the other hand, knows why we are unable to understand the miracle. It is because of Sin. Sin beclouds the human mind and makes it incapable of understanding the paradox. Sin separates man from the truth by making the two unlike each other.

The author, Climacus, points out that if a person's understanding and the paradox can agree on their complete unlikeness, then there takes place "a happy encounter," which results in faith. However, if a person cannot accept the paradox, and the encounter is "unhappy," then the person is offended. This offense does not come from reason; there is so much that reason cannot grasp. Rather, it comes directly from the paradox. This offense Climacus calls "an acoustic illusion."

Faith is not an act of will in the same way as conduct is such an act. Faith is given by the God who acts freely and miracu-

lously, creating the conditions and setting the time. Hegel had
juxtaposed the two categories, possibility and necessity, but
Climacus insists that as a category, possibility is much stronger
and larger than necessity. From the learner's point of view, the
necessary is neither in the past nor in the future, but always in
the present, or in what he prefers to call *actuality*. With the
help of "necessity," we can neither prophesy the future (nothing
"must" happen), nor interpret the past (nothing "had to" happen). Present, past, and future are instead all encompassed within
the realm of possibility, moving into actuality. We can never
understand what happened in the past except the fact that it
happened. The past holds no certainty about itself, how it
happened. Climacus speaks of an "apprehension of the past."
In order to interpret the past, we need faith in its having
happened a certain way. However, the faith needed for *the
Event* in history, the Incarnation, has to be of a special kind,
since here we encounter the Paradox that God, the eternal,
revealed himself in time.

When the learner asks if it would not have been an advantage
to have been one of Christ's contemporaries, the answer is
given: since this cannot be grasped with ordinary faith, "apprehension of the past," it makes no difference whether the person
lived then, is alive now, or will live a hundred years from
now. No human being is born with faith, but what can happen
is that faith can be born in a person and can become that
person's second nature. A new being is formed. An eternal
happiness cannot be based merely on historical knowledge. It
can only be based on faith in the Paradox, that the eternal God
entered time in a historical event.

Socrates is the very best of teachers. But something extraordinary has happened in history since Socrates' time: the Incarnation. This event should either be taken seriously—which
means dealing with the Paradox, or the same Paradox should
be rejected. To adapt the Incarnation to speculative philosophy
constitutes a false mixture, which results in unacceptable confusion. Climacus maintains that if we take Christianity at
its word, then we see that history has taken a decisive turn
for us, and that the human condition has radically changed.

The highest truth can be known—in faith. The seeking spirit can find the answer to what is truth.

When the annoyed reader breaks into the book's dialogue saying that this is nothing new, this is the old catechism, then Climacus defends himself by saying that he never intended to say anything new. If there is anything "new" to it, it is precisely that it goes against the idea of progress. We cannot progress beyond either one of the two members of the dialogue, Socrates or Christ, the two greatest teachers. But they are qualitatively different. Socrates teaches us about ourselves and our conduct. Christ teaches us about God and the conduct of God. Socrates makes us concentrate on memory and recollection of the past while God makes us concentrate on the future and the repetition of the miracle. The moral of *Fragments*, printed on the last page (as was the custom for comedies or fairy tales) is worded thus:

The projected hypothesis indisputably makes an advance upon Socrates, which is apparent at every point. Whether it is therefore more true than the Socratic doctrine is an entirely different question, which cannot be decided in the same breath, since we have here assumed a new organ: Faith; a new presupposition: the consciousness of Sin; a new decision: the Moment; and a new Teacher: the God in Time. Without these I certainly never would have dared present myself for inspection before that master of Irony, admired through the centuries, whom I approach with a palpitating enthusiasm that yields to none. But to make an advance upon Socrates and yet say essentially the same things as he, only not nearly so well—that at least is not Socratic.[4]

When Kierkegaard finished *Fragments*, he had in a sense reached the summit. For the previous four years, he had worked feverishly day and night. Thoughts had just kept pouring out of him. His dialectical training since childhood had been an enormous asset. His body was frail and awkwardly out of control, but his mind was a nimble climber. From the top, he could survey the landscape and take delight in its clarity, depth, and scope.

Fragments was published in 1844, that is, before *Stages*, and Kierkegaard was at that time teeming with new ideas and settings, and it did not then occur to him that he might have lost his audience. The motto for *Fragments*, "Better well hung than ill wed"—selected from a German translation of Shakespeare's *Twelfth Night*—indicates that he envisioned the academic community reading him, and that he expected to be strongly rejected by all the learned scholars.[5] What happened was a deafening silence.

From *Stages* we remember the comment that there might not be a single reader left. Kierkegaard had labored so hard and had been so absorbed in his own theater and the performance he staged that the crucial audience had almost vanished from his consciousness. He had somehow taken for granted— after the success with *Either/Or*—that the audience was out there in rapt attention. But the lights came on, and the house was empty.

III   Concluding Unscientific Postscript

Kierkegaard's problem now changed. He had to go back and explain his works with a thoroughly interpretative postscript. Then he would retire to a country parsonage, his authorship completed. Concluded.

Postscript is therefore a very important book, but it is a postscript and not very useful if we are not familiar with the other works. Furthermore, it is primarily a postscript to *Fragments*, although in this case—as in many such cases—the explanatory postscript is far longer than the work it is meant to explain, spinning off on its own.

The enigmatic word "unscientific" in the title ties *Postscript* with *Fragments*, in which Climacus had promised a sequel that would deal with the objective truth of Christianity. *Postscript* does so in Book One, but it is Book Two that takes up the subjective problem, the unscientific problem of becoming a Christian, and that is where Climacus makes his major contribution.

The motto, "But really, Socrates, what do you think this all amounts to? It is really scrapings and parings of systematic thought, as I said a while ago, divided into bits," shows us right from the start that *Postscript* is a descendant of *Fragments*, "scrapings and parings of systematic thought."[6]

It is not that Kierkegaard is against science or that he thinks that scientific data are not both valid and interesting. But science belongs in the aesthetic category. Human beings endanger themselves by mistaking scholarly enterprise for the ultimate truth, thereby forgetting how to live in the realms of the ethical and the religious categories. People can wallow in facts and construe systems and philosophies from new facts and pursue with exhausting energy every whim of their curiosity. But Kierkegaard held the view that if this cast of mind prevails in the future, then the natural sciences will corrupt the world.[7] Technology will outrun the truth.

In Book One, Climacus deals with all the new findings and theories concerning Christianity that were floating around in his day. He points out that in the end such theories do not advance or impede the search for the truth of Christianity one iota.

Climacus first turns to the learned exegetes who critically examine the documentation and the sources of Christianity and debate the truth of the Bible. Can one build one's eternal happiness on a book? Speaking about "inspiration," many scholars answer yes. But Climacus maintains his skepticism. Inspiration has nothing to do with scholarly investigation. It is solely a matter of faith, and faith cannot be proved. By listening to opponents or proponents debating inspiration, faith tires and loses its passion. The debating scholars grow old and die, never having found out anything about themselves and their eternal happiness because they never made a firm decision regarding themselves. Objectively, the Bible is a book like other books. But subjectively read and subsequently admired, it stands out for us, demanding action on our part.

What goes for the Bible goes for the Church. Christianity's staying power through the centuries does not prove its eternal truth. Many other things have lasted. Many traditions have grown with time. Objective historical scholarship does not open the possibility of reaching the truth about Christianity. Outward, approximate "truth" falls helpless before Christianity's claim to the truth.

Climacus finally turns to speculative philosophy for help in his search for the truth in Christianity. But the philosophers also seem to limit their interest to objective truth, and they can give no answer to the question of eternal happiness, which they consider merely a subjective and rather nonsensical question. Climacus ends Book One with a homey illustration typical of that swift, original Kierkegaardian style that demolishes opponents with a single stroke:

This contradiction between the subject who is in passion infinitely interested, and philosophical speculation viewed as something that might assist him, I shall permit myself to illustrate by means of an image from the sensible world. In sawing wood it is important not to press down too hard on the saw; the lighter the pressure exerted by the sawyer, the better the saw operates. If a man were to press down with all his strength, he would no longer be able to saw at all. In the same way it is necessary for the philosopher to make himself objectively light; but everyone who is in passion infinitely interested in his eternal happiness makes himself subjectively as heavy as possible. Precisely for this reason he prevents himself from speculating. Now if Christianity requires this interest in the individual subject (which is the assumption, since this is the point on which the problem turns), it is easy to see that he cannot find what he seeks in speculation. This can also be expressed by saying that speculative philosophy does not permit the problem to arise at all; and it follows that all its pretense of answering the problem constitutes only a mystification.[8]

Climacus on Lessing

As human documents, few of Kierkegaard's passages move us as much as the tribute of gratitude that Climacus pays to Lessing. If only Kierkegaard's contemporaries could have understood and reviewed him in that manner! What would have happened if suddenly a reader had appeared who could grasp the intention of Kierkegaard's works and appreciate his style in that way? We can speculate about such an imaginary encounter and imagine how grateful and happy it would have made Kierkegaard—at first. But we must subsequently also imagine him trying in all manner of ways to shake this admirer loose.

At any rate, this piece reveals the kind of review of his own work that Kierkegaard would have liked to see. In "Something

About Lessing," Climacus does not touch on Lessing as a scholar, an aesthetician or a sage, but focuses on his subjectivity, his person:

> ...that he did not permit himself to be deceived into becoming world-historic and systematic with respect to the religious, but understood and knew how to hold fast to the understanding that the religious concerned Lessing, and Lessing alone, just as it concerns every other human being in the same manner; understood that he had infinitely to do with God, and nothing, nothing to do with any man directly.[9]

And Climacus feels that Lessing understood the meaning of indirect communication. In its deepest sense, a person can communicate directly only with God; only in that encounter does full openness occur. Only before God can we tell everything, revealing all our drudgery through prayer and repentance, through fear and trembling, for all of which there is no coherent language. No one can ever take this relationship away from another person. Nobody can live anybody else's life. The struggle and the suffering are private. We can communicate this to others only through hints, jests, and stories. Therefore, Climacus praises Lessing's style:

> And now his style! This polemic tone, which every instant has unlimited leisure to indulge in a witticism, and that even in a period of ferment; for according to an old newspaper I have found, the age was then precisely as now in such a ferment of change that the world has never seen the like. This stylist equanimity, which develops a simile in minutest detail, as if the literary expression had a value in itself, as if peace and safety reigned; and that although perhaps the printer's devil and world-history and all mankind stood waiting for him to have it finished. This systematic slackness, which refuses to obey the paragraphic norm. This mingling of jest and earnest, which makes it impossible for a third party to know which is which—unless indeed the third party knows it by himself. This artfulness, which perhaps even sometimes puts a false emphasis upon the indifferent, so that the initiated may precisely in this manner best grasp the dialectically decisive point, while the heretics get nothing to run with. This form of his, so completely an expression of his individuality, spontaneously and refreshingly cutting its own

path, not dying away in a mosaic of catchwords and authorized phrases and contemporary slogans, which in quotation marks give evidence that the writer keeps up with the times, while Lessing on the other hand confides to the reader *sub rosa* that he keeps up with the thought. This adroitness in teasingly using his own ego, almost like Socrates, excusing himself from all fellowship; or rather insuring himself against fellowship in relation to all that truth, whose chief feature it is, that one must be alone about it; not wishing to have others with him for the sake of the triumph, since there is here no triumph to win, unless indeed one thinks of the infinite, where the triumph consists in becoming nothing before God; not wishing to have other men about him when struggling in the deadly perils of solitary thought, since it is just this solitariness which is the way.[10]

In short, here is Kierkegaard's own program found in and projected onto Lessing: Direct communication would be to defraud God. Kierkegaard has Climacus say of Lessing, "And then I should understand, if no one else, that he had the best of me."

The chapters on Lessing open and set the pace for Book Two, the section dealing with "The Subjective Problem," "The Relation of the Subject to the Truth of Christianity," and "The Problem of Becoming a Christian." Here in Lessing we are given a model, a prototype, a hero for the purpose of a more concrete discussion. It impresses on us the fact that our concern centers on people who live, breathe, think, develop, and die, rather than on isolated concepts, theories, and systems. "An existing individual is constantly in the process of becoming"; the existential thinker "constantly reproduces this existential situation in his thoughts, and translates all his thinking into terms of process." In this respect, the existential thinker wrestles with his style like an author: "for he only has a style who never has anything finished, but 'moves the waters of the language' every time he begins, so that the most common expression comes into being for him with the freshness of a new birth."[11]

Climacus ties the idea of the famous "leap" (forever associated with Kierkegaard's name) to Lessing. He places it in a significant situation. In Lessing's last hours, his friend Jacobi discovers to his horror that Lessing is a Spinozist and a pantheist.

Jacobi proceeds with diligence and anxiety in his attempts to persuade Lessing to take the leap, the *salto mortale,* into the "true faith." But Lessing, understanding that in the hour of death there can be no assistance in the leap, jokes with Jacobi and, as once Socrates did, he then quietly slips away. "When one is to leap, one must be alone about it and hence also alone about understanding its impossibility.... The last thing that human thinking can will to do is to will to transcend itself in the paradoxical. And Christianity is precisely the paradoxical.... Christianity is a desperate way out for everyone who really accepts it."[12]

The irony here is aimed at the Hegelians and their System. A logical system is always possible, but what is it then but mere mathematics and illusion? On the other hand, it is impossible to construct an existential "system." Individuals can either forget their identity as existing human beings under the obligation to struggle to find out what existence entails and go their way unquestioning and unquestioned, or they can give their whole energy to concentrating on and grappling with the meaning of life. Lessing had deliberately chosen this latter course, and he defined the task of becoming subjective as "constant striving."

Climacus understands that his praise of Lessing would not sit well with an age enamored with the word "objective," meaning progress, a higher and higher reaching, and an ever-expanding hope. Climacus aims to put this escalating process into reverse. His hope is to teach people to get a perspective on its limitations and on the way the individual gets lost in the shuffle of these blocks of progress. He wants to point out how a delight in the System often obscures that most important and difficult task of becoming subjective. It is far more difficult to think about the simple than the complicated. Science forgets about subjectivity, and philosophy shuns it. Climacus feels that an "objective lunacy" has become the teacher, and that in such a scheme we all end as observers, rather than participants in life. The absence of inwardness becomes a common malady. But as soon as an individual begins to contemplate truth and appropriate it inwardly, probing himself, he sees the madness which the objective researcher often foregoes.

Objectivity exists in the aesthetic. There it has its end in itself.

To count as subjective individuals, we must leave the aesthetic realm and get to know ourselves and our personal history in the ethical. Only in the ethical can we deal with "immortality" and "eternal life." What does it mean to be immortal? Do we become immortal, or are we immortal? We must wrestle with such questions as individuals in total subjectivity. Now Lessing as a model is overtaken by the great Socrates.

What does it mean to die? People know about it in a general way, but do they understand it? What is it to be reconciled with life? To become truly human? What is suicide? What does it mean? In contrast to objective truth, subjective truth shows that these questions become essential to the individual and are appropriated by him. Inwardness becomes the truth. Socrates came this far. He believed that a god exists. And he held onto the objective uncertainty "with the whole passion of his inwardness, and it is precisely in this contradiction and in this risk that faith is rooted." Thus Socrates came as close to faith as one can come. Climacus shows a far higher appreciation of Socrates' reach than Kierkegaard had done in *The Concept of Irony*.

But we also know that Climacus remains convinced that our position differs from that of Socrates; the world has changed, and we must deal with the truth of Christianity. The Incarnation cannot be thought. The Paradox that the eternal truth has entered time cannot be explained—only proclaimed. And a relationship between an existing individual and eternal truth can only be *believed*. A little bit of understanding—or a huge amount: it makes no difference. Understanding has no inroad. It is decision that counts. The passionate act. Passion and Paradox have to hit it off.

It is precisely when he has arrived at this point that Climacus inserts an appendix: "A Glance at a Contemporary Effort in Danish Literature." "A Glance" reviews every single one of the pseudonymous books from *Either/Or* onward. This piece of writing is often praised as the best introduction to Kierkegaard's works. But we must keep in mind that it was written for the purpose of *Postscript*, and therefore this review stresses the necessity of indirect communication in expressing existential inwardness. Climacus climbs from book to book, turning them into dialectical stepping-stones that support the thesis of truth as subjectivity. Climacus is very pleased with this literary effort, especially *Stages* because it complements his thesis from *Fragments* and his position as a humorist:

> My thesis was that subjectivity, inwardness, is the truth. This principle was for me decisive with respect to the problem of Christianity, and the same consideration has led me to pursue a certain tendency in the pseudonymous books, which to the very last have honestly abstained from doctrination. Particularly I thought I ought to take cognizance of the last of these books, because it was published after my *Fragments*, recalling the earlier publications by means of a free reproduction, and determining the religious stage through humor as *confinium*.[13]

Climacus's great concern is that if Christianity is the truth, then the Classical categories and thought patterns must have changed radically. Religion is not sentimental private business without consequence. Tragedy and comedy as defined by Aristotle are not adequate definitions any more. That is why Climacus is so pleased with the story of suffering, "Guilty/Not Guilty?" because in it these categories are pressed much closer together. If suffering is religiously understood, then laughing and weeping are molded together, and the old division putting them wide apart seems naïve:

> A principle propounded by Lord Shaftesbury, which makes laughter a test of truth, was the occasion during the last century for the appearance of one or another little inquiry as to whether this is so or not. In our time the Hegelian philosophy has desired to give preponderance to the comical, which might seem a particularly strange thing for the Hegelian philosophy to do, since this philosophy is surely least of all equipped to withstand an attack from that side. In ordinary life we laugh when something is made to seem ridiculous, and after having laughed we sometimes say: but one is really not justified in making such a thing ridiculous. But if the comic interpretation is well done, one cannot restrain oneself from laughingly spreading the story further—naturally accompanied by the edifying afterthought: but it is not right to make such a thing ridiculous. It goes unnoticed how ridiculous this is, that there is a contradiction in the fictitious attempt to act ethically by means of an edifying

afterthought, instead of renouncing the illegitimate antecedent. Now when this is so, when the advance and wider dissemination of culture and polished manners, when the refinement of life contributes to develop a sense for the comic, so that an overwhelming partiality for the comical is characteristic of our time, which both in the correct and the incorrect sense seems to rejoice in the Aristotelian view that lays stress on a sense for the comic as a distinguishing mark of man's nature—in such circumstances the religious address must long since have taken note of how the comical stands related to the religious. For what occupies the minds of men so much, what constantly recurs in conversation, in intercourse, in books, in the modifications of the entire view of life, that is something that the religious dare not ignore; unless indeed the Sunday performances in church are meant to constitute a kind of indulgence, where at the price of a grumpy devotionalism for an hour's time, one buys immunity to laugh unchecked the whole week through. The question of the legitimacy of the comic, of its relationship to the religious, of whether it does not have a place in the religious address itself— this question is of essential significance for a religious existence in our times, where the comical everywhere runs away with the victory. To cry alas and alack over this tendency only proves how little the champions of religion respect what they fight for. It is surely an indication of far greater respect for the religious to demand that it be given its proper place in daily life, than to keep it at a Sunday-distance away from life, in high-flown eccentricity.

The matter is quite simple. The comical is present in every stage of life (only that the relative positions are different), for wherever there is life, there is contradiction, and wherever there is contradiction, the comical is present. The tragic and the comic are the same, in so far as both are based on contradiction; *but the tragic is the suffering contradiction, the comical, the painless contradiction.* That something which the comic apprehension envisages as comical may entail imaginary suffering for the comical individual, is quite irrelevant. In that case, for example, it would be incorrect to apprehend the hero of Holberg's "The Busy Man" as comical. Satire also entails pain, but this pain has a dialectic which gives it a teleology in the direction of a cure. The difference between the tragic and the comic lies in the relationship between the contradiction and the controlling idea. The comic apprehension evokes the contradiction or makes it manifest by having in mind the way out, which is why the contradiction is painless. The tragic apprehension sees the contradiction and despairs of a way out.[14]

Climacus tells us that the aim behind using pseudonyms and creating heroes and naming prototypes must be to stir the imagination of the readers and encourage them to take hold of existence: to enable them to transform an *esse* (to be) into a *posse* (to be able to). These heroes and models act on the reader's behalf.

According to Climacus, the greatest danger to the two existential categories, the ethical and the religious, comes from modern philosophy, which has brought about confusion by letting thought reach for reality instead of remaining in lofty disinterest. Philosophy and poetry should stick to possibility. Thought has great validity, but it should not be confused with reality. Thought and imagination gain their importance in that they enhance and beautify existence. The true and the good and the beautiful belong together. But they are united in existence, not in thought.

"Existing is an art." It is vital for Climacus to point out that the subjective thinker is not a kind of scientist, but an artist experimenting with himself. All existential problems are "passionate problems."

The last section of *Postscript* deals with the religious category. It includes a clarification and an expansion of *Fragments* that makes an important delineation between "religiousness A," which is general and immanent, and "religiousness B," which is specifically Christian, paradoxical, and transcendent.

If there has been change in history as a result of the Incarnation, then a change awaits all individuals. Their development moves not merely from a state of disinterested "aesthetic-pathetic" observation to the interested and active-ethical mode of existence, but more important, it goes beyond to complete transformation in Christian religiousness where the individual depends "absolutely on the Absolute." If we as individuals accept Christ (the God in Time) as our Teacher, then we need a complete reschooling and transformation.

Religiousness A is still paganism and immanent. In religiousness A, individuals stand before God in submission and guilt-consciousness. Humor is the expression of this stance in which the persons have arrived inwardly at a position of self-annihilation of their own understanding, losing themselves in prayer like Job.

The paradox occurs in religiousness B. Just as the eternal once entered time, so also are individuals given access to eternal happiness through suffering. We have here the "double" movement from *posse* to *esse*. The Christian has it *now*.

Repulsive to thought, suffering is nevertheless only too familiar in existence. Experience teaches us about guilt, suffering, and death, crushingly huge chunks of life that we conveniently label "morbid" and stash away. But Climacus refuses to do so. The larger part of *Postscript* deals with these phenomena and how they affect inwardness and are transformed by Christianity.

Postscript does not pretend that it is easy to become a Christian. Some interpret the phrase, "becoming like little children because the kingdom of God belongs to them," as meaning that we should imitate little children, and this infuriates Climacus. He finds nothing childish about Christianity and thinks that a child has no use for it. He sees the Christianity taught to children as "idyllic mythology." Childish Christianity may well be cute in the little ones, but in adults it constitutes tasteless fantasy. Becoming a Christian involves a strong decision, an important choice; the age of childhood is not the time to grasp the gravity of the situation. The labor of inwardness in becoming a Christian is a hard, maturing process. Culture offers no help by making it child's play. Climacus discusses this fearsome business at length:

Thus a strict upbringing in Christianity may perhaps have made life too hard for a man without helping him in turn; in his heart he may perhaps feel a desire like that of the people who besought Christ to depart from their country because He made them afraid. But the son whom the father made unfortunate, if he is high-minded, will continue to love the father, and when he suffers from the consequences he sometimes maybe will sigh despondently, "Would this had never happened to me," but he will not abandon himself to despair, he will labor against the suffering by laboring through it. And as he labors the sorrow will be assuaged; he soon will be more sorry for the father than for himself, he will forget his own pain in the profound sympathetic sorrow of the reflection how hard it must be for the father if he understood it—so he will strive more and more mightily, his salvation will be important to him for his own sake, and now almost more precious for the father's sake—thus he will labor, and it will succeed surely. And if it succeeds, he will be, as it were, out of his wits with the joy of enthusiasm; for after all what father has done so much for his son, what son can be so much indebted to his father! And so it is with Chrsitianity. Even if it has made him unhappy, he does not for this cause give it up; for it never occurs to him that Christianity might have come into the world to do men harm; it constantly remains venerable to him. He does not let it go, and even if he sighs despondently, "Would I had never been brought up in this doctrine," he does not let it go. And despondency becomes sadness, as though almost it must be hard on Christianity that such a thing could occur; but he does not let it go, in the end Christianity must make it good to him. In the end—yea, that is not little by little, it is much less, and yet infinitely much more. But only slatternly men let go of that which once has made an absolute impression upon them, and only paltry souls practise despicable usury with their own suffering by seeking to get out of it the miserable profit of being able to unsettle others, and by becoming self-important with the basest presumption which wants to prohibit others from finding comfort because one has not found it himself. If there be any man in our time whom Christianity has unsettled (as I have no doubt is the case, and as can be proved factually), one thing can be required of him, that he keep silent. For his talk, ethically regarded, is a thievish assault, and in its consequences still worse than that, for it ends with neither of them having anything, neither the robber nor the victim.[15]

The enormous merit of the investigation in *Postscript* rests in the manner in which it distinguishes between true religious experience and pious jibberish. With precision and care, endless patience and matchless humor, Climacus leads us forward to an understanding of religion in general and of Christianity in its highest paradoxical potential. Climacus himself does not proclaim himself to be such a Christian. Neither does he deny that he speaks on his own behalf.

IV *"Responsible for Publication: S. Kierkegaard"*

Postscript and *Fragments* list Johannes Climacus as author. But printed underneath on the title pages in both cases we find this note: "Responsible for Publication: S. Kierkegaard." This makes us suspect that Kierkegaard felt a greater kinship to the pseudonym "Climacus" than to some of the others he used. Climacus is almost an alter ego. At the end of *Postscript*, Kierkegaard includes "A First and Last Declaration," in which he openly acknowledges his authorship of the various pseudonymous works, explaining why he has chosen such a method of "polynymity":

... it has an *essential* ground in the character of the *production*, which for the sake of the lines ascribed to the authors and the psychologically varied distinctions of the individualities poetically required complete regardlessness in the direction of good and evil, of contrition and high spirits, of despair and presumption, of suffering and exultation, etc., which is bounded only ideally by psychological consistency, and which real actual persons in the actual moral limitations of reality dare not permit themselves to indulge in, nor could wish to. What is written therefore is in fact mine, but only in so far as I put into the mouth of the poetically actual individuality whom I *produced*, his life-view expressed in audible lines. For my relation is even more external than that of a poet, who poetizes characters, and yet in the preface is himself the author. For I am impersonal, or am personal in the second person, a *souffleur* [prompter] who has poetically produced the *authors*, whose preface in turn is their own production, as are even their own names. So in the pseudonymous works there is not a single word which is mine, I have no opinion about these works except as a third person, no knowledge of their meaning except as a reader, not the remotest private relation to them, since such a thing is impossible in the case of a doubly reflected communication. One single word of mine uttered personally in my own name would be an instance of presumptuous self-forgetfulness, and dialectically viewed it would incur with one word the guilt of annihilating the pseudonyms.[16]

Kierkegaard declares himself that whereas he is only "figuratively" the author of the aesthetic works, he is "quite literally the author of the Edifying Discourses, and of every word in them."

V Edifying Discourses

As yet we have not touched upon the edifying, "upbuilding" works. But without this very important piece in the puzzle, the dialectic becomes one-sided and demonic.

For Kierkegaard, one must use his own will and strength to pay for the inward journey. Although he never ventured outside the Christian religion, Kierkegaard well understoood the drive behind autonomous search. He did not take the given tradition for granted. As a young man of eighteen (in 1831), he wrote:

It takes some time before we really settle down and feel at home (know where everything has its place) in the divine economy. We grope around amid a multiplicity of moods, do not even know how we should pray; Christ does not take on any definite configuration in us—we do not know what the cooperation of the Spirit means, etc.[17]

Kierkegaard acts from such a perspective in his edifying works. The configuration of Christ or Christ's image needs to be built up. Kierkegaard's aesthetic authorship is pseudonymous, because it deals with situations in which readers are supposed to recognize themselves. There Kierkegaard wants as much as possible to be personally accidental, only aiding the individual in a Socratic-maieutic manner to get to know himself, to get an image of himself. In his edifying books, however, his aim is to strengthen the religious and eventually to build up the image of Christ. It is not that these discourses are not personal. On the contrary. They are in his own name, and they are the record of such a pilgrimage of appropriation of the image of Christ, the given. Therefore, the central message in each one of them is taken from texts in the Bible. The vision is on the meeting between the personal and incidental with the divine and eternal.

Each time Kierkegaard published a pseudonymous work, he also published edifying discourses in order to illustrate for his readers how a person's growth in self-understanding relates directly to his intensified relationship to God. Moreover, these discourses progress through the same stages that he develops in the aesthetic works. The earliest discourses are therefore designed for people in the aesthetic sphere on their way to the realization that there can be fixed points in this oscillating world. The seeker will find that everything is a gift from God, that one must forgive one's neighbor, and that suffering should be borne with patience. These discourses do not dramatize the unusual, but emphasize the common. So, for instance, in *Three Discourses on Imagined Occasions,* these occasions are: going to confession—which indicates the distance between Kierkegaard's time and ours when this is no longer common practice (at least not in the Protestant churches); attending a wedding; and taking part in a funeral. From such situations existential questions naturally arise: What does it mean to seek God? What is it to make a resolution to love? What is the meaning of death?

Weddings and funerals give us occasion to reflect on these situations that are in store for all of us. We live and get into trouble. We marry. We die. Through these discourses Kierkegaard wants to help us to a greater awareness and a deeper religiosity; he wants to lead us toward the ability to focus on the essential significance of these occasions, without lapsing into mere sentimentality. The religiousness Kierkegaard speaks about in these earlier discourses can be described as general religiousness, or "religiousness A" in a lower case.

In his ethical discourses addressed to people who have become aware of the choice, Kierkegaard stresses "purity of heart." In this, his second layer of "upbuilding" discourses, he is aiming at strengthening "the individual," the person who has taken the decisive step into the ethical, making the decision to self will. The table of contents to *Purity of Heart* indicates his plan for edification:

Live as an "Individual"
Occupation and Vocation; Means and End
Conclusion:
Man and the Eternal

The title of a series of discourses aimed at aiding the persons who have become "the exception" is *The Gospel of Suffering*. When "the individuals" finds themselves bogged down in intolerable compromise and sordid settlement, the only way out is through turning to God in repentance. But renewal is impossible without outside help. That help comes from Christ, the innocent Christ who suffered. To suffer is the human condition. Suffering is unavoidable and often comes to people through no fault of their own. By becoming Christians, however, people undergo suffering, because they experience in their lives a renewed consciousness that makes them realize their guilt. When individuals link their lives more closely to Christ's, then the very gospel is suffering.

Aware that he might well be criticized for slighting social problems in his deep concern for the individual and for inwardness, Kierkegaard states in his journal:

In spite of everything men ought to have learned about my maieutic carefulness, in addition to proceeding slowly and continually letting it seem as if I knew nothing more, not the next thing—now on the occasion of my new Edifying Discourses they will probably bawl out that I do not know what comes next, that I know nothing about sociality. The fools! Yet, on the other hand, I owe it to myself to confess before God that in a certain sense, there is some truth in it, not only as men understand it, namely that always when I have first presented one aspect sharply and clearly, then I affirm the validity of the other even more strongly. Now I have the theme of the next book. It will be called *Works of Love*.[18]

Not until *Works of Love* does Kierkegaard present the new ethic that Christianity offers. He knew how very important it was to avoid misunderstanding and sentimentality when he stated in so many words: You shall love as God loves. Since God loves everyone, Christians should love their neighbors—meaning all people.

Many scholars would deny that Kierkegaard has developed a Christian ethic. They claim that he is essentially uninterested in social ethics. They think that he leaves it all up to God and thus does not demand involvement in human affairs. What Kierkegaard refutes so sharply, however, is false belief in human solutions, in progress and evolution, development and expansion. He advocates instead an educational process that would lead to a heightened awareness of the meaning of loving one's neighbor. He reiterates that Christ has given the commandment to love, and that only someone who has lived a long time in the Christian school, like Saint Paul, can speak about such Christian love. Beginners can easily make a "flirtatious" mistake. Indeed, the whole purpose of these discourses is to provide a heightened awareness of religion and point to a way of living for others.

Seekers begin to form an image of "the Christian." An understanding develops, a grasp of the meaning of choosing that way and becoming sensitive to God. Seeking Christians begin to see that Christian action aligns them with Christ. First with *The Lilies of the Fields and the Birds of the Air,* Kierkegaard finally enters what Climacus calls religiousness B, the paradoxical-Christian mode of being. Here he writes as a Christian poet speaking of the joy of being with God who takes care of all sorrow.

The aesthetic works describe ways of becoming inwardly aware and "conscious of self." The edifying discourses present a countermethod that leads to becoming "conscious of Christ." Kierkegaard held that a personality is formed by its encounters and conversations—not only with other people, other personalities, but also inwardly with the eternal. Eternal values shape the consciousness of "*the* individual."[19] Kierkegaard reflected on the "upbuilding" enterprise of consciousness. He discovered another way, wholly outside the intellectual part of the self. That way begins with Christ.

As he worked on the religious discourses, Kierkegaard discovered how the two images had grown in him. One had his own name and took its shape in reflection before God. The other was the image of Christ. The image of Christ came to overwhelm him, eclipsing the self-image that had emerged first.

The noteworthy fact for the reader is that Kierkegaard when he writes under his own name writes edifyingly of what he wants to become. He preaches just as much to himself as to the reader. One has to "interiorize" the image of Christ and "appropriate" the Christian tradition. Only in that manner can God get hold of a person and effect the metamorphosis.

During the years 1847–1848, Kierkegaard felt the time was approaching when the "metamorphosis" that he anticipated could happen at any moment, and he held himself prepared in prayer and expectation. A frequently quoted passage from his journals in Easter Week of 1848 refers to such an experience of new birth: when his old being with its melancholy, its tormenting memories, its haughtiness and concealment would fall away, and he could speak freely and directly:

My whole nature is changed. My concealment and reserve [*Indesluttethed*] are broken—I am free to speak.
Great God, grant me grace![20]

On Easter Monday, however, he was already hesitant. This did not yet seem to be the moment when his reserve would finally be broken. His life was to continue unaltered, but the books that he now planned to write would be concerned with the appropriation of Christianity; they were not going to describe it from the outside as Climacus had done, but would describe how it was to be on the inside—at the very center of Christianity. For this task he could not use his own name. Not yet. He was still imagining what it would be. For this reason he settled on the pseudonym Anti-Climacus—the counterpart to Climacus.

VI *Anti-Climacus*

When we say that Anti-Climacus is the antithesis of Climacus, this should not be taken to mean they have different personalities. Anti-Climacus is every bit as intelligent, as humorous and bitingly ironic as is Climacus. But Climacus remains within human intellectuality, while Anti-Climacus rests within faith in Christ. Climacus climbs upward, so to speak, while Anti-Climacus descends.

VII   Training in Christianity

Anti-Climacus speaks from within the sphere that Climacus clinically describes as "religiousness B." He tells what it means to have faith and to have received grace, which is beyond the grasp of the will. Two books are ascribed to Anti-Climacus: one deals with the negative reactions to faith: despair and offense; the other describes the happy encounter between the Paradox and the self, and that book is called *Training in Christianity,* a somewhat unfortunate English translation, since the very point is "training into" (*Indøvelse*) or the appropriation of the Christ image. Here we find Christ depicted as one who was like God but who humbled himself and became like human beings (Phil. 2). The image of God has grown within the self of the mature individual to such an extent that it can now be accepted in faith.

The fact of the Incarnation, that God became a poor and lowly man, can only be recognized by faith. Christ remained "incognito" to the world at large. But he became the prototype for all Christians, whose duty it is to imitate him. In the process of becoming Christians, that is, on the way to faith, the disciples slowly discover the similarities between their path and the stations of the cross.

In this process of becoming a Christian, faith holds fast to the image of Christ, and in the moment of grace, selfhood touches Godhood. Faith is the meeting place where body, soul, and spirit can be overtaken by the Spirit, and where the whole self can come to rest. This is where the seemingly endless dialectical process ends. Grace ends the struggle, unites the finite and the infinite, heals the divided self. God reveals himself in the individual. That is "the Moment."

VIII   The Sickness unto Death

Training in Christianity is Anti-Climacus's description of a happy encounter between the two images: the one we form ourselves and the one we receive from God. The positive response is faith. The negative response, the unhappy encounter, despair, is the subject of *The Sickness unto Death.* For our understanding of Kierkegaard's aesthetic works, *The Sickness unto Death* is a crucial commentary, because it deals with all the stages and their responses in the defense of the ego. Anti-Climacus is a superb psychologist who stresses that the life of an individual must be seen as being composed of both stages and a whole.

The Sickness unto Death has a most deterrent beginning:

Man is spirit. But what is spirit? Spirit is the self. But what is the self? The self is a relation which relates itself to its own self, or it is that in the relation [which accounts for it] that the relation relates itself to its own self; the self is not the relation but [consists in the fact] that the relation relates itself to its own self. Man is a synthesis of the infinite and the finite, of the temporal and the eternal, of freedom and necessity, in short it is a synthesis. A synthesis is a relation between two factors. So regarded, man is not yet a self.[21]

Through careful examination, this seemingly hopeless repetition of words gradually becomes clear. We find here an obscure way of speaking about the images, the image of self and its relation to God, "that Power which constituted the whole relation."

Anti-Climacus follows the formation of self through the five stages. He underscores the possibility of remaining within, as opposed to developing out of, each particular stage. Such stagnation is all too common:

That this condition is nevertheless despair and is rightly so denominated may be taken as an expression for a trait which we may call, in a good sense, the opinionativeness of truth. *Veritas est index sui et falsi.* But this opinionativeness of truth is, to be sure, held in scant honor, as also it is far from being the case that men in general regard relationship to the truth, the fact of standing in relationship to the truth, as the highest good, and it is very far from being the case that they, Socratically, regard being under a delusion as the greatest misfortune; their sensuous nature is generally predominant over their intellectuality. So when a man is supposed to be happy, he imagines that he is happy (whereas viewed in the light of the truth he is unhappy), and in this case he is generally very far from wishing to be torn away from that delusion. On the contrary, he becomes furious, he regards the man who does this

as his most spiteful enemy, he considers it an insult, something
near to murder, in the sense that one speaks of killing joy. What is
the reason of this? The reason is that the sensuous nature and the
psycho-sensuous completely dominate him; the reason is that he
lives in the sensuous categories agreeable/disagreeable, and says
goodbye to truth etc.; the reason is that he is too sensuous to have
the courage to venture to be spirit or to endure it. However vain
and conceited men may be, they have nevertheless for the most
part a very lowly conception of themselves, that is to say, they have
no conception of being spirit, the absolute of all that a man can
be—but vain and conceited they are . . . by way of comparison. In
case one were to think of a house, consisting of cellar, ground-floor
and *premier étage,* so tenanted, or rather so arranged, that it was
planned for a distinction of rank between the dwellers on the several
floors; and in case one were to make a comparison between such a
house and what it is to be a man—then unfortunately this is the
sorry and ludicrous condition of the majority of men, that in their
own house they prefer to live in the cellar. The soulish-bodily synthesis
in every man is planned with the view to being spirit, such is the
building, but the man prefers to dwell in the cellar, that is, in the
determinants of sensuousness. And not only does he prefer to dwell
in the cellar; no, he loves that to such a degree that he becomes
furious if anyone would propose to him to occupy the *bel étage*
which stands empty at his disposition—for in fact he is dwelling
in his own house.

No, to be in error or delusion is (quite un-Socratically) the thing
they fear the least.[22]

Hedonistic aesthetes posit pleasure as their goal; aesthetes
in this category live from moment to moment without reflection,
in a childish manner. Although they do not know it, such aesthetes live in despair, for they have no consciousness of meaning in their life. They have nothing to look forward to except
what their environment can offer them. These persons live in
the immediate, failing to sort out the essential from the unessen-
tial, the important from the trivial, and the helpful from the
harmful.

Next Anti-Climacus gives an example of another sort of
aesthete. These persons do reflect, so much in fact that they
become totally absorbed in dreams and fantasies or obsessed
and infatuated with knowledge. Such romantic people seek

infinity outside themselves and consequently always run away from their own selves. At this stage, we find the Philistines who lose their selves "by getting engaged in all sorts of worldly affairs, by becoming wise about how things go in this world." They distract themselves either by the finite or by the infinite.

It is Anti-Climacus's opinion that these aesthetes do not give enough attention to the categories of possibility and necessity. The dreamers do not recognize necessity and survey—in leisurely fashion—the infinite blur of possibilities; but because they can neither discriminate among them nor attach their self to any one of them, they end by doing nothing and feeling worthless in their despair. On the other hand, we also have the persons who see no ways out of environment and heritage; they can see no possibility of accomplishing what they would like to accomplish; they despair, and their lives become endless series of trivial events.

A true consciousness of one's worth is born with self-reflection. Reflection gives the insight that an individual constitutes something separate from the environment, something in itself. When such consciousness is born, individuals gain a new strength, but also a new chance to despair. With consciousness of self, persons lose their immediacy and—being once removed—begin to judge themselves and their performance. Then two new possibilities for despair appear: "Despair at not willing to be oneself," and "Despair of willing despairingly to be oneself." Here we recognize the situation of the ironists. The despair is not over something exterior, but over oneself. "With every increase in the degree of consciousness, and in proportion to that increase, the intensity of despair increases."

Even though they have committed themselves at one point, persons in the ethical stage may yet fall into the ambush of despair; for since they have formed the consciousness of their "infinite," immortal, eternal, ideal self so weakly, they can relapse into immediacy through various methods of distraction. Either they can keep mindlessly busy all the time—or they can become the type that wallows in self-pity. "This despair is that of weakness, a passive suffering of the self."

Anti-Climacus then proceeds further into the ethical, introducing persons who have decided to become themselves, but have mistaken somebody else's self for their own simply because they cannot recognize the validity of their own self. Thus they despair because they cannot become another self. This type offers innumerable complications. Some resign themselves to the impossibility of becoming themselves. They obscure their chosen standards and alter their self-image and then fall hopelessly into melancholy.

So the despairing self is constantly building nothing but castles in the air, it fights only in the air. All these experimented virtues make a brilliant showing; for an instant they are enchanting like an oriental poem: such self-control, such firmness, such ataraxia, etc., border almost on the fabulous. Yes, they do to be sure; and also at the bottom of it all there is nothing. The self wants to enjoy the entire satisfaction of making itself into itself, of developing itself, of being itself; it wants to have the honor of this poetical, this masterly plan according to which it has understood itself. And yet in the last resort it is a riddle how it understands itself; just at the instant when it seems to be nearest to having the fabric finished it can arbitrarily resolve the whole thing into nothing.[23]

With careful descriptions Anti-Climacus climbs from the "lower," less-developed stages of self-consciousness and their related forms of despair, up to the "higher" forms that are manifested in people who have come to understand that the self is the only important thing in this world. They have knowledge of self and of the world. They have grown independent, so independent that they are able to renounce everything in order to seek out their "selves."

The most high-strung form of despair he calls "demonic." Individuals caught in "demonic" despair are conscious of everything, including "the Power that posited the image." Such despair "wills to obtrude upon this Power in spite, to hold onto it out of malice." Persons in this form of despair deliberately offend God, but at the same time, they are the closest to becoming pleasing to God. "Pride and confidence in self served to free this man from being dependent on anything earthly. Now he is free but at the same time he is in despair. He has tried every possibility and only got negative results."[24]

Anti-Climacus is describing the stage of humor, the point on the way to faith at which individuals gain "imagination," which here means, not dream or illusion, but rejection of reality in favor of something more real. Such persons are ready for the leap because they realize that God is the only meaning of life. But they also hold back, realizing that the leap into faith means an abandonment of intellectuality for self, a death of a self-ordered image in exchange for a resurrected self which they fear. They know that this self-image must die, but they cling to it in despair.

The sickness unto death is despair, but at the same time despair is what propels the spirit, keeping it moving and searching. To sin is to remain in despair. To repent is to realize one's despair and to live in expectancy of God. Of course, deeds that harm others can constitute sin, but because everything relates to God, the chief sin is to cling to one's own despair: "To understand that, humanly, it is his own destruction and then nevertheless to believe in the possibility, is what is meant by faith."

The gravest sin is to despair of the forgiveness of sin, which for Anti-Climacus means the inability to give in to grace, i.e., exchanging one's self-image that was born in rationality, justice, and order for the image of Christ.

IX   *Climacus, S. Kierkegaard and Anti-Climacus: A Conclusion*

Anyone reading only the Anti-Climacus books, *The Sickness unto Death* and *Training in Christianity,* must conclude that Kierkegaard was an irrationalist. But these two are books about psychology, Christian psychology. They form a positive and a negative response to the life cycle. They describe the path Kierkegaard himself traveled. They make important contributions to the understanding of religious experience. As a psychologist, Anti-Climacus knows how terribly important it is for persons to know what they are going to become. It is terribly important that persons do what is right for them and that they do it in their own way—that they feel it is right for them. It is also terribly important for persons to be able to leave what they are doing, to retire. The most difficult times in life require that persons have an image of their essential nature. To feel good and right even when suffering—that is to be Christ-like.

Kierkegaard believed that Christianity had introduced into history a model, a paradigm, to which all people could make their selves conform. It is human defiance that jars this process.

In *The Sickness unto Death*, Anti-Climacus, the psychologist, astutely describes many different states of despair in which spirit and intellect are at odds. The pressures upon intellect generated by culture make people desire too many things, among them to be someone other than themselves. Their spirit cannot accept this pressure. The diagnosis is despair.

Anti-Climacus, the Christian psychologist, tells people that what they actually fail to understand in the various situations of despair is that they do not want to accept the fact that they come from God. He believes that the memory of this makes their spirits unruly. To be divorced from God is the hardest suffering for the human spirit to bear. The message from *Training in Christianity* enters at the point at which the two books coalesce in precisely this situation. It assists each individual reader. Christ stands as the Inviter:

The Moral
And what does all this mean? It means that everyone for himself, in quiet inwardness before God, shall humble himself before what it means in the strictest sense to be a Christian, admit candidly before God how it stands with him, so that he might yet accept the grace which is offered to everyone who is imperfect, that is, to everyone. And then no further; then for the rest let him attend to his work, be glad in it, love his wife, be glad in her, bring up his children with joyfulness, love his fellow men, rejoice in life. If anything further is required of him, God will surely let him understand, and in such case will also help him further; for the terrible language of the Law is so terrifying because it seems as if it were left to man to hold fast to Christ by his own power, whereas in the language of love it is Christ that holds him fast. So if anything further is required of him, God will surely let him understand; but this is required of everyone, that before God he shall candidly humble himself in view of the requirements of ideality. And therefore these should be heard again and again in their infinite significance. To be a Christian has become a thing of naught, mere tomfoolery, something which everyone is as a matter of course, something one slips into more easily than into the most insignificant trick of dexterity.

"But if the Christian life is something so terrible and frightful, how in the world can a person get the idea of accepting it?" Quite simply, and, if you want that too, quite in a Lutheran way: only the consciousness of sin can force one into this dreadful situation—the power on the other side being grace. And in that very instant the Christian life transforms itself and is sheer gentleness, grace, loving-kindness, and compassion. Looked at from any other point of view Christianity is and must be a sort of madness or the greatest horror. Only through the consciousness of sin is there entrance to it, and the wish to enter in by any other way is the crime of lèse-majesté against Christianity.

But sin, the fact that thou and I are sinners (the individual), people have abolished, or they have illicitly abated it, both with respect to life (the domestic, the civic, the ecclesiastical life) and to learning, which has invented the *doctrine* of . . . sin in general. As a compensation they have wanted to help men into Christianity and keep them in it by means of all that about world-history, all that about the gentleness of this teaching, its exalted and profound character, etc., all of which Luther would have called bosh, and which is blasphemy, since it is impudence to wish to fraternize with God and Christ.

Only the consciousness of sin is the expression of absolute respect, and just for this reason, i.e. because Christianity requires absolute respect, it must and will display itself as madness or horror, in order that the qualitative infinite emphasis may fall upon the fact that only consciousness of sin is the way of entrance, is the vision, which, by being absolute respect, can see the gentleness, loving-kindness, and compassion of Christianity.

The simple man who humbly confesses himself to be a sinner—himself personally (the individual)—does not need at all to become aware of all the difficulties which emerge when one is neither simple nor humble. But when this is lacking, this humble consciousness of being personally a sinner (the individual)—yea, if such· a one possessed all human wisdom and shrewdness along with all human talents, it would profit him little. Christianity shall in a degree corresponding to his superiority erect itself against him and transform itself into madness and terror, until he learns either to give up Christianity, or else by the help of what is very far remote from scientific propaedeutic, apologetic, etc.—that is, by the help of the torments of a contrite heart (just in proportion to *his* need of it) learns to enter by the narrow way, through the consciousness of sin, into Christianity.[25]

The invitation is to become Christ's "contemporaries," to let everything in the world be secondary to becoming a Christian.

The two pseudonyms, Climacus and Anti-Climacus, are so close to S. Kierkegaard that often in books and articles about Kierkegaard, their views are not distinguished from his. This is both right and wrong.

"Anti-Climacus has something in common with Climacus, but the difference is in Johannes Climacus' having placed himself so low that he even declares himself not to be a Christian and Anti-Climacus' supposing himself to be a Christian to an extraordinary degree, . . . I considered myself above Joh. Climacus and below Anti-Climacus," wrote Kierkegaard in his Journal.[26]

Climacus is a philosopher who, on the grounds of careful observation and reasoning, propounds the thesis that "truth is subjectivity." Anti-Climacus is a Christian psychologist whose concern is with the appropriation of Christianity by individuals. In the middle is Kierkegaard, the person, suffering the tension. These books are records of his pilgrimage, supporting him from below and above. The books written under his own name, S. Kierkegaard, are "edifying," strengthening the religious. He has not yet stepped forth as a "witness," speaking "in character," speaking directly, in the now. That step was taken with the journal, "The Instant." The moment had come. It had been thoroughly prepared.

CHAPTER 8

Repetition

RELIGIOUS experience is nothing to trifle with. It is dangerous. It touches a live wire in the center of human beings and sends them off. Nobody knew that better than Kierkegaard and that is why he was so infinitely careful in describing and defining what he considered to be the real thing. He was absolutely clear on the fact that it was real. First and foremost, he himself had experienced it, and second, from reading and observing he knew that other people shared the experience. Just as there is no way to command people to stop dreaming, so is there no way to demand that people stop having religious experiences. It is part and parcel of human experience, of "existing."

In order to distinguish what for him marked the truly religious experience, Kierkegaard hit upon the category of "repetition." He wrote a novel that has "Repetition" as its title and its theme.[1] This book has been praised as containing the finest, most poetic writing that Kierkegaard ever produced, but it has also been regarded as something of a failure, because it is reported that he changed the ending when he heard of Regine's engagement to Mr. Schlegel.

We can be sure that Kierkegaard would never have published this book had he not been convinced that it contained "the real thing." This real experience, however, is not easily accessible. We encounter two characters in this novel who have both had heightened existential experiences: the one resembles religious experience; the other is genuine religious experience.

The first character is by no means a fool or a simpleton. He is a sophisticated aesthete, and he describes his levitation, his *Himmelsreise*, like this:

I got up in the morning feeling uncommonly well. This sense of well-being increased out of proportion to all analogy during the

195

forenoon. Precisely at one o'clock I was at the highest peak and surmised the dizzy maximum which is not indicated on any scale of well-being, not even on the poetical thermometer. The body had lost all its earthly heaviness, it was as though I had no body, just for the reason that every function enjoyed its completest satisfaction, every nerve tingled with delight on its own account and on account of the whole, while every pulsation, as a disquietude in the organism, only suggested and reported the sensuous delight of the instant. My gait became a glide, not like the flight of a bird that cleaves the air and leaves the earth behind, but like the billows of the wind over a field of grain, like the yearning bliss of the cradling waves of the sea, like the dreamy gliding of the clouds. My very being was transparent, like the depths of the sea, like the self-contented silence of the night, like the quiet monologue of midday. Every feeling of my soul composed itself to rest with melodious resonance. Every thought proffered itself freely, every thought proffered itself with festal gladness and solemnity, the silliest conceit not less than the richest idea. Every impression was surmised before it arrived and was awakened within me. The whole of existence seemed to be as it were in love with me, and everything vibrated in preordained *rapport* with my being. In me all was ominous, and everything was enigmatically transfigured in my microcosmic bliss, which was able to transform into its own likeness all things, even the observations which were most disagreeable and tiresome, even disgusting sights and the most fatal collisions. When precisely at one o'clock I was at the highest peak, where I surmised the ultimate attainment, something suddenly began to chafe one of my eyes, whether it was an eye-lash, a mote, a speck of dust, I do not know; but this I know, that in that selfsame instant I toppled down almost into the abyss of despair—a thing which everyone will understand who had been so high up as I was, and when he was at that point has been engaged with the generic question how nearly absolute contentment can be attained. Since that time I have given up every hope of ever feeling myself content absolutely and in all ways, have given up the hope I once cherished, not indeed of being absolutely content at all times, but at least at particular instants, even if these units of instants were not more numerous than, as Shakespeare says, "a tapster's arithmetic was capable of summing up."[2]

It was a marvelous experience, but "a mote, a speck of dust" made it topple. Since then he has lived with a memory of that druglike morning, but it is intertwined with the memory of the despair that followed, and he has abandoned the search for "absolute contentment." He settles in the ironic position.

The other character has a very different kind of journey. When the marvelous experience of falling in love comes to him, he accepts it body, soul, and spirit. It transforms him. He is lifted to the heavens. Yet he too comes tumbling down into despair. His spirit begins to wage war. Yet he refuses to become "demoniacal," telling himself that his suffering is only a figment of his imagination. He struggles on, searching for a model, a person who has experienced something similar and will not lie to him. He finds Job, and during his months of struggle he holds on to Job in order to find meaning for his existence, to wring it out of God. The outcome is "repetition," which is a truly religious mode of living.

The Danish word *"Gentagelse"* means repetition but has a very special nuance, which the English equivalent is too general to catch. It means "retake"—in the sense that a film director can order a retake. The scene is going to be played again, but the positions, the lighting, the accents are changed; it becomes not just a dull repetition but a "double take" on the situation, which captures the actors because suddenly the structure of the whole play becomes evident: it fills the scene with what has been before and apprehension of what will come in the future. The unity between past and future makes the scene revelatory, and the actors come through with new energy.

Repetition was published the same day as *Fear and Trembling*: October 16, 1843. In *Fear and Trembling* we were exposed to the intensity of the religious, to its suspension of the ethical, to the dreadful silence, to Abraham who made the double movement into faith, and to the God who acts. We witnessed the abandonment of the rational for the paradoxical. The author of *Fear and Trembling*, Johannes de Silentio, openly gives us the whole mysterious story without taking away its awesome majesty. Johannes di Silentio, however, is himself a highly reflective person who stands at the border of the religious. He can admire Abraham, yet he cannot follow him. We left Johannes as a knight of resignation, praising Abraham, but in need of understanding. Abraham represents to him the highest, but there is an unbridgeable gulf between them.

We have every reason to consider *Repetition* to be the dialectical counterpart to *Fear and Trembling* and to expect that in this book we shall find an opposite inroad to the religious that must be considered along with the message of the double movement "in the power of the absurd."

The subtitle of *Repetition* is *An Essay in Experimental Psychology*, which indicates that we are aligned with Vigilius Haufniensis, Frater Taciturnus, and Anti-Climacus. The author here is Constantine Constantius, familiar to us from *Stages* in which he figured as the character who ventured to arrange a perfect banquet. He is the kind of person who will go to any length to prepare for a situation that might render some interesting insight into human behavior. Not a young man, he has considerable experience and knowledge and likes to reflect, pen in hand, on whatever comes his way. His speech at the banquet revealed him as well-read both in literature and in philosophy; as an observer of women, he made the point that though woman is aesthetically very lovely, regarded ethically she becomes merely "jest." For a man to become involved with a woman inevitably results in utter confusion. To illustrate the point he told a comic anecdote about a woman who tells her lover she will not be able to endure his going away on a long journey; she will die of sorrow. Yet when he anxiously returns, she is not only not dead, but is happily married to another.

This short story is the plot of *Repetition*, though everything is rearranged, as is the poet's license. Thus, it is another version of the love stories described in Kierkegaard's works. What Constantine had told in a few rapid lines in *Stages* is the full-blown plot in *Repetition*. The slower tempo here increases the tragic impact, even though the events are still comic. We cannot dissociate ourselves from the real suffering that the episode inflicts on the young man. We notice similarities with Frater Taciturnus's experiment in *Stages*, but the differences are quite marked. This time the structure of the story telling is conventional in the sense that it has a beginning, a middle, and an end.

There are only two characters: Constantine and the young man. Possibly we have already met the young man. He could be the same intelligent but immature and inexperienced young man who was the first speaker at the banquet in *Stages;* there he spoke of woman as ridiculous, though he admitted that he did not really know what he was talking about, for he had never had the experience of being in love. Here in *Repetition,* however, he is immersed in that experience and in its consequences. That *Repetition* was written earlier than *Stages* does not prove that the two characters are not the same. On the contrary, they are the same—simply another example of Kierkegaard's playing with "marionettes," his way of employing theater. In the aesthetic stage there is no "time," no necessary development, only possibility.

Both Constantine and the young man speak in the first person. Throughout the book Constantine, the commentator and experimenter, remains within the aesthetic category, while the young man—because of the love story—suddenly "leaps" out of that category and begins speaking and acting in a manner that Constantine cannot understand. One obvious point of the book is the confusion between the two, their "heterogeneity," as, increasingly, they talk on different levels. The difference does not result from the fact that an older man is opposed to an inexperienced youth; Kierkegaard does not use this device—so common as a source of misunderstanding in ordinary fiction. The difference lies in the fact that through an experience of love that shakes the foundation of his being, the young man soars beyond the older man, who will not allow this to happen to him.

The motto of *Repetition* wonderfully expresses the ambiguity that arises because of the different levels: "On wild trees the flowers are fragrant; on cultivated trees the fruits." At first, we would assume that the cultivated tree is the versatile Constantine Constantius, who writes with such sophistication; but we also know that Kierkegaard intended to illustrate the futility of such an aesthetic approach to life. A tree has to bear fruit; the process involves painful inward movement. In the story, it is the young man who develops and produces the fruit. Constantine can only detect the fragrance, not taste the real thing.

The book has two parts. In the first part, Constantine is the main spokesman. The book opens with him writing a small essay on the theme of "repetition." He is enthusiastic; he sees repetition as a decisive expression for what the Greeks called "recollection," but with a difference. The Greeks taught that all knowledge was recollection. Modern philosophy, he thinks, will teach that "the whole of life is a repetition." The difference:

Repetition and recollection are the same movement, only in opposite directions; for what is recollected has been, is repeated backwards, whereas repetition properly so called is recollected forwards.[3]

A little later on he states that it takes courage to will repetition:

If God himself had not willed repetition, the world would never have come into existence. He would either have followed the light plans of hope, or he would have recalled it all and conserved it in recollection. This he did not do, therefore the world endures, and it endures for a fact that it is a repetition. Repetition is reality, and it is the seriousness of life.[4]

Intrigued by the idea of repetition, Constantine is reminded of an experiment. A young man recently came to him to confide that he was in love. He needed "a confidant in whose presence he could talk aloud to himself."[5] Constantine describes the young man as glowing with love:

As a grape when it is at the point of perfection becomes transparent and clear, while the juice bubbles through its fine veins, as the husk of a fruit breaks when the fruit ripens to all its fullness, so did love break forth almost visibly in his being. I could hardly forbear to snatch a sidewise glance at him now and then, almost as though I were in love with him; for such a youth is as alluring a sight as a young girl.[6]

Constantine finds himself almost afraid, when he sees what effect the love affair has upon this basically melancholy man who paces the floor, reciting a love poem over and over. His fears prove reasonable; the young couple has hardly become engaged when the young man breaks off the relationship. Observing him, Constantine has the impression that the young man had at once "leapt over the whole of life." The young woman whom he worshiped suddenly became a burden to him. His melancholy increased with every meeting. He made her unhappy and felt guilty because of her unhappiness—even though he had nothing to confess to her. He could not give a reason for his own unhappiness. He used his whole poetic ability to entertain her.

In his analysis, Constantine describes what went wrong:

> The young girl was not his love, she was the occasion of awakening the primitive poetic talent within him and making him a poet . . . she had made him a poet, and thereby she had signed her own death warrant.[7]

The young man suffers. His dilemma involves being unable to go through with the partnership, the dependence required in marriage. He cannot realize such an ideal, nor can he imagine entering a relationship that—from the beginning—is founded on a mismatch and not on a match made in heaven, on the ideal. Thus he is quickly transported into limbo. He is an outsider, an exception. He stands outside the universal.

The psychologist Constantine coins a phrase for the young man's inability to compromise and just get married: "His soul lacked the elasticity of irony." The phrase is twice repeated. Constantine first makes his observation when the young man declares that he is unable to go through with the marriage, and he finds cause to repeat it when the young man balks at a proposed plan that would make the young woman detest him and result in her breaking the engagement herself. This plan, which is Constantine's, would free the young man from her, while allowing him to retain her as his "poetic Genius." Going through with such deception would require irony and silence about the actual motive. But the young man is unable to pronounce "irony," or, as Constantine puts it, in a clever metaphor, to speak "thieves' Latin." Much too serious, he will not deceive. He flees the scene and disappears. Nobody knows his whereabouts. Maybe he has committed suicide.

At this point Constantine resumes his essay on "repetition":

> The dialectic of repetition is easy; for what is repeated has been, otherwise it could not be repeated, but precisely the fact that it has been gives to repetition the character of novelty. When the

Greeks said that all knowledge is recollection they affirmed that all that is has been; when one says that life is a repetition one affirms that existence which has been now becomes. When one does not possess the categories of recollection or of repetition the whole of life is resolved into a void and empty noise. Recollection is the pagan life-view, repetition is the modern life-view; repetition is the *interest* of metaphysics, and at the same time the interest upon which metaphysics founders; repetition is the solution contained in every ethical view, repetition is a *conditio sine qua non* of every dogmatic problem.[8]

This passage impresses more than it enlightens us. Our confusion grows when we learn that Constantine's next move is to experiment with "Gentagelse" by taking a trip to Berlin, where he had been once before and where he had thoroughly enjoyed himself. During his first visit to Berlin, he especially liked to go to the theater. He was young, and the theater gave him an insight into his own inner development. The theater made him see his possibilities as an emerging personality:

Surely there is no young man with any imagination who has not at one time been captivated by the enchantment of the theater, and desired to be himself carried away into the midst of that fictitious reality in order to see and hear himself as an *alter ego,* to disperse himself among the innumerable possibilities which diverge from himself, and yet in such a way that every diversity is in turn a single self. Of course it is only at a very early age such a desire can express itself. Only the imagination is awake to this dream of personality, all the other faculties are still sound asleep. In such a dream of imagination the individual is not a real figure but a shadow, or rather the real figure is invisibly present and therefore is not content with casting one shadow, but the individual has a multiplicity of shadows, all of which resemble him and for the moment have an equal claim to be accounted himself. The personality is not yet discovered, its energy announces itself only in the passion of possibility; for it is true in the life of the spirit as it is in the case of many plants that the germinal sprout comes last.[9]

Suddenly we hear Constantine speaking about the image-forming process, about the importance of heroes and models for the young imagination to test its empathy. We pay attention because we feel we are very near the heart of the Kierkegaardian psychology. As always, Constantine gets carried away, but he returns to the "as yet unformed" personality, which he calls "the cryptic individual":

So does the possibility of the individual stray at random amongst its own possibilities, discovering now one and now another. But the possibility of the individual does not want merely to be heard; it is not merely an onrushing force like the wind, it also assumes shape, therefore at the same time it wants to be seen. Every possibility of the individual is therefore a sounding shadow. The cryptic individual no more believes in the great noisy feelings than he does in the crafty whisper of malice, no more in the blissful exultation of joy than in the infinite sigh of sorrow; the individual only wants to hear and see with pathos, but, be it observed, to hear and see himself. However it is not really himself he wants to hear. That is not practicable. At that instant the cock crows, and the figures of the twilight flee away, the voices of the night fall silent. If they continue, then we are in an entirely different domain, where all this goes on under the alarming observation of moral responsibility, then we are on the border of the demoniacal. In order not to get an impression of his real self, the cryptic individual requires that the environment be as light and ephemeral as the figures, as the frothy effervescence of the words which sound without echo. Such an environment is the theatrical stage, which for this reason precisely is appropriate to the shadow-play of the cryptic individual.[10]

Constantine, then, is a person with great insight, and we catch ourselves wondering how he can be childish enough to try this experiment with repetition by going back to Berlin. The whole trip is a disaster. Exterior changes immediately sidetrack him. Nothing is quite the same and "the rank weed of memory strangled every thought at birth." He gets bored and annoyed with the concept of repetition. All he learns from the whole undertaking is that the older people become, the less content they are with life.

So we find ourselves at the end of Part One of the book without any notion of what repetition can be. Constantine is bored and now patterns his life after the advice we found in "The Rotation Method." The young man may, or may not, have committed suicide. The idea of repetition has been strangled to death by the thought process.

It is when we turn to Part Two that we discover how carefully we have been prepared for what happens next. It is Part Two that bears the title "Repetition." What has gone before was background. The focus changes to the young man, who had disappeared, causing Constantine to fear he had committed suicide. He had not. But the burden of his love for the woman and his surprise discovery of self had become intolerable to him. He fled the country. He deserted.

We find him in Sweden, living in utter despair. He writes to Constantine, but begs him not to answer. Actually, he has come to despise Constantine and his schemes, but he needs him as a confidant. Constantine and his style of living once struck him as exemplary. The young man knows that Constantine will read with interest without being "ethically severe."

About once a month Constantine receives one of these letters. They describe how the young man moves rapidly inward while outwardly remaining quiet: eating, drinking, keeping order around him, sleeping by day, and lying awake at night.

The first letter discusses Constantine's plan, which he admits was aesthetically flawless:

Your plan was capital, indeed peerless. Even yet at certain moments I grasp like a child at the heroic shape you once held up to my admiring gaze with the declaration that it was my future destiny, the heroic shape which was to have made me a hero if I had had the strength to assume it. At that time it carried me away with all the power of illusion into a complete imaginative intoxication.[11]

But the young man was not "the artist" who would be capable of sustaining this "heroic" role. He fled in silence, and by doing so, he lost his "self." He signs the letter: "Your devoted nameless friend."

The next letter reveals that now he passionately reads the book of Job, finding his only solace in the figure of Job. Job defied his friends' advice and stood up for himself, saying: Not guilty. Likewise, the young man wants to maintain his own innocence.

He could not marry, and therefore he left her. Why, then, must she be in the right in the eyes of the world, and he in the wrong?

My love cannot express itself in a marriage. If I were to marry her, she would be crushed. Perhaps the possibility of marriage appeared alluring to her. I cannot help that—so it was to me. The very instant reality comes into question, all is lost, it is then too late.[12]

Constantine seems to have been wrong in his opinion that the young man was not really in love with the young woman, that she was merely the occasion for his love. He is in love, and it is out of sympathy for her that he cannot go through with the marriage. That would have killed her. But perhaps, by deserting her, he has killed her in any case. Reflection upon the cause of this sudden change in his life shows the young man that Constantine can no longer remain his hero. By presenting that devious plan, he has forfeited his heroic role. But Job! He is in the right position. Everything that he loved and valued most was taken away from him.

Just as Johannes de Silentio in *Fear and Trembling* tries to understand Abraham, the young man here clings to Job. He cannot quote him, but he appropriates him. Job is human. "He lies upon the confines of poetry. Nowhere in the world has the passion of pain found such an expression."[13] Job claimed to be right and by doing so he made himself "an exception to all the juridical interpretations of his time." Job did not take a false expression into his mouth. By persevering before God he earned his right to become a hero.

What Job lets the young man discover is that God cannot be conceived under ethical categories. Such attempts make God a tyrant. The greatness of Job as a model is that he did not cry out against God or abandon him. Nor did he become "demoniacal," saying that God was right though in his innermost being he felt that he was right himself. No, Job held on to the claim that he was right, and then he waited and waited for God to speak.

... Job does not tranquilize like a hero of faith, but he provides temporary relief. Job represents as it were the whole weighty plea presented on man's behalf in the great suit between God and man, the prolix and dreadful process of justice which had its ground

in the fact that Satan raised a suspicion against Job, and which
ends with the explanation that the whole thing is a trial of probation.

This category, "trial of probation," is neither aesthetic, nor ethical,
nor dogmatic, it is entirely transcendent. Not until it is known to
be a trial could a place be found for it in a dogmatic work. But
so soon as this knowledge is at hand the elasticity of trial is
weakened, and the category is really a different one. This category
is absolutely transcendent and places man in a purely personal
relationship of contradiction to God, in such a relationship that he
cannot rest content with any explanation at second hand.[14]

While this testing takes place, ethics falters, becomes helpless and insufficient. The self floats on the deep, deep waters
of the unknown. Even the category of "faith" does not catch it:

Job is not a hero of faith, he gives birth with prodigious pains
to the category of "trial"—precisely because he is so developed that
he does not possess this category in childish immediacy.[15]

Here lies the difference between Job and Abraham. The hero
of faith, Abraham, the model in *Fear and Trembling*, was naïve.
Abraham made the double movement from resignation to faith
without resistance to God. He resigned. Faith took him over.
He moved again. Likewise, "the knight of faith" acted alertly at
every moment. These provide two examples of the positive, the
happy encounter with the paradoxical. In *Repetition*, the model,
Job, has a strongly built self-image, a reflective consciousness,
and is not like the primeval Abraham. Job is a religious poet.
The encounter with God is a confrontation, and Job is put on
"trial of probation."

In the letter of January 13, the young man indicates that he
has understood "for himself" the case of Job. "When God passes
judgement a man loses himself and forgets the pain in the love
which is intent upon educating." Job won his case eternally because he lost *before God*, not before any temporal court or
human judgments. Thus Job was blessed and received everything back in double measure. Job held out in his plea. God
acted, and Job was "blessed."

In the February letter, the young man alludes to Job on his
ash pile: "Here I sit. On the plea of innocent." He expects a

thunderstorm that will transform him. He has resigned his self. He is ready. If it means that he shall marry the young woman, he will do so.

At this point Constantine enters the remark that he is no longer able to follow what his young friend is writing. They seem to speak different languages. Constantine had been able to foresee a religious crisis and to describe how the young man would move closer to the border of the marvelous. But when the young man actually arrives and crosses the border, he becomes ludicrous to Constantine.

The final letter, dated May 31, is jubilant. The crisis is over. A miracle has occurred. The young woman has married another man, and the young man is free. He has his self again. "I am again unified." He moves again, having gained immensely in inwardness. He has earned his right to be a poet. He has got back his self doubly increased:

Is there not then a repetition? Did I not get everything doubly restored? Did I not get myself again, precisely in such a way that I must doubly feel its significance? . . . I am again myself, the machinery has been set in motion. The snares in which I was entangled have been hewn asunder, the magic spell which bewitched me so that I could not return to myself has now been broken.[16]

The sympathy that the young man had felt for the young woman and the responsibility for her well-being have not blown away. She still means everything to him. But the situation has entirely changed. He can move again. He has the freedom to be himself, to be a poet. Not by fraud did this happen, but by trial and blessing.

A Second Glance at the Experiment in Literature

In *Repetition*, Kierkegaard draws heavily upon his own experience with Regine. This was the experience that made *him* a poet, and here he tells what he means by saying so. The shock effect of the experience was tremendous. His life was as before; yet everything was changed. Nobody understood better than Kierkegaard that, from the outside, the whole affair looked like a rather comic story. Yet he knew the passion involved. During the whole testing period everything had been on trial "before God." That Job had been with him we understand not only from his handling of the Job story here in *Repetition,* but also from his use of it in the sermon in "Ultimatum," and in one of the early edifying discourses, "The Lord Gave and the Lord Hath Taken Away, Blessed Be the Name of the Lord," which treats the Job story with an empathy very similar to that bestowed upon the Abraham story in *Fear and Trembling.*

If we turn to "A Glance at a Contemporary Effort in Danish Literature," in *Concluding Unscientific Postscript,* we find that in this review Climacus stresses the fact that the suspension of the ethical is prolonged in *Repetition,* compared with the Abraham story in *Fear and Trembling,* and that here the young man returns to duty, but "retains an everlasting impression of the fearfulness" through which he has gained "imagination raised to the second power."

Slowly we understand that Kierkegaard is really describing something that cannot readily be put into words. In *Fear and Trembling* and in *Repetition,* Kierkegaard, the religious poet, takes care that we will not forget the fearfulness of entering that highest category and that we will not confuse it either with sentimentality or with ethical commandments. There is much too much so-called religion around that should be exposed for what it is: deception and wishful thinking. But there is also the real thing, which Kierkegaard knows and which he wishes to transmit. The only way it can be done is through "midwifery," or to use another metaphor from *On Authority and Revelation:*

. . . it is one thing to be a physician beside a sickbed, and another thing to be a sick man who leaps out of his bed by becoming an author, communicating bluntly the symptoms of his disease. Perhaps he may be able to express and expound the symptoms of his illness in far more glowing colors than does the physician when he describes them; for the fact that he knows no resource, no salvation, gives him a peculiar passionate elasticity in comparison with the consoling talk of the physician who knows what expedients to use. But in spite of that there remains the decisive qualitative difference between a sick man and a physician. And this difference is precisely the same decisive *qualitative difference* between being a premise-author and an essential author.[17]

This passage and many others like it help us to understand the amazing end of *Repetition,* which is a postscript to the reader. In it Constantine describes the whole story as his own experiment, as his "double take" as an author. He says of the young man:

He has retained an ideal conception of the whole love affair, to which he is able to give any expression whatever, but as sentimentally defined, because he possesses no factual evidence. He has therefore a fact of consciousness, or rather he has no fact of consciousness but a dialectical elasticity which will make him productive in the realm of sentiment. While this productivity remains his utmost attainment, he is sustained by something unutterably religious. Thus in the earlier letters, in some of them especially, the movement came much closer to a really religious conclusion; but the instant the temporary suspension is lifted he gets himself again, now however as a poet, and the religious sinks down to the bottom, that is, it remains as an unutterable substratum.[18]

The religious did not break through. It sank down—becoming a substratum. This man became the physician, the clinician, who can diagnose "the sickness" and describe the symptoms. He split himself into a Constantine who is trying to describe the experience, using familiar tools, saying what the term "repetition" means in Greek philosophy, what it should be in contemporary philosophy, what it would perhaps look like as a psychological experiment. But the book fails, and we fail the book if we do not comprehend that what Kierkegaard is trying to do is also to transmit the experience of the "patient," the young man, who was healed.

It becomes quite clear if we read the book of Job that the friends of Job are "levelers"—people who explain the experience too quickly and too wisely. Job, however, remains in suspense. He does not let his position be translated into wisdom. The stance of the author to the book of Job is that of a "genuine" author, the true poet.

In *Repetition* Job is appropriated by the young man, who repeats his trial. He affirms and affirms and affirms possibility without accepting actuality. If the young man had been religious, then he might have gone right ahead like an Abraham.

However, since he was not like Abraham but like Job, he remains in affirming possibility. What we witness in *Repetition* is the birth of the religious poet, and repetition means—to use a metaphor that is familiar yet not readily appropriated—a burning bush that is not consumed.

Dolan Hubbard

633-8796

201 Elm Street

Salisbury N.C.

Notes and References

Chapter One

1. The Danish *"Sandhedsvidne"* is a rather common word, without the somewhat pretentious ring of "witness for/to the truth." It means a person who tells the truth, or who has the irresistible urge to tell the truth, or who loves to tell the truth, especially when it shocks or even hurts others. For S.K. truth was more than wisdom; and just as the philosopher was a lover of wisdom (Greek, *philos* + *sophia*), so the Christian was to have a passion for the truth and with his life to be a witness to it. "Every time a witness for the truth makes the truth a heart-felt matter of inwardness (and this essentially is the business of the witness for the truth), every time a genius with primitive force makes the truth inwardly vivid—then also the established order will be offended in him." *Training in Christianity*, p. 88. This book was written in 1848 but published by S.K. in 1850. Later S.K. wished to eliminate its pseudonymous author (Anti-Climacus), its three prefaces, and its "Moral"—which goes to show how heavily the burden of his insight weighed upon him and how he developed with it (see below, chapters 3 and 7).

2. Søren Kierkegaard, *Armed Neutrality* and *An Open Letter*, Howard V. Hong and Edna H. Hong, eds. and trans. (Bloomington, Ind. and London: University of Indiana Press, 1968), p. 71. This compilation from his Journals and Papers is useful in order to understand how S.K. resolved the question of what to become: poet or pastor?

3. Ibid., pp. 90ff., 108ff., 117ff., 124, 169 give pertinent citations concerning S.K.'s relationship to Bishop Mynster.

4. One such penetrating study is Karl Löwith's *From Hegel to Nietzsche: The Revolution in Nineteenth-Century Thought*, David E. Green, trans. (Garden City, N.Y.: Anchor Books, 1967). Löwith has pointed out the difference between, on the one hand, S.K.'s interpretation of becoming a Christian, and Hegel's rational interpretation and Goethe's humanistic interpretation, on the other. Of Goethe's words, 'We shall all grow gradually from a Christianity of word and faith to a Christianity of disposition and deed," Löwith writes (p. 19), "The contrasting attempts of Nietzsche and Kierke-

gaard, once more to force the decision between paganism and Christianity, are determined reactions to that amorphous Christianity represented by Hegel and Goethe."

5. W. H. Auden published "Knight of Doleful Countenance," *The New Yorker* 44 (1968): 141 ff.; Genêt: "Letter from Paris," *The New Yorker* 40 (1964): 170; John Updike: "The Fork," *The New Yorker* 42 (1966): 115 ff.; Julian N. Hartt: "Christian Freedom Reconsidered: The Case of Kierkegaard," *Harvard Theological Review* 60 (1967): 133–44; Geoffrey Clive: "The Sickness unto Death in the Underworld: A Study of Nihilism," *Harvard Theological Review* 51 (1958): 135–67.

On the "Kierkegaard and——" theme there are articles aplenty, of which a few can be mentioned here: "Auden and Kierkegaard," by Edward Callan, *The Christian Scholar* 48 (1965): 211–23; "Goethe and Kierkegaard," by August Closs, *Modern Language Quarterly* 10 (1949): 264–80; "Herzen and Kierkegaard," by R. M. Davison, *Slavic Review* 25 (1966): 191–209; "Kierkegaard and Schweitzer: An Essay in Comparison and Contrast," by E. M. Dodd, *London Quarterly and Holborn Review* 170 (1945): 148–53; "Kafka and Kierkegaard: A Reassessment," by Brian F. M. Edwards, *German Life and Letters* 20 (1967): 218–25; "Observations on Unamuno and Kierkegaard," by Oscar A. Fasel, *Hispania* 38 (1955): 443–50. Ronald Grimsley takes the prize with: "Kierkegaard and Descartes," *Journal of the History of Philosophy* 4 (1966): 31–41; "Kierkegaard and Leibniz," *Journal of the History of Ideas* 26 (1965): 383–96; "Kierkegaard and Scribe," *Revue de littérature comparée* 38 (1964): 512–30; "Kierkegaard, Vigny, and 'the Poet,'" *Revue de littérature comparée* 34 (1960): 52–80; "Rousseau and Kierkegaard," *Cambridge Journal* 7 (1954): 615–26. "Isak Dinesen, Søren Kierkegaard, and the Present Age," by Eric O. Johannesson, *Books Abroad* 36 (1962): 20–24; "Kierkegaard and Sartre," by Howard Johnson, *American-Scandinavian Review* 35 (1947): 220–25; "Hume and Kierkegaard," by Richard H. Popkin, *Journal of Religion* 31 (1951): 274–81; "Ibsen, Nietzsche, and Kierkegaard," by Angelo S. Rappoport, *New Age* 3 (1908): 21 ff.; "Kierkegaard and Shakespeare," by James E. Ruoff, *Comparative Literature* 20 (1968): 343–54.

A study on "Kierkegaard and Nabokov" should be a fascinating project, for Nabokov as a writer also hides, yet insists that his readers know his entire body of writing because he makes constant allusions to individual works. Indeed, there seems to be no clue to Nabokov's method if one forgets S.K.'s influence.

6. The one theologian of these who perhaps have reached farthest

outside the theological ghetto is Martin Buber with his often quoted I-Thou concept. In *Two Types of Faith: A Study of the Interpretation of Judaism and Christianity* (New York: Harper & Brothers, Torchbook, 1961), Buber quotes S.K. (p. 167) in order to illustrate the way in which S.K. has understood *emunah* (Hebrew for "faith"), another kind of faith than the Pauline *pistis* (Greek for "faith").

7. It is understandable that positivist philosophy would have no interest in a philosopher who stresses the paradoxical so strongly as S.K. does. During the early part of the twentieth century, he all but disappeared from philosophical discourse in the Anglo-American academic community. He reappeared when Wittgenstein in his later years began to speak in a similar vein, and the seriousness of his choice of expression became better understood. See Stanley Cavell: *Must We Mean What We Say?* (New York: Scribner's, 1969), the chapters "The Availability of Wittgenstein's Later Philosophy" (pp. 44–72) and "Kierkegaard's 'On Authority and Revelation'" (pp. 163–79).

8. The existentialists stress the difference between *"Dasein"* and *"Existenz."* Karl Jaspers puts his emphasis on *"Existenz,"* and Heidegger centers his investigation on *"Dasein."* S.K. uses the terms *"Eksistens"* and *"Tilværelse"* but does not give priority to either as being "higher" than the the other. See Ralph Henry Johnson: *The Concept of Existence in the Concluding Unscientific Postscript* (The Hague: Martinus Nijhoff, 1972).

9. For a study of "self," see Mark C. Taylor, *Kierkegaard's Pseudonymous Authorship: A Study of Time and Self* (Princeton, N.J.: Princeton University Press, 1975). The Israeli scholar Adi Schmuëli (*Kierkegaard and Consciousness*, Princeton, N.J.: Princeton University Press, 1971) boldly discusses a key concept in S.K.'s writings using the contemporary "consciousness raising" as an interpretative translation.

10. Norman O. Brown in his *Life Against Death: The Psychoanalytical Meaning of History* (Middletown, Conn.: Wesleyan University Press, 1959) comments (on p. 109): "Kierkegaard speaks like a psychoanalyst when he says, 'Time does not really exist without unrest; it does not exist for dumb animals who are absolutely without anxiety.'" Sigmund Freud does not seem to know of S.K.; in *The Problem of Anxiety,* he makes no mention of S.K.'s *The Concept of Dread,* nor of his *The Sickness unto Death.*

11. Constantino V. Riccardi, *Christ and Freedom: A Christocentric Analysis of Suicidal Behavior* has recently (1972) surveyed thinkers

who have dealt—well or badly—with the topic of suicide, including S.K.

12. Northrop Frye, *Anatomy of Criticism* (Princeton, N.J.: Princeton University Press, 1957), pp. 15, 313, 345. This influential work of criticism is perhaps the best tool for students of literature trying to grasp the scope of S.K.'s aesthetic works, which most other methods tend to atomize.

13. Jens Himmelstrup has compiled the terminological dictionary to S.K.'s *Samlede Værker* (Copenhagen: Gyldendal, 1962). Niels Thulstrup has edited *Kierkegaardiana*, the publication of Søren Kierkegaard Selskabet (Copenhagen: Munksgaard, 1955–69). Gregor Malantschuk has written the definitive study of S.K.'s dialectics: *Kierkegaard's Thought*, ed. and tr. by Hong and Hong (Princeton, N.J.: Princeton University Press, 1971).

14. The three original translators were Walter Lowrie, David Swenson, and Alexander Dru. Of these, Lowrie pulled the heaviest load (see Selected Bibliography, p. 225). Lee M. Capel did a magnificent piece of work on *The Concept of Irony*. The job of translating is now carried out by Howard and Edna Hong who won the National Book Award for their first volume, *Kierkegaard's Journals and Papers*, and who deserve maximal support to enable them to finish all seven volumes. Two have been completed; but if all are not finished, the worth of the project is lost, since S.K.'s strength lies in the consistency with which he works his themes over and over.

15. See F. J. Billeskov Jansen: *Studier i Søren Kierkegaards Literære Kunst* (Copenhagen: Rosenkilde og Bagger, 1951), which emphasizes the two styles of S.K.

16. The introduction to *On Authority and Revelation, The Book on Adler*, Walter Lowrie, trans. (Princeton, N.J.: Princeton University Press; also New York: Harper & Brothers, Torchbooks, 1966), pp. 3–11.

17. Søren Kierkegaard, *The Present Age and Of the Difference between a Genius and an Apostle*, tr. by Alexander Dru, Introduction by Walter Kaufmann (New York and Evanston, Ill.: Harper & Row, Publishers, Inc., Torchbooks, 1962). All quotations refer to this edition.

18. Ibid., p. 33.

19. Ibid., p. 43.

20. Ibid., p. 40.

21. Ibid., p. 83.

22. For the distinction between a genius and an apostle, see second essay, ibid., pp. 89–108.

23. *The Corsair* is referred to in *The Present Age* as "the dog," see ibid., p. 66; see also below, chapter 3.

24. Danish *Øjeblikket,* sometimes also translated "The Instant."

25. See Chapter 3, p. 70.

Chapter Two

1. H. C. Andersen's autobiography, *Mit Livs Eventyr* (Copenhagen, 1855).

2. H. C. Andersen: *Kun en Spillemand,* first published in 1836. See *Andersen's Works* (Boston: Houghton Mifflin, 1898). "En Comœdie i det Grønne" was the play that satirized S.K.

3. *From the Papers of One Still Living*: Published against his will by S. Kierkegaard, 1838. So for instance Walter Lowrie, in *Kierkegaard* (p. 92), explains the title with S.K.'s surprise that he had survived his father (New York and Evanston, Ill.: Harper & Row, Publishers, Torchbook 1962). Emanuel Hirsch has given special attention to this book (which is usually neglected) in his *Kierkegaardstudien,* 2 vols. (Gütersloh, 1930), 1: p. 10 ff. G. Malantschuk in *Kierkegaard's Thought,* stresses the consistency in S.K.'s thinking that is apparent from the very beginning: pp. 182 ff.

4. S.K. has written much on the idea of the genius (Danish, *Geni*). The most important passages of what he has to say are to be found in this pamphlet, in *The Concept of Dread,* and in *The Difference between a Genius and an Apostle.* Genius is an innate power, *ingenium.*

5. See above, p. 30.

6. A good collection of Andersen's Tales is: *The Snow Queen and Other Tales* (A Signet Classic). Particularly "The Snow Queen" (pp. 141–69) displays his distrust of science and mathematics and his trust in love and goodness.

7. *Om Begrebet Ironi,* 1841. *The Concept of Irony* (Bloomington, Ind.: Indiana University Press, 1965), Lee Capel's excellent translation, introduction, and comments are invaluable contributions to the S.K. research. He gives a historical survey, a *Stand der Forschung,* plus a glossary with key terms in correlation between Danish, English, and German.

8. Ibid., p. 50.

9. Professor Heiberg and Docent Martensen in particular receive many challenges that are veiled to a modern reader but were understood by S.K.'s contemporaries.

10. Ibid., his petition is appended to the text, p. 350.

11. Ibid., p. 63.

12. Ibid., p. 156.

13. See above p. 35.

14. Ibid., p. 180.

15. Ibid., p. 202. Separate thyself from the state, the establishment. S.K. here describes the birth of an individual conscience.

16. Ibid., p. 280.

17. Ibid., p. 320.

18. Ibid., p. 341.

19. Ibid., p. 306.

20. Ibid., p. 307.

21. In spite of his praise of Goethe, S.K. considers him—along with Hegel—the chief seducer of the age. He came to speak of the Goethe-Hegelian fallacy. They saw irony as "the mastered moment"—not as a way of obtaining truth. They were not "missionaries" like Socrates. See Carl Roos, *Kierkegaard og Goethe* (Copenhagen: G.T.C. Gads Forlag, 1955).

22. *The Concept of Irony*, p. 341.

Chapter Three

1. See p. 38.

2. *Armed Neutrality*, p. 4.

3. For information on the Heiberg family see Henning Fenger: *The Heibergs*, Twayne's World Authors Series, No. 105 (New York: Twayne Publishers, Inc., 1971).

4. S.K.'s own renderings of his meetings with King Christian VIII are fascinating. Mutual sympathy arose between the two men, and S.K. quickly concluded that he ought to dissociate himself from the king. *The Journals of Kierkegaard*, ed. with an introd. by Alexander Dru (New York: Harper & Row, Torchbooks, 1959), pp. 153–61.

5. For S.K. biographies see Walter Lowrie, *Life of Kierkegaard*, 2 vols. (New York and Evanston, Ill.: Harper & Row, Publishers, Torchbooks, 1962), and Josiah Thompson, *Kierkegaard* (New York: Knopf, 1973). There are many more, and almost every introduction to S.K.'s works includes a biographical note. See also S.K.'s *The Point of View for My Work as an Author: A Report to History*, ed. with a preface by Benjamin Nelson (New York and Evanston, Ill.: Harper & Row, Publishers, Torchbooks, 1962).

6. *The Journals of Kierkegaard* (Harper Torchbooks), pp. 81–82.

7. Ibid., p. 39.

8. Ibid., pp. 59–60.

9. Ibid., p. 67.

10. See Chapter 4.

11. *The Journals of Kierkegaard* (Harper Torchbooks), pp. 69–70. This account of his engagement was sent to Regine Olsen on S.K.'s death with all the papers relating to their engagement. They were published after her death, in 1904, under the title, *Kierkegaardske Papirer: Forlovelsen*, ed. by Raphael Meyer.

12. The term is S.K.'s own description of melancholy. Neither melancholy nor despondency are active enough terms to bring across the hyperactivity of mind versus body that characterizes this state. Parts of this account are incorporated word for word in *Stages*.

13. *The Journals of Kierkegaard*, p. 73.

14. Lowrie: *Kierkegaard*, p. 236.

15. See "the exception" below, Chapter 6, p. 147.

16. S.K.'s recurrent deliberations in seeking a position as a minister are treated in Villads Christensen's *Søren Kierkegaard: Det centrale i hans Livssyn* (Copenhagen: 1964). See also the introduction to *The Crisis and A Crisis in the Life of an Actress* (New York: Harper & Row, Publishers, 1967), tr. and introduction by Stephen Crites.

17. Danish *"Corsaren"* means "pirate," "privateer," or in a freer translation "gadfly."

18. See Lowrie, *Kierkegaard*, p. 350.

19. Quoted from ibid., p. 356.

20. Danish *"Metamorphose,"* an expression that S.K. uses in connection with melancholy, meaning to get rid of it in the same manner as the butterfly rises from the cocoon.

21. See Chapter 7.

22. Lowrie, *Kierkegaard*, pp. 392–93.

23. Ibid., pp. 368–69.

24. *The Journals of Kierkegaard*, p. 165: "On each of the later works there is, on the title page: *Poetic*, in order to show that I do not proclaim myself to be an exceptional Christian, or to be what I describe. *Without authority*, in order to denote that I do not lay others under an obligation, or judge them. *A spiritual revival*, in order to show that I have nothing to do with outward changes, or that kind of reformation. One man alone cannot help or save the age in which he lives, he can only express the fact that it will perish."

25. *The Point of View for My Work as an Author* (New York: Harper & Row, Torchbooks, 1962), p. 58.

26. P. Rodhe: *Søren Kierkegaard* (New York: Humanities Press, 1971), p. 124.

27. See Chapter 1.

28. Lowrie: *Kierkegaard,* p. 384.

29. *The Journals of Kierkegaard,* p. 231.

30. *Øjeblikket* was the first writing by S.K. that was translated into French and Italian and used for anticlerical propaganda.

31. Lowrie, *Kierkegaard,* pp. 573-75.

32. Ibid., p. 581.

33. *The Point of View for My Work,* p. 61.

34. Compare for instance the Kierkegaard of Walter Lowrie with the Kierkegaard of Josiah Thompson (see Selected Bibliography).

Chapter Four

1. *Either/Or,* 2 vols. (Princeton, N.J.: Princeton University Press, 1959, Princeton Paperbook) 1: p. 9.

2. Ibid., p. 13.

3. The question of a motto was one to which S.K. gave the utmost significance. The motto is not supposed to be a witty and cleverly found "bon mot," but to set the tone for the work, an introduction and a summing up, an anticipatory hint that puts the reader in the right receptive mood.

4. *Either/Or,* 1: p. 19.

5. Ibid., p. 37.

6. "Whichever you do you will repent it" [Diogenes Laertius, *Socrates.* Sec. 16].

7. Ibid., p. 59.

8. Ibid., p. 67. The argumentation is not original. It echoes both Aristotle and Hegel.

9. Ibid., p. 88.

10. Aristotle's word is *"hamartía,"* which means "error" and "guilt." See his *Poetics,* Chapter 3. In Christianity *"hamartía"* means "sin" and "guilt," and there is a completely different world view implied in the two meanings, which S.K. has perceptively picked up and explained.

11. *Either/Or* 1: p. 188.

12. The "Goethe-Hegelian" became a catch-phrase which S.K. applied to the modern speculative age. They were the prime seducers. For S.K.'s relationship to Goethe, see Carl Roos: *Kierkegaard og Goethe* (Copenhagen: G.E.C. Gads Forlag, 1955).

13. *Either/Or* 1: p. 213.

14. Ibid., p. 228. See also below, Chapter 8.

15. J. L. Heiberg, S.K.'s teacher, admired friend, yet adversary, translated Scribe's comedies for The Royal Theater.

16. S.K. was particularly interested in the idea of misunderstanding, as it implies a breakdown of communication that is simultaneously comic and tragic.

17. *Either/Or* 1: p. 271.

18. In the ancient myth Ixion wanting to seize Hera was deceived by a cloud in her form.

19. The motto in Vol. 2 is from Chateaubriand's novel *Atala* (1801): "The great passions are hermits and to transport them to the desert is to hand over to them their proper domain." It answers indirectly the question posed by Young. To be baptized passion must be brought from isolation into communal and marital life. To remain a hermit is to invite the demons.

20. *Either/Or* 2: p. 10.

21. Ibid., p. 29 ff.

22. Ibid., p. 58 ff.

23. Ibid., p. 96.

24. Ibid., p. 126.

25. Ibid., pp. 133–34.

26. Ibid., pp. 139–40.

27. See p. 185.

28. *Either/Or* 2: p. 150.

29. The "Equilibrium" is an attack upon Hegel's philosophy which S.K. loosely calls "the System." He is particularly angered that Hegelianism is trying to abolish the principle of contradiction. See *The Present Age*; see above, Chapter 1.

30. *Either/Or* 2: p. 333.

31. "The exception" is an extremely important term. We have also "the ordinary" and "the extraordinary." These never appear in the aesthetic category, only in the ethical and beyond. See *Stages*, below, p. 147.

32. *Either/Or* 2: p. 341.

33. "Only the truth that edifies is the truth for you" are the last words of *Either/Or*. This comes to be the major theme in S.K.'s writing; see p. 165 and p. 194.

Chapter Five

1. See Shalom Spiegel, *The Last Trial* (New York: Pantheon Books, 1967), a fascinating account of various interpretations of the Abraham-Isaac story in the Jewish tradition.

2. Erich Auerbach, *Mimesis* (Princeton, N.J.: Princeton University Press, 1953). Auerbach makes a comparison between Homeric epic style and the epic style in the account of Abraham's sacrifice of

Isaac. Certain features of his reading remind one of S.K.'s. For instance: "But even the human beings in the Biblical stories have greater depths of time, fate and consciousness than do the human beings in Homer; although they are nearly always caught up in an event engaging all their faculties, they are not so entirely immersed in its present that they do not remain continually conscious of what has happened to them earlier and elsewhere; their thoughts and feelings have more layers, are more entangled" (Quoted from p. 12 in the 1968 paperback edition). Whereas Abraham remembers, Homer's heroes "wake every morning as if it were the first day of their lives" (ibid., p. 13). According to Auerbach, Homer's heroes are aesthetes, and the biblical heroes are ethical. Auerbach stresses the underlying passion of the biblical stories which is absent in the Homeric. Auerbach makes no reference to Kierkegaard, however.

3. *Fear and Trembling and The Sickness unto Death* (Princeton, N.J.: Princeton University Press; Princeton Paperback, 1968), p. 31.

4. Ibid., p. 23. S.K.'s first treatise which remained unpublished, a refutation of Descartes's method, is called "Johannes Climacus, or *De Omnibus Dubitandum Est.*" See Selected Bibliography.

5. Ibid., p. 29.

6. Ibid., p. 28.

7. Ibid., p. 31.

8. Ibid., p. 69.

9. Ibid., p. 84.

10. Ibid., p. 82. In his eagerness to demonstrate the faults of such exegetes, S.K. has purposely made a mistake himself, since the word *meisein* does not exist. But the method does. S.K. is correct in his basic hermeneutical approach.

11. Ibid., p. 54.

12. Ibid., p. 49–51.

13. Ibid., p. 97.

14. Ibid., p. 103–104. See p. 90: "The true knight of faith is a witness, never a teacher and therein lies his deep humanity. . . ."

15. Ibid., p. 107 ff.

16. Ibid., pp. 108–109.

Chapter Six

1. *The Concept of Dread*, translated into English and published during World War II, made an instant impact. Among others, President Roosevelt read it and commented on its significance. See Frances Perkins, *The Roosevelt I Knew* (New York: Viking Press, 1946), p. 148.

2. S.K.'s term is *"Dogmatik,"* which in English is called "systematic theology."

3. *Stages on Life's Way* (New York: Schocken Books, paperback, 1967), pp. 39–41.

4. The young man and Constantine appear in *Repetition*; see Chapter 8.

5. *Stages,* p. 48.

6. Ibid., p. 56.

7. Ibid., p. 76.

8. Ibid., p. 79–80.

9. Ibid., p. 141.

10. Ibid., p. 136.

11. Ibid., p. 145.

12. Ibid., p. 147. At this point follows a discussion of Goethe's apprehension of love in his *Aus meinem Leben.*

13. Ibid., p. 170.

14. It is a technique that has been highly successful in films. It consists of "flashbacks," but used sophistically as in Robbe-Grillet's "Last Year in Marienbad."

15. *Stages,* p. 13. Paul Sponheim has also written a useful introduction to this edition.

16. Ibid., pp. 382–83.

17. Ibid., pp. 416–18. Frater Taciturnus is referring to Aristotle's *Poetics,* Chapter 6; Börne, *Collected Works* (Hamburg, 1829), 2: p. 144 ff.; "The Docents" that S.K. so often refers to in a derogative manner are "assistant" professors, eager to prove their scholarly acumen.

18. For a comprehensive study of "love" in the Classical and Christian tradition, see M. C. D'Arcy, *The Mind and Heart of Love: Lion and Unicorn. A Study in Eros and Agape* (New York: Henry Holt, 1947). This book is extremely useful as background reading. It makes us understand the history behind the so-called male and female principles. But its highest merit is to make comprehensible the split in self, concerning love vs. the self-love with which we have trouble in *Stages.* See especially Chapters 3, 6, 10, and 11.

19. *Stages,* pp. 443–44.

Chapter Seven

1. *Concluding Unscientific Postscript* (Princeton, N.J.: Princeton University Press, 1941, Princeton paperback), p. 259.

2. Ibid., p. 545.

3. Niels Thulstrup has provided an excellent introduction and

a thorough commentary to *Philosophical Fragments* (Princeton, N.J.: Princeton University Press, 1962). For background of the theological and philosophical discussion, see his commentary, pp. 146–52.

4. Ibid., p. 139.

5. Act I, Scene 5.

6. From *Hippias Major*, a dialogue attributed to Plato.

7. For an interesting schematic division between "the scientific community" and "the individual," see Ralph Henry Johnson, *The Concept of Existence in the Concluding Unscientific Postscript* (The Hague: Martinus Nijhoff, 1972).

8. *Concluding Unscientific Postscript*, p. 55.

9. Ibid., p. 61.

10. Ibid., pp. 64–65.

11. Ibid., p. 79. See also the relationship between S.K. and Pastor Boesen at the time of S.K.'s approaching death.

12. Ibid., p. 93.

13. Ibid., p. 266.

14. Ibid., p. 458 ff.

15. Ibid., pp. 522–23.

16. Ibid., p. 551.

17. *Journals and Papers* II, A, 756. The translation quoted from G. Malantschuk: *Kierkegaard's Thought* (Princeton, N.J.: Princeton University Press, 1971), p. 308.

18. Quoted from the translators' introduction to *Works of Love* (New York: Harper & Row, Harper Torchbooks, 1962), p. 17.

19. *"Hin Enkelte"* means "that single individual," but now we begin to see that "single" means *"monachos"* in the sense of having one goal and becoming one with the goal.

20. *Armed Neutrality*, p. 58.

21. *Fear and Trembling and The Sickness unto Death*, p. 146.

22. Ibid., pp. 175–76.

23. Ibid., p. 203.

24. Ibid., p. 257.

25. *Training in Christianity* (Princeton, N.J.: Princeton University Press, 1944), pp. 71–72. S.K. later wanted to eliminate the Moral, together with the prefaces and the pseudonym. See above, pp. 192–94.

26. *Journals and Papers*, V [X¹ A 517].

Chapter Eight

1. In this, the last chapter, an attempt is made to give an analysis of one of S.K.'s books, using the tools we have acquired. In reading

S.K., one must take the following steps: First, one must locate the work in S.K.'s whole body of writing and ascertain its dialectical functioning point—to aid us in this process, S.K. has given his own guides, both in *Concluding Unscientific Postscript* and in *My Point of View as an Author*. Second, one must never forget "indirect communication," which makes it essential to be familiar with the stages and to locate all characters in the stage to which they belong. Third, one must investigate the heroes in order to understand what is supposed to be "appropriated." S.K.'s style is a by-product of his conception of the whole; its unevenness is part of his eagerness to be absolutely clear and yet concealed. There is much to praise and much to blame. For a view by a literary critic, see Henning Fenger in his article, "Kierkegaard—A Literary Approach," *Scandinavica* 3 (1964): 1–16.

2. *Repetition* (Princeton, N.J.: Princeton University Press, 1941; also, New York: Harper & Row, 1964, Torchbooks). Quoted from Torchbooks edition, pp. 78–79. In the Princeton Paperback pp. 74–76.

3. Ibid., p. 33.

4. Ibid., p. 35.

5. Ibid., p. 37.

6. Ibid., p. 38.

7. Ibid., p. 40.

8. Ibid., pp. 52–53.

9. Ibid., p. 58. In the Princeton Paperback pp. 42–43.

10. Ibid., pp. 59–60.

11. Ibid., p. 94.

12. Ibid., p. 105.

13. Ibid., p. 115.

14. Ibid., p. 115. In the Princeton Paperback   p. 130.

15. Ibid., p. 116.

16. Ibid., p. 126.

17. *On Authority and Revelation*, p. 11.

18. *Repetition*, p. 135; compare the relationship between Frater Taciturnus and Quidam. See Chapter 6. In both cases we deal with "heterogeneity" in self or a divided self.

Selected Bibliography

PRIMARY SOURCES

1. In Danish

Søren Kierkegaard. *SAMLEDE VÆRKER,* 1–20 (3. udgave), udgivet af A. B. Drachmann, J. L. Heiberg og H. O. Lange. *Terminologisk Ordbog* ved Jens Himmelstrup. Sammenlignende Register til første, anden og nærværende udgave af *Samlede Værker.* Copenhagen: Gyldendal, 1962–64.

2. In English Translations

Søren Kierkegaard's Journals and Papers. Translated by Howard V. Hong and Edna H. Hong. Bloomington, Ind., and London: Indiana University Press, vol. 1, 1967; vol. 2, 1970; vols. 3–7 forthcoming. (From *Papirer* I–XI, suppl. vols. XII, XIII, 1969–70, and *Breve og Aktstykker vedrørende Søren Kierkegaard,* Niels Thulstrup, ed., I–II, 1953–54.)

The following are listed in order of time of writing, with Danish titles in parenthesis. The various introductions to the English editions are usually very enlightening.

The Concept of Irony. Translated by Lee Capel. New York: Harper & Row, Publishers, 1966. Bloomington: Indiana University Press, 1968. (*Om Begrebet Ironi* by S. A. Kierkegaard. 1841.)

Either/Or. 2 vols. Vol. 1 translated by David F. Swenson and Lillian Marvin Swenson; Vol. 2 translated by Walter Lowrie; 2nd ed. revised by Howard A. Johnson. Princeton, N.J.: Princeton University Press, 1959. (*Enten-Eller,* I–II. Edited by Victor Eremita. 1843.)

Johannes Climacus, or De omnibus dubitandum est, and *A Sermon.* Translated by T. H. Croxall. London: Adam and Charles Black, 1958. ("*Johannes Climacus eller* De omnibus dubitandum est," written 1842–43, unpublished, *Papirer* IV B I. *Demis-Prædiken,* 1844, unpublished, IV C I.)

Edifying Discourses. 4 vols. Translated by David F. Swenson and Lillian Marvin Swenson. Minneapolis: Augsburg Publishing

House, 1943–46. (*Opbyggelige Taler* by S. Kierkegaard. 1843, 1844.)

Fear and Trembling (with *The Sickness Unto Death*). Translated by Walter Lowrie. Princeton, N.J.: Princeton University Press, 1954. (*Frygt og Bæven* by Johannes de Silentio. 1843.)

Repetition. Translated by Walter Lowrie. Princeton, N.J.: Princeton University Press, 1941. (*Gjentagelsen* by Constantine Constantius. 1843.)

Philosophical Fragments. Translated by David F. Swenson. 2nd ed. rev. by Howard V. Hong. Princeton, N.J.: Princeton University Press, 1962. (*Philosophiske Smuler* by Johannes Climacus. Edited by S. Kierkegaard. 1844.)

The Concept of Anxiety [Dread]. Translated by Walter Lowrie. 2nd ed. Princeton, N.J.: Princeton University Press, 1957. (*Begrebet Angest* by Vigilius Haufniensis. Edited by S. Kierkegaard. 1844.)

Thoughts on Crucial Situations in Human Life. Translated by David F. Swenson. Edited by Lillian Marvin Swenson. Minneapolis: Augsburg Publishing House, 1941. (*Tre Taler ved tænkte Leiligheder* by S. Kierkegaard. 1845.)

Stages on Life's Way. Translated by Walter Lowrie. Princeton, N.J.: Princeton University Press, 1940. (*Stadier paa Livets Vej.* Edited by Hilarius Bogbinder. 1845.)

Concluding Unscientific Postscript. Translated by David F. Swenson and Walter Lowrie. Princeton, N.J.: Princeton University Press for American Scandinavian Foundation, 1941. (*Afsluttende uvidenskabelig Efterskrift* by Johannes Climacus. Edited by S. Kierkegaard. 1846.)

The Present Age [part of *Two Ages: the Age of Revolution and the Present Age. A Literary Review*] and *Two Minor Ethico-Religious Treatises.* Translated by Alexander Dru and Walter Lowrie. London and New York: Oxford University Press, 1940. (*En literair Anmeldelse, To Tidsaldre* by S. Kierkegaard, 1846; *Tvende ethisk-religieuse Smaa-Afhandlinger* by H. H., 1849.)

On Authority and Revelation, The Book on Adler. Translated by Walter Lowrie. Princeton, N.J.: Princeton University Press, 1955. ("Bogen om Adler," written 1846–47, unpubl., *Papirer* VII² B 235.)

Purity of Heart. Translated by Douglas Steere. 2nd ed. New York: Harper & Brothers, 1948. (*Opbyggelige Taler i forskjellig Aand* by S. Kierkegaard, pt. I. "*En Leiligheds-Tale,*" 1847.)

The Gospel of Suffering and *The Lilies of the Field.* Translated by David F. Swenson and Lillian Marvin Swenson. Minneapolis:

Augsburg Publishing House, 1948. (*Opbyggelige Taler i forskjellig Aand* by S. Kierkegaard, pt. 3, "*Lidelsernes Evangelium*"; pt. 2; "*Hvad vi lære af Lilierne paa Marken og af Himmelens Fugle*," 1847.)

Works of Love. Translated by Howard V. Hong and Edna H. Hong. New York: Harper & Row, Publishers, Inc., 1962. (*Kjærlighedens Gjerninger* by S. Kierkegaard. 1847.)

The Crisis and The Crisis in the Life of an Actress. Translated by Stephen Crites. New York: Harper & Row, Publishers, Inc., 1967. (*Krisen og en Krise i en Skuespillerindes Liv,* by Inter et Inter, *Fædrelandet,* Nos. 188–91. 24–27 July 1848.)

Christian Discourses, including also *The Lilies of the Field and the Birds of the Air* and *Three Discourses at the Communion on Fridays.* Translated by Walter Lowrie. London and New York: Oxford University Press, 1939. (*Christelige Taler* by S. Kierkegaard, 1848; *Lilien paa Marken og Fuglen under Himlen* by S. Kierkegaard, 1849; "*Ypperstepræsten*"–"*Tolderen*"–"*Synderinden*," *Tre Taler ved Altergangen om Fredagen* by S. Kierkegaard, 1849.)

The Sickness Unto Death (with *Fear and Trembling*). Translated by Walter Lowrie. Princeton, N.J.: Princeton University Press, 1954. (*Sygdommen til Døden* by Anti-Climacus. Edited by S. Kierkegaard. 1849.)

Training in Christianity, including also *The Woman Who Was a Sinner.* Translated by Walter Lowrie. Princeton, N.J.: Princeton University Press, 1944. (*Indøvelse i Christendom* by Anti-Climacus, S. Kierkegaard, ed., 1850; *En opbyggelig Tale* by S. Kierkegaard, 1850.)

Armed Neutrality and An Open Letter. Translated by Howard V. Hong and Edna H. Hong. Bloomington and London: Indiana University Press, 1968. (*Den bevæbnede Neutralitet,* written 1848–49, published 1965; *Foranledigt ved en Yttring af Dr. Rudelbach mig betræffende, Fædrelandet,* No. 26. 31 January 1851.)

The Point of View . . . , including "Two Notes about 'the Individual' " and *On My Work as an Author.* Translated by Walter Lowrie. London and New York: Oxford University Press, 1939. (*Synspunktet for min Forfatter-Virksomhed,* by S. Kierkegaard, written 1848, published 1859; *Om min Forfatter-Virksomhed* by S. Kierkegaard, 1851.)

For Self-Examination. Translated by Howard V. Hong and Edna H.

Hong. Minneapolis: Augsburg Publishing House, 1940. (*Til Selvprøvelse* by S. Kierkegaard. 1851.)
Judge for Yourselves! in *For Self-Examination* and *Judge for Yourselves! ...*, with *Two Discourses at the Communion on Fridays*. Translated by Walter Lowrie. Also includes *The Unchangeableness of God* (David F. Swenson, tr.). Princeton, N.J.: Princeton University Press, 1944. (*Dømmer Selv!* by S. Kierkegaard, 1852; *To Taler ved Altergangen om Fredagen* by S. Kierkegaard, 1851; *Guds Uforanderlighed* by S. Kierkegaard, 1855.)
Kierkegaard's Attack upon "Christendom," 1854–1855. Translated by Walter Lowrie. Princeton, N.J.: Princeton University Press, 1944 (*Bladartikler I–XXI* by S. Kierkegaard, *Fædrelandet*, 1854–55; *Dette skal siges, saa være det da sagt* by S. Kierkegaard, 1855; *Øieblikket* by S. Kierkegaard, 1–9, 1855; 10, unpublished, S.V., XIV; *Hvad Christus dømmer om officiel Christendom* by S. Kierkegaard, 1855.)
The Journals of Søren Kierkegaard ... a Selection .... Translated by Alexander Dru. London and New York: Oxford University Press, 1938. (From *Søren Kierkegaards Papirer*, I–XI. 18 vols. 1909–36.)

SECONDARY SOURCES

General works on Kierkegaard are listed in the bibliography of *Søren Kierkegaard's Journals and Papers* (see above), 1967, pp. 482–88.

CHRISTENSEN, VILLADS. *Søren Kierkegaard: Det centrale i hans Livssyn*. Copenhagen, 1964.

COLLINS, JAMES. *The Mind of Kierkegaard*. Chicago: Henry Regnery Co., 1953.

CROXALL, T. H. *Kierkegaard Commentary*. New York: Harper and Row, 1956.

DIEM, HERMANN. *Kierkegaard's Dialectic of Existence*. London: Oliver and Boyd, 1959.

HENRIKSEN, AAGE. *Kierkegaard Studies in Scandinavia*. Copenhagen: Munksgaard, 1951.

HIRSCH, EMANUEL. *Kierkegaard-Studien*, 2 vols. Gütersloh: Druck und Verlag von C. Berteismann, 1930.

JANSEN, F. J. BILLESKOV. *Studier i Søren Kierkegaards Literære Kunst*. Copenhagen: Rosenkilde og Bagger, 1951.

JOHNSON, RALPH HENRY. *The Concept of Existence in the Concluding Unscientific Postscript*. The Hague: Martinus Nijhoff, 1972.

LOWRIE, WALTER. *Kierkegaard.* New York and London: Oxford University Press, 1938.

MACKEY, LOUIS. *Kierkegaard: A Kind of Poet.* Philadelphia: University of Pennsylvania Press, 1971.

MALANTSCHUK, GREGOR. *Kierkegaard's Thought.* Edited and translated by Howard V. Hong and Edna H. Hong. Princeton, N.J.: Princeton University Press, 1971.

MESNARD, P. *Le vrai visage de Kierkegaard.* Paris: Beauchesne et ses Fils, 1948.

RODHE, P. *Søren Kierkegaard.* New York: Humanities Press, 1971.

ROOS, CARL. *Kierkegaard og Goethe.* Copenhagen: G.E.C. Gads Forlag, 1955.

SWENSON, DAVID. *Something About Kierkegaard* (Revised and enlarged edition), edited by Lillian Marvin Swenson. Minneapolis: Augsburg Publishing House (1945), 1956.

SCHMUËLI, ADI. *Kierkegaard and Consciousness.* Princeton, N.J.: Princeton University Press, 1971.

TAYLOR, MARK C. *Kierkegaard's Pseudonymous Authorship: A Study of Time and Self.* Princeton, N.J.: Princeton University Press, 1975.

THOMTE, REIDAR. *Kierkegaard's Philosophy of Religion.* 1948; New York: Greenwood Press, 1969.

THULSTRUP, NIELS. *Kierkegaards Verhältnis zu Hegel und zum spekulativen Idealismus.* Stuttgart, Berlin, Köln, Mainz: Kohlhammer, 1972.

Index

231

double movement, 126, 127, 178, 197, 198, 206
doubt, 109, 110, 111, 117, 154
drama, 35, 83, 84, 127
dread, 132, 133, 147, 160
Dru, A., 22, 214n14
duty, 98, 106, 111, 120, 121, 122, 186, 208

earthquake, 52
empathy, 23, 85, 202
empiricism, 39, 46
encounter, happy and unhappy, 165, 186
enthusiasm, 26, 27
envy, 27
epic, 35
erotic, the, 79-83, 95, 138, 143
eternal, 100, 101, 103, 107, 119, 124, 163, 164, 169, 174, 181, 183, 184, 187; eternal consciousness, 164; eternal happiness, 87, 164, 169, 170, 178
ethical, the (the category of), 20, 107, 109, 114, 115, 120, 121, 139, 148, 151, 154, 159, 160, 169, 189
ethics, 122, 127, 129, 132, 183, 184, 206
exception, the, 61, 69, 112, 121, 129, *147*, 149, 150, 160, 161, 182, 201, 205
existence, 116, 160, 173
existentialism, 20

faith, 53, 101, 117, 120-31, 143, 165, 166, 174, 185, 186, 191, 206
fate, 84, 98, 155-57
Faust, 24, 82, 87, 88, 93, 96, 129
Fenger, H., 216n3, 222n1
finiteness, 103, 124
"first love," 55, 89-91, 98, 99, 100, 101, 102, 105, 144
Frater Taciturnus, 149-59, 161, 162, 198
freedom, 91, 101, 103, *108*, 133, 187

Freud, S., 20, 213n10
Frye, N., 22, 214n12

genius, 34, 36, 73, 214n22, 215n4
"genuine author," 24, 209
God in Time, the, 165, 177
Goethe, 44, 86, 117, 129, 216n21, 221n12
Goldsmith, M., 62, 63
Governance, 35, 66
grace, 186, 191, 192, 193
grief, reflective, 88
guilt, 84, 85, 129, 130, 151, 157, 183
Guilty/Not Guilty, 59, 62, 149-51, 153, 175

Hamann, J. G., 21
Hegel, 20, 21, 38, 68, 89, 117, 166, 216n21
Heiberg, J. L., 47
Heiberg, Mme J. L., 65
hero, 21, 28, 73, 87, 117, 172, 177; aesthetic, 155; religious, 153, 154, 155; tragic, 41, 121, 130, 153, 157
heterogeneousness, 152, 199
heterogeneity, 124, 153, 199, *223n18*
Himmelstrup, J., 214n13
Hirsh, E., 215n3
history, 100, 103, 105, 106, 108, 111, 148, 165, 192
Hong, E., & H., 22, 214n14
humor, 21, 44, 134, 149, 160, 161, *163*, 175, 177, 190

idea, 39, 83, 142
ideal, 103, 201
imagination, 21, 23, 47, 65, 88, 91, 98, 118, 123, 131, 177, 191, 202, 208
immanent, 163, 177
immediacy, 87, 101, 103, 128, 140, 143, 144, 149, 151-52, 189, 206
immortality, 140, *174*
incarnation, 19, 165, 166, 174, 177, 186
incognito, 153, 186

DATE DUE

MAY 1 5 '78	MAY 10 '78		
MAY 9 '78	MAY 11 '78		
GAYLORD			PRINTED IN U.S.A.